Configuring Windows Devices Exam 70-697

Lab Manual

Patrick Regan

WILEY

SENIOR EXECUTIVE EDITOR	Bryan Gambrel
MARKET SOLUTIONS ASSISTANT	Jessy Moor
EXECUTIVE MARKETING MANAGER	Michele Szczesniak
CONTENT MANAGER	Nichole Urban
PRODUCTION COORDINATOR	Nicole Repasky
PRODUCTION EDITOR	Loganathan Kandan

www.wiley.com/college/microsoft

ISBN 978-1-119-12620-1

BRIEF CONTENTS

Lab 1: Supporting Windows Store and Cloud Apps

Lab 2: Supporting Authentication and Authorization

Lab 3: Migrating and Configuring User Data

Lab 4: Configuring Hyper-V

Lab 5: Supporting Mobility Options

Lab 6: Supporting and Managing Devices with Microsoft Intune

Lab 7: Deploying Software Updates by Using Microsoft Intune

Lab 8: Configuring IP Settings

Lab 9: Configuring Network Settings

Lab 10: Configuring and Maintaining Network Security

Lab 11: Supporting Data Storage

Lab 12: Supporting Data Security

Lab 13: Configuring Shared Resources

Lab 14: Configuring File and Folder Access

Lab 15: Configuring Remote Connections

Lab 16: Configuring Mobility Options

Lab 17: Deploying and Managing Azure RemoteApp

Lab 18: Supporting Desktop Apps

Lab 19: Configuring System Recovery

Lab 20: Configuring File Recovery

Lab 21: Configuring and Managing Updates

CONTENTS

1. Supporting Windows Store and Cloud Apps 1

Exercise 1.1: Signing Up for Office 365 3
Exercise 1.2: Installing Office 2016 from Office 365 5
Exercise 1.3: Signing Up for Microsoft Intune 7
Exercise 1.4: Sideloading Windows Store Apps to Microsoft Intune 9
Lab Challenge: Creating and Integrating a Microsoft Account 12

2. Supporting Authentication and Authorization 17

Exercise 2.1: Managing Local User Passwords 18
Exercise 2.2: Using a PIN and Picture Password 22
Exercise 2.3: Creating and Managing Domain User Accounts 25
Exercise 2.4: Using Credential Manager 27
Exercise 2.5: Creating and Supporting HomeGroups 29
Lab Challenge: Managing Account Policies 30

3. Migrating and Configuring User Data 33

Exercise 3.1: Configuring and Managing User Profiles 35
Exercise 3.2: Configuring Folder Locations 37
Exercise 3.3: Installing the User State Migration Tool 39
Exercise 3.4: Migrating User Profiles 40
Lab Challenge: Creating a Roaming User Profile 45

4. Configuring Hyper-V 49

Exercise 4.1: Installing and Configuring Hyper-V 50
Exercise 4.2: Creating and Managing Virtual Machines 51
Exercise 4.3: Creating and Managing Virtual Switches 53
Exercise 4.4: Creating and Managing Virtual Disks 56
Lab Challenge: Creating and Managing Checkpoints 58

5. Supporting Mobility Options 59

Exercise 5.1: Configuring Power Settings 60
Lab Challenge: Using Powercfg.exe 62

6. Supporting and Managing Devices with Microsoft Intune 65

Exercise 6.1: Managing Microsoft Intune Users and Devices 67
Exercise 6.2: Managing Microsoft Intune Groups 71
Exercise 6.3: Managing Microsoft Intune Policies 73
Exercise 6.4: Configuring Microsoft Intune Monitoring and Alerts 75
Lab Challenge: Running Microsoft Intune Reports 76

7. Deploying Software Updates by Using Microsoft Intune 79

Exercise 7.1: Identifying, Approving, and Declining Updates Using Microsoft Intune 80
Exercise 7.2: Configuring Automatic Updates in Microsoft Intune 82
Lab Challenge: Deploying Third-Party Updates with Microsoft Intune 84

8. Configuring IP Settings 87

Exercise 8.1: Configuring IPv4 Settings 88
Exercise 8.2: Configuring IPv6 Settings 91
Exercise 8.3: Configuring Advanced Shared Settings and Network Locations 93
Lab Challenge: Troubleshooting IP Network Problems 94

9. Configuring Network Settings 97

Exercise 9.1: Configuring Network Adapters 98
Lab Challenge: Configuring Wi-Fi Networking 100

10. Configuring and Maintaining Network Security 103

Exercise 10.1: Configuring Windows Firewall 104
Exercise 10.2: Configuring Connection Security Rules (IPsec) 106
Lab Challenge: Creating an Authentication Exception Rule 110

11. Supporting Data Storage 113

Exercise 11.1: Creating a Simple Volume 114
Exercise 11.2: Creating a Storage Pool and a Storage Space 117
Exercise 11.3: Installing and Configuring BranchCache on a File Server 118
Exercise 11.4: Creating a DFS Namespace 122
Lab Challenge: Using OneDrive to Manage Files/Folders 126

12. Supporting Data Security 129

Exercise 12.1: Managing NTFS and Share Permissions 130
Exercise 12.2: Encrypting Files with Encrypting File System (EFS) 133
Exercise 12.3: Encrypting a Volume with BitLocker 136
Lab Challenge: Using Dynamic Access Control 137

13. Configuring Shared Resources 143

Exercise 13.1: Configuring Printers 144
Lab Challenge: Configuring Libraries 147

14. Configuring File and Folder Access 149

Exercise 14.1: Enabling Disk Quotas 150
Exercise 14.2: Enabling Auditing 152
Lab Challenge: Implementing Advanced Auditing 156

15. Configuring Remote Connections 159

Exercise 15.1: Configuring a VPN Client 160
Exercise 15.2: Using the Connection Manager Administration Kit (CMAK) 163
Exercise 15.3: Using Remote Desktop 167
Lab Challenge: Configuring Split Tunneling 170

16. Configuring Mobility Options 173

Exercise 16.1: Syncing Your Computer 174
Lab Challenge: Using a Work Folder 177

17. Deploying and Managing Azure RemoteApp 181

Exercise 17.1: Using Remote Applications 182
Lab Challenge: Removing Remote Desktop Services 188

18. Supporting Desktop Apps 191

Exercise 18.1: Installing and Using the Application Compatibility Toolkit (ACT) 192
Exercise 18.2: Deploying Desktop Applications Using Microsoft Intune 195
Lab Challenge: Removing the Microsoft Intune Client 197

19. Configuring System Recovery 199

Exercise 19.1: Configuring and Using a Restore Point 200
Lab Challenge: Rolling Back a Device Driver 202

20. Configuring File Recovery 205

Exercise 20.1: Scheduling a Windows 10 Backup 206
Exercise 20.2: Performing a File Restore 209
Exercise 20.3: Using File History 210
Lab Challenge: Recovering Files from OneDrive 212

21. Configuring and Managing Updates 215

Exercise 21.1: Configuring Windows 10 Updates 216
Lab Challenge: Configuring Windows Update Policies 218

LAB 1
SUPPORTING WINDOWS STORE AND CLOUD APPS

THIS LAB CONTAINS THE FOLLOWING EXERCISES AND ACTIVITIES:

Exercise 1.1	Signing Up for Office 365
Exercise 1.2	Installing Office 2016 ProPlus from Office 365
Exercise 1.3	Signing Up for Microsoft Intune
Exercise 1.4	Sideloading Windows Store Apps to Microsoft Intune
Lab Challenge	Creating and Integrating a Microsoft Account

BEFORE YOU BEGIN

The lab environment consists of student workstations connected to a local area network, along with a server that functions as the domain controller for a domain called adatum.com. The computers required for this lab are listed in Table 1-1.

Table 1-1
Computers required for Lab 1

Computer	*Operating System*	*Computer Name*
Client	Windows 10	A machine running Windows 10 that is connected to the Internet.

In addition to the computers, you will also require the software listed in Table 1-2 to complete Lab 1.

Table 1-2
Software required for Lab 1

Software	*Location*
Lab 1 student worksheet	Lab01_worksheet.docx (provided by instructor)
PowerPointViewer.exe	Downloaded from https://www.microsoft.com/en-us/download/details.aspx?id=13.

Working with Lab Worksheets

Each lab in this manual requires that you answer questions, shoot screen shots, and perform other activities that you will document in a worksheet named for the lab, such as Lab01_worksheet.docx. You will find these worksheets on the book companion site. It is recommended that you use a USB flash drive to store your worksheets, so you can submit them to your instructor for review. As you perform the exercises in each lab, open the appropriate worksheet file, fill in the required information, and then save the file to your flash drive.

SCENARIO

After completing this lab, you will be able to:

- Sign up for an Office 365 account
- Sign up for a Microsoft Intune account
- Install Office 365 ProPlus from Office 365
- Sideload a Windows Store app to Microsoft Intune
- Create and integrate a Microsoft account

Estimated lab time: 110 minutes

NOTE	*If you are using the MOAC Labs Online system, you will not be able to perform this exercise. Instead, you need to use a computer running Windows 10 with access to the Internet. If your classroom has a dedicated Windows Server 2012 R2 or Windows Server 2016, you can use a virtual machine running Windows 10.*

Exercise 1.1	Signing Up for Office 365
Overview	In this exercise, you will first create an account for Office 365 and then you will create a group consisting of one user and send a test email to the group.
Mindset	Office 365 is a subscription-based online office and services offered through a website aimed at organizations. It allows you to create and manage users and groups.
Completion time	20 minutes

1. Log into a Windows 10 computer that is connected to the Internet.

2. On the taskbar, click the **Start** button. When the Start page opens, type **IE** and then click **Internet Explorer**.

3. Open the following web page:

   http://office.microsoft.com/en-us/business/

4. Click **See plans & pricing** and then click **See more plans & pricing**. Review some of the plans and look at the differences between the Business plans and the Enterprise plans.

Question 1	*Which program does Office 365 Enterprise E5 offer that Enterprise E3 does not offer?*

Question 2	*Which option does E5 have for advanced eDiscovery?*

Question 3	*Which option allows you to make, receive, and transfer calls across a wide range of devices?*

5. Click the **Office 365 Enterprise E5** option at the top of the window. Then review what options Office 365 Enterprise E5 has to offer.

Question 4	*Which collaboration software does Office 365 offer that allows employees to connect with up to 10,000 users in order to share information across teams?*

6. Near the top of the window, click **Office 365 Enterprise E3** and then click the **Free trial** option. The Office 365 Enterprise E3 Trial signup page opens as shown in Figure 1-1.

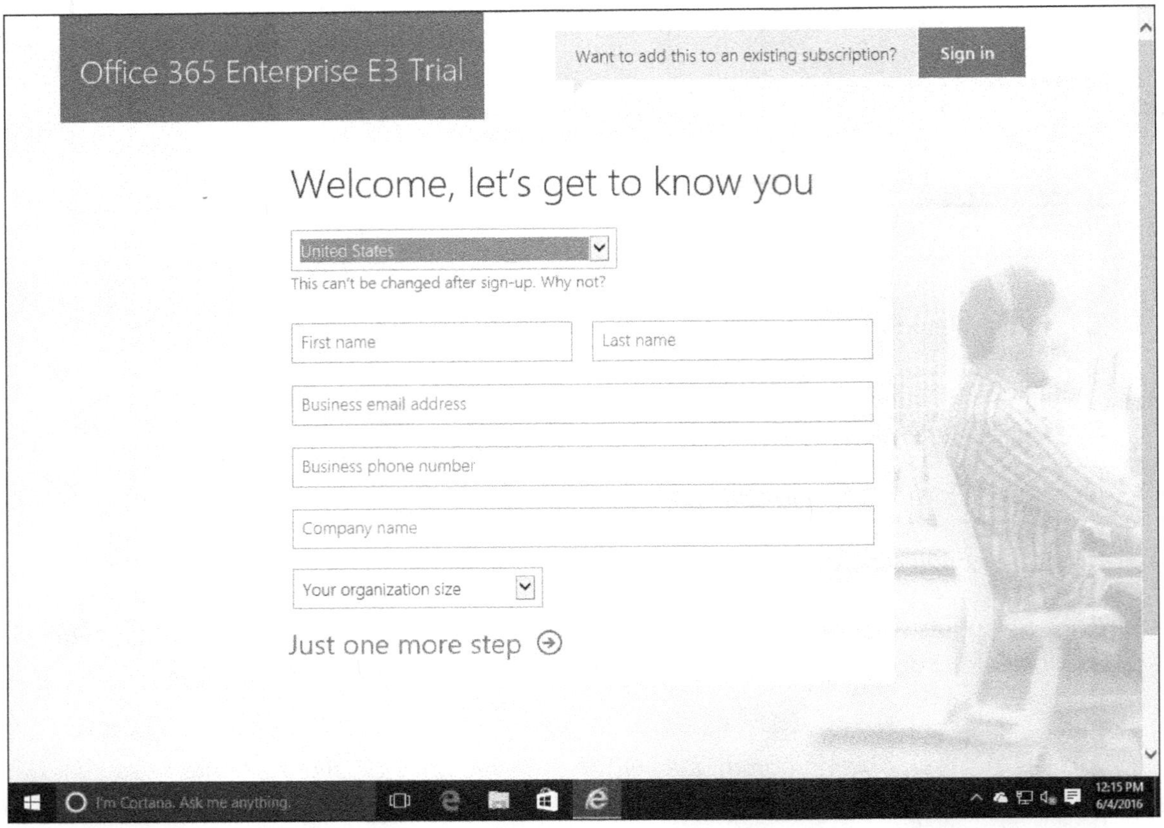

Figure 1-1
The Office 365 Enterprise E3 Trial sign-up page

7. On the Welcome, Let's get to know you page, type the following information:

   First name: **<Your first name>**

   Last name: **<Your last name>**

   Business email address: **<Your email address>**

   Business phone number: **<Your phone number>**

   Company name: **<FirstName><LastName>Office365<Month><Year>**

   Therefore, if your name is John Smith and you are performing this lab in November 2016, you would type:

   JohnSmithOffice365112016, which produces a login domain of JohnSmithOffice365112016 .onmicrosoft.com

8. For the organization size, select **25-49 people**. Then click **Just one more step**.

9. On the Create your user ID page, for the User ID, type the following:

    <FirstInitial><LastName>

    Therefore, if your name is John Smith, you would type:

    JSmith

10. For Your company, type:

    <FirstName><LastName>Office365<Month><Year>

    Therefore, if your name is John Smith and you are performing this lab in November 2016, you would type:

    JohnSmithOffice365112016.

11. For the Password text box and the Confirm password text box, type **Pa$$w0rd**. Click **Create my account**.

12. In the Prove. You're. Not. A. Robot page, Text me is already selected. Type a name of a cell phone in the Phone number text box and then click **Text me**.

13. When you get the code in the text message, type the code in the **Enter your verification code** text box. Click **Next**.

Question 5	*What is the URL to the sign-in page?*

14. When the account is created, take a screen shot showing a successful configuration of a Windows desktop by pressing **Alt+PrtScr** and then paste it into your Lab01_worksheet file in the page provided by pressing **Ctrl+V**.

15. Close Internet Explorer.

Exercise 1.2	Installing Office 2016 from Office 365
Overview	In this exercise, you will install Office 2016 from Office 365.
Mindset	Office 365 Enterprise E3 (unlimited users) plans include a subscription for Office 2016 for as many as five PCs/Macs. Microsoft Office 2016 includes desktop versions of the following applications. When you deploy Office 2016 from Office 365, you are deploying the 32-bit version of Office 2016.
Completion time	30 minutes

1. On the computer running Windows 10 that is connected to the Internet, open **Internet Explorer**.
2. Go to **http://portal.office.com** and log in with your credentials. After you log in, you should see a screen similar to Figure 1-2.

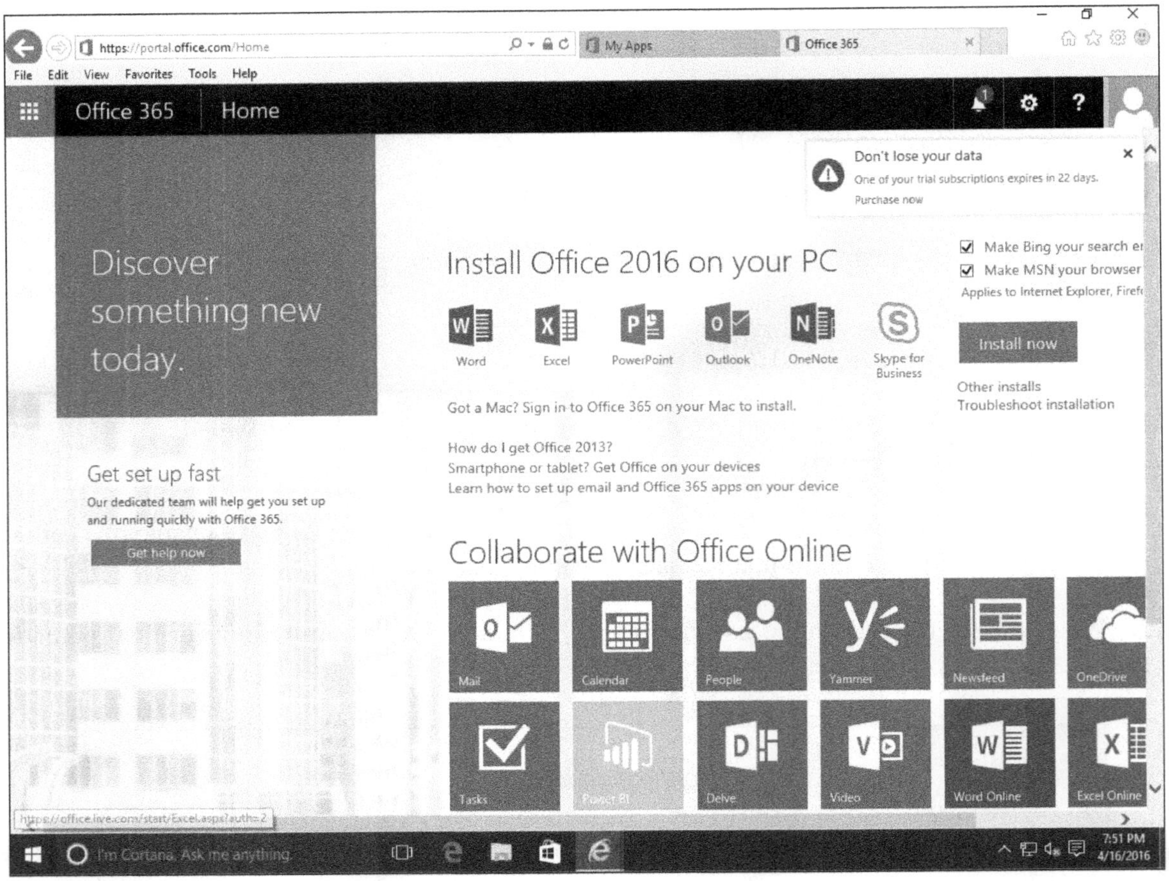

Figure 1-2
Accessing the Office 365 Portal

Question 6	*Which programs are included with Office 2016?*

3. Click **Install now**.
4. When you are prompted to run or save the executable file, click **Run**. If you are prompted to make changes to your PC, click **Yes**. It will take several minutes to install Office 2016.

5. When Office 365 is installed, take a screen shot by pressing **Alt+PrtScr** and then paste it into your Lab01_worksheet file in the page provided by pressing **Ctrl+V**.

6. Click **Close**.

7. Close **Internet Explorer**.

Exercise 1.3	Signing Up for Microsoft Intune
Overview	In this exercise, you will sign up for a Microsoft Intune account.
Mindset	Microsoft Intune is a cloud-based management solution that allows you to manage your computers and mobile devices when they are connected to or not connected to the corporate network. Microsoft Intune helps you manage your computers and mobile devices through a web console.
Completion time	20 minutes

1. On the computer running Windows 10 that is connected to the Internet, open **Internet Explorer**.

2. Go to **http://www.microsoft.com/en-us/server-cloud/products/microsoft-intune/** and then click **Try Now**.

3. On the signup page (as shown in Figure 1-3), type the following and then click **Next**:

   Country or Region: **<Your country or region>**

   First name: **<Your first name>**

   Last name: **<Your last name>**

   Business email address: **<Your email address>**

   Business phone number: **<Your phone number>**

   Company name: **<Your last name> Corporation**

   Your organization size: **25-49 people**

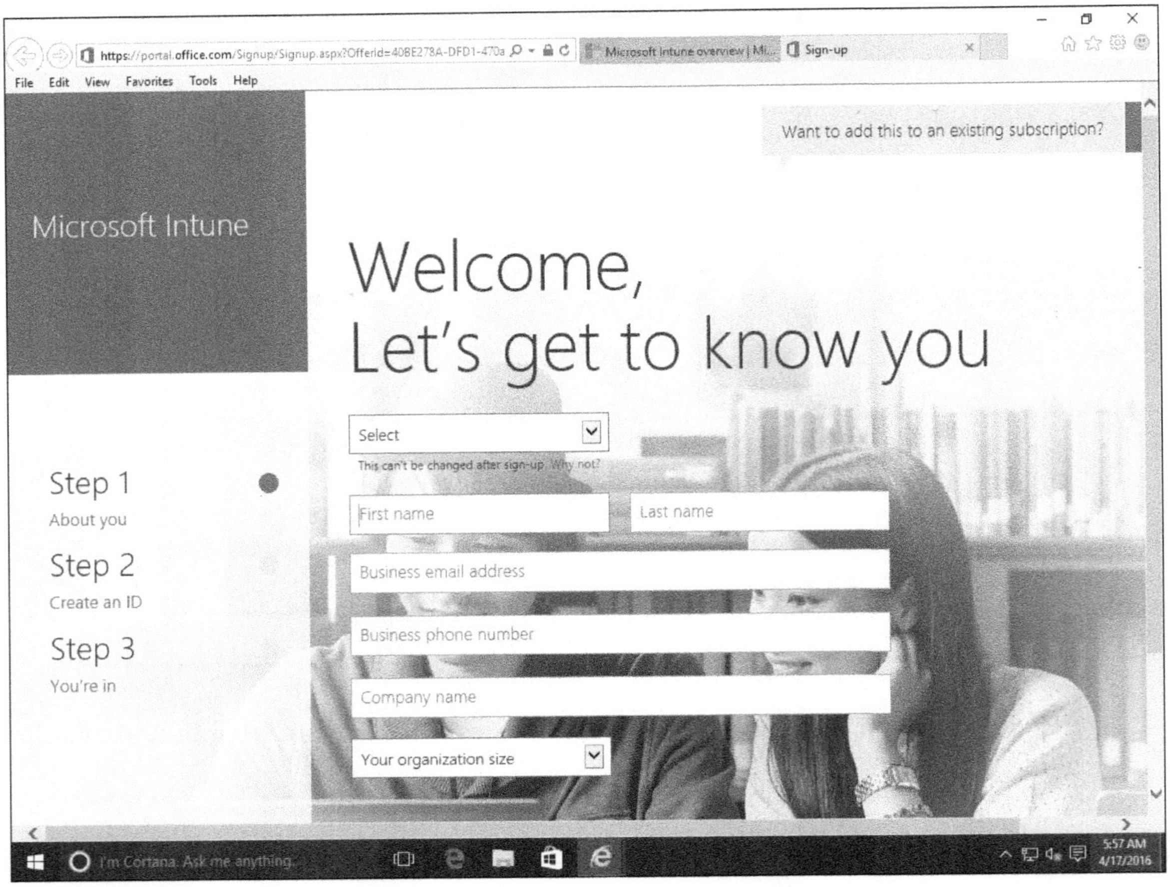

Figure 1-3
Creating a Microsoft Intune account

4. On the Create your user ID page, type the following:

   User name: **<FirstInitial><LastName>**

   Therefore, if your name is John Smith, you would type:

   JSmith

5. For your company, type:

   <FirstName><LastName>Training<Month><Year>

   Therefore, if your name is John Smith and you are performing this lab in June 2015, you would type:

   JohnSmithTraining062015 (in front of .onmicrosoft.com)

Question 7	*What is your company name?*

6. For the Create new password text box and the Confirm new password text box, type **Pa$$w0rd**. Click **Next**.

7. On the Prove. You're. Not. A. Robot. page, type your phone number and then click **Text me**.

8. In the Enter your verification code text box, type the code that you received on your phone and then click **Create my account**.

9. On the Save this info page, record the sign-in page and user ID. Click **You're ready to go**.

10. On the Get Started with Microsoft Intune page, click **Start**.

11. When the Office 365 Admin center preview page opens, click the Admin centers icon and then log in to **Intune**.

12. If a message appears, indicating the application requires Microsoft Silverlight, click **Get Microsoft Silverlight**. When you are prompted to run or save Silverlight_x64.exe, click **Run**. If the User Account Control dialog box displays, click **Yes**.

13. In the Install Silverlight dialog box, click **Install now**. When you are prompted to enable Microsoft Update, click **Next**. Click **Close**.

14. If you are prompted to log in, type **Pa$$w0rd** in the Password text box.

15. Click the **Admin** icon.

16. Take a screen shot of the Administration Overview page by pressing **Alt+PrtScr** and then paste it into your Lab01_worksheet file in the page provided by pressing **Ctrl+V**.

17. Close **Internet Explorer**.

Exercise 1.4	Sideloading Windows Store Apps to Microsoft Intune
Overview	In this exercise, you will download the PowerPoint Viewer, upload the executable to Microsoft Intune, and then configure Microsoft Intune so that it can be deployed to your Microsoft Intune clients.
Mindset	There are several ways in which you can install applications using Microsoft Intune. One method is Sideloading, which is the process of installing Windows Store applications without using the Windows Store.
Completion time	20 minutes

1. Open File Explorer by clicking the **File Explorer** icon on the taskbar.

2. Navigate to the **C:** folder.

3. At the top of the window, click the **New folder** button. For the folder name, type **Software**.

4. On the computer running Windows 10 that is connected to the Internet, open **Internet Explorer**.

5. Go to **https://www.microsoft.com/en-us/download/details.aspx?id=13** and download **PowerPoint Viewer**. Save the PowerPoint Viewer to the **C:\Software** folder.

6. Go to the Microsoft Intune website (**https://manage.microsoft.com**) and log in to Microsoft Intune.

7. Click the **Apps** workspace. The Apps workspace is shown in Figure 1-4.

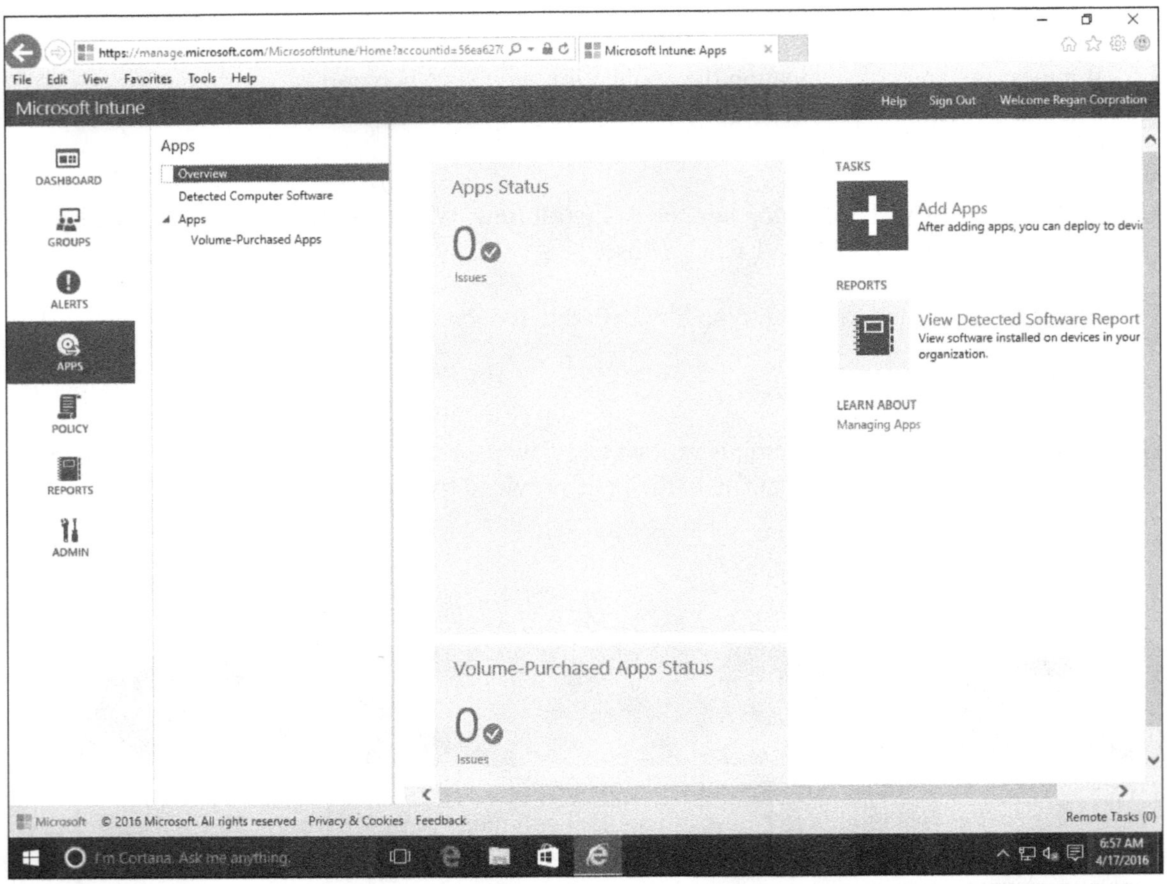

Figure 1-4
Accessing the Apps workspace

8. Under Tasks, click **Add Apps**. If you are prompted to confirm that you want to run Microsoft Intune Software Publisher, click **Run**. If you are prompted to sign in, log in with an administrator account for Intune.

9. In the Add Software Wizard, on the Before you begin page, click **Next**. The Software Setup page opens.

Question 8	*What are the default software installer file types?*

10. In the Specify the location of the software setup files text box, type **C:\Software \PowerPointViewer.exe** and then click **Next**.

11. On the Software description page, in the Publisher text box, type **Microsoft**. Click **Next**.

12. On the Requirements page, answer the following question and then click **Next**.

Question 9	*What is the default architecture and the default operating system?*

13. On the Detection rules page, select the Use the **default detection rules** option and then click **Next**.

14. On the Command line arguments page, click **Next**.

15. On the Returns codes page, click **Next**.

16. On the Summary page, click **Upload**.

17. When the software is uploaded, take a screen shot showing that the data was uploaded successfully by pressing **Alt+PrtScr** and then paste it into your Lab01_worksheet file in the page provided by pressing **Ctrl+V**.

18. Click **Close**.

19. Click the **Apps** workspace and then click **Apps Status**.

20. At the top of the window, click **Manage Deployment**.

21. In the Deploy Software Wizard, on the Select Groups page, click **All Computers** and then click **Add**. Click **Next**.

22. On the Deployment Action page, under Approval, select **Required Install** from the pull-down menu. For the Deadline, select **One month**, displaying one month from now.

23. Click **Finish**.

24. Take a screen shot showing Apps, including the Deployed column, by pressing **Alt+PrtScr** and then paste it into your Lab01_worksheet file in the page provided by pressing **Ctrl+V**. You may need to readjust the columns to show the Deployed colum.

25. Close **Internet Explorer**.

Lab Challenge	Creating and Integrating a Microsoft Account
Overview	In this exercise, you will create a Microsoft Account using Windows 10 Settings on a system that has access to the Internet. To use a Microsoft Account with Windows 10, the system cannot be part of a domain. For you to create this account, you will need a Hotmail, MSN, or Outlook email account.
Mindset	A user account is used to identify a user or other identity on a system, which can be used in authentication, authorization, and auditing. Microsoft accounts enable you to synchronize your desktop across multiple Windows 10 devices.
Completion time	20 minutes

1. On a computer that has an Internet connection, ensure that the server is not part of a domain. If the system is part of a domain, follow these instructions:

   a. Right-click the **Start** button and choose **System**.

   b. On the System page, click **Change settings**.

   c. In the System Properties dialog box, click the **Change** button.

   d. In the Computer Name/Domain Changes dialog box, select **Workgroup**. In the Workgroup text box, type **WG** and then click **OK**.

   e. Read the warning and then click **OK**.

   f. In the Welcome dialog box, click **OK**.

   g. When a message indicates that you must restart your computer to apply these changes, click **OK**.

   h. Click **Close** to close the System Properties dialog box.

   i. When a message indicates that you must restart your computer to apply these changes, click **Restart Now**.

   j. Log in as administrator with the password of **Pa$$w0rd**.

2. Click the **Start** button to open the Start Menu and then click **Settings**.

3. Click **Accounts**.

Question 10	*If the Family & other users option does not appear, what is the problem?*

4. Click the **Family & other users** option, as shown in Figure 1-5.

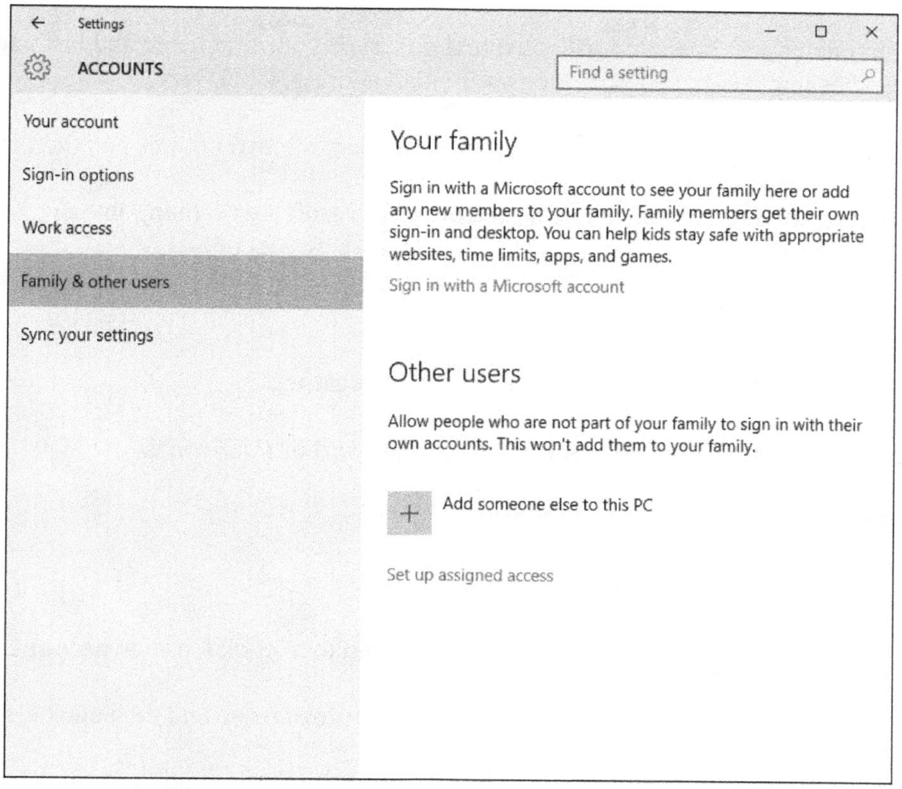

Figure 1-5
Managing Family and other users on a standalone Windows 10 computer

5. Click the **Add someone else to this PC** option.
6. On the How will this person sign in? page, to use an existing Microsoft Account, in the Email or phone text box, click **I don't have this person's sign-in information** link.
7. On the Let's create your account page, type your First name and Last name in the appropriate text boxes.
8. In the someone@example.com address, type the following:

   <FirstName>.<LastName>.Training<Month><Year>@Outlook.com

   Therefore, if your name is John Smith, and it is April 2016, you would type:

   John.Smith.Training042016@Outlook.com
9. For the Password, type **Pa$$w0rd**.
10. In the Birthmonth, Day, and Year boxes, specify your birthday. Click **Next**.

11. On the Add security info page, in the Phone number text box, type your phone number and then click **Next**.

12. In the First name text box and Last name text box, type your first name and last name. In the someone@example.com text box, type your email address. Click **Next**.

13. On the See what's most relevant to you option, deselect the two options and then click **Next**.

    a. **Enhance my online experience by lettings Microsoft Advertising use my account information.**

    b. **Send my promotional offers from Microsoft.**

14. Click the **Start** button, click **Power**, and then click **Restart**.

15. Log in to Windows as **administrator** with the password of **Pa$$w0rd**.

16. Click the **Start** button and then click **Settings**.

17. Click **Accounts > Family & other users.**

18. Click the new Microsoft account that you created and then click **Change account type**.

19. Change the Account type from Standard User to **Administrator** and then click **OK**.

20. Take a screen shot of the Accounts page by pressing **Alt+PrtScr** and then paste it into your Lab01_worksheet file in the page provided by pressing **Ctrl+V**. You may need to readjust the columns to show the Deployed colum.

21. To remove the account, click **Remove**.

22. When you are prompted to confirm that you want to delete the account and data, click the **Delete account and data** button.

23. Close the **Control Panel**.

24. If the computer was part of a domain, join the PC back to the domain.

    a. Right-click the **Start** button and choose **System**.

    b. On the System page, click **Change settings**.

    c. In the System Properties dialog box, click the **Change** button.

    d. Click the Domain option and in the Domain text box, type **adatum.com** (or the name of the school domain).

    e. In the Windows security dialog box, in the User name text box, type administrator. In the Password text box, type **Pa$$w0rd**. If your school domain does not use this account, specify the appropriate username and password. Click **OK**.

f. When you are welcome to the domain, click **OK**.

g. When it a message indicates that you must restart your computer to apply these changes, click **OK**.

h. To close the System Properties dialog, click **Close**.

i. When you are prompted to restart your computer, click **Restart Now**.

End of lab.

LAB 2
SUPPORTING AUTHENTICATION AND AUTHORIZATION

THIS LAB CONTAINS THE FOLLOWING EXERCISES AND ACTIVITIES:

Exercise 2.1 Managing Local User Passwords

Exercise 2.2 Using a PIN and Picture Password

Exercise 2.3 Creating and Managing Domain User Accounts

Exercise 2.4 Using Credential Manager

Exercise 2.5 Creating and Supporting HomeGroups

Lab Challenge Managing Account Policies

BEFORE YOU BEGIN

The lab environment consists of student workstations connected to a local area network, along with a server that functions as the domain controller for a domain called adatum.com. The computers required for this lab are listed in Table 2-1.

Table 2-1
Computers required for Lab 2

Computer	*Operating System*	*Computer Name*
Server	Windows Server 2012 R2	LON-DC1
Client	Windows 10	LON-CL1
Client	Windows 10	LON-CL4

In addition to the computers, you will also require the software listed in Table 2-2 to complete Lab 2.

Table 2-2
Software required for Lab 2

Software	*Location*
Lab 2 student worksheet	Lab02_worksheet.docx (provided by instructor)

Working with Lab Worksheets

Each lab in this manual requires that you answer questions, shoot screen shots, and perform other activities that you will document in a worksheet named for the lab, such as Lab02_worksheet.docx. You will find these worksheets on the book companion site. It is recommended that you use a USB flash drive to store your worksheets, so you can submit them to your instructor for review. As you perform the exercises in each lab, open the appropriate worksheet file, fill in the required information, and then save the file to your flash drive.

SCENARIO

After completing this lab, you will be able to:

- Create a local and domain user account
- Manage local and domain user passwords
- Manage PIN and picture passwords
- Manage credentials with Credential Manager
- Create and support a HomeGroup
- Manage account policies

Estimated lab time: 110 minutes

Exercise 2.1	Managing Local User Passwords
Overview	In this exercise, you will create a new local user account. You will then manage the new user's password by using Settings and the Computer Management console.
Mindset	Authentication represents the way that security principals (users, computers, and processes) prove their identity before they are allowed to connect to your network. The most common authentication method is passwords.
Completion time	25 minutes

1. Log in to **LON-CL1** as **adatum\administrator** with the password of **Pa$$w0rd**.
2. Right-click the **Start** button and choose **Computer Management**.
3. In the Computer Management console, expand the **Local Users and Groups** node and click the **Users** node, as shown in Figure 2-1.

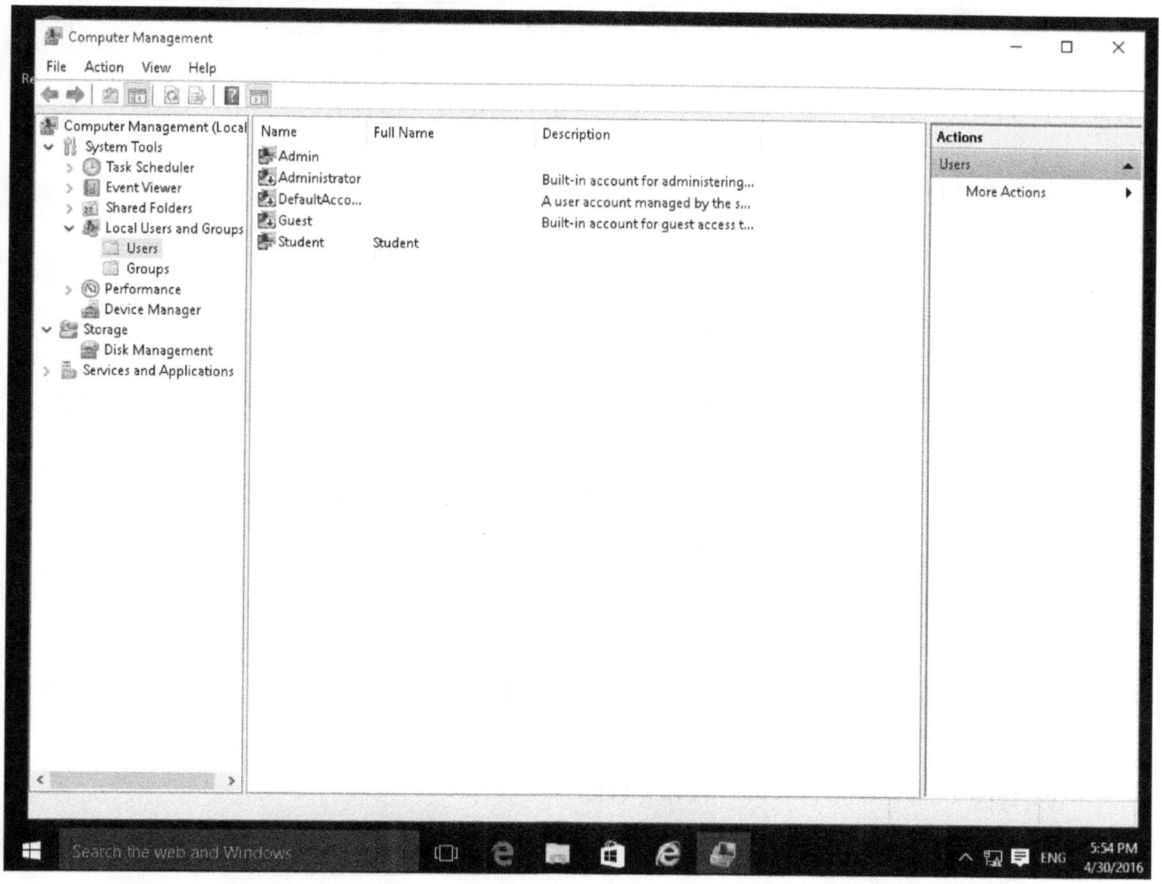

Figure 2-1
Managing local user accounts

4. Right-click the **Users** node and choose **New User**.
5. In the New User dialog box, type the following information and then click the **Create** button.

   User name: **JSmith**

   Full Name: **John Smith**

   Password and Confirm password: **Pa$$w0rd**
6. Click the **Close** button to close the New User dialog box.

7. Take a screen shot showing the Computer Management console showing the new user by pressing **Alt+PrtScr** and then paste it into your Lab02_worksheet file in the page provided by pressing **Ctrl+V**.

8. Double-click the **JSmith** account.

9. In the JSmith Properties dialog box, click the **Member Of** tab.

Question 1	*Which group is JSmith a member of?*

10. Click the **Add** button.

11. In the Select Groups dialog box, answer the following question.

Question 2	*What location will the group come from based on the From this location field?*

12. In the Enter the object names to select text box, type **Administrators** and then click **OK**.

13. To close the JSmith Properties dialog box, click **OK**.

14. Right-click the JSmith account and choose **Set Password**.

15. In the Set Password for JSmith dialog box, click **Proceed**.

16. In the Set Password for JSmith dialog box, in the New password and Confirm password text boxes, type **Password01** and then click **OK**.

17. When a dialog box opens stating the password is set, click **OK**.

18. Close the Computer Management console.

19. Click the **Start** button and then click **Settings**.

20. In the Settings window, click **Accounts**.

21. Click **Other users**. You should see the John Smith account.

22. Log out of Windows 10 by clicking the **Start** button, right-clicking **Administrator**, and choosing **Sign out**.

23. At the bottom of the screen, click **Other user**. Then log in as **Lon-CL1\JSmith** with the password of **Password01**. It will take a couple minutes to create a profile for JSmith.

24. Click the **Start** button. Right-click **John Smith** and choose **Change account settings**.

25. Click **Sign-in options**.

26. In the Password section, click the **Change** button.

27. When you are prompted to provide the Current password, type **Password01** and then click **Next**.

28. In the New password and Reenter password text boxes, type **Pa$$w0rd**. In the Password hint text box, type **Default**. Click **Next**.

29. Take a screen shot showing that the password was changed, by pressing **Alt+PrtScr** and then paste it into your Lab02_worksheet file in the page provided by pressing **Ctrl+V**.

30. Click the **Finish** button.

Question 3	*Which message appears?*

Question 4	*Since the password includes all four types of characters (complex password) and is 8 characters long, what is the real reason this message appears?*

31. Click **Close**.

32. Right-click the **Start** button and choose **Computer Management**.

33. In the Computer Management console, expand the **Local Users and Groups** node and then click the **Users** node.

34. Right-click the **JSmith** and account and choose **Set Password**.

35. In the Set Password for JSmith dialog box, click the **Proceed** button.

36. In the New password and Confirm password text boxes, type **Pa$$w0rd** and then click **OK**.

37. When the password has been set, click **OK**.

38. Close **Computer Management**.

On LON-CL1, stay logged in as LON-CL1\JSmith for the next exercise.

Exercise 2.2	Using a PIN and Picture Password
Overview	In this exercise, you will configure a PIN and picture password for the new account you just created in Exercise 2.1.
Mindset	Two other forms of authentication based on what you know is the personal identification number (PIN) and picture password. A PIN is a short numeric password used to authenticate a user to a system. A picture password consists of two components: a picture and a gesture that you draw on it. You can pick the image from a default set included with the Windows 10 installation or select your own.
Completion time	20 minutes

1. On **LON-CL1**, with you logged in as JSmith, click the **Start** button and then click **Settings**.
2. Click **Accounts**.
3. Click **Sign-in options**, as shown in Figure 2-2.

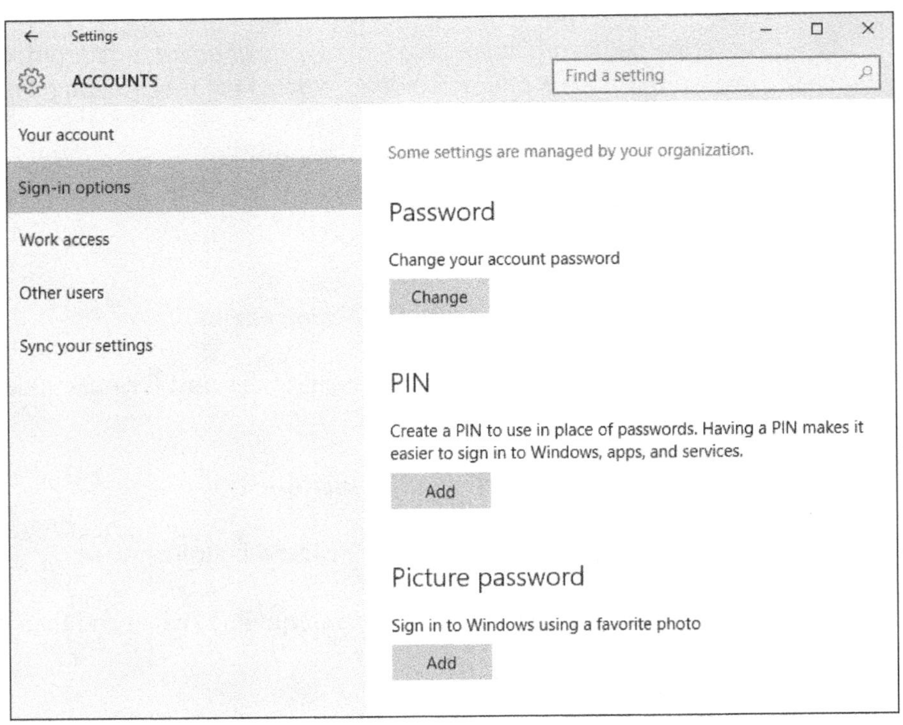

Figure 2-2
Accessing sign-in options

4. In the PIN section, click the **Add** button.
5. On the First, verify your account password page, in the text box, type **Pa$$w0rd** and then click **OK**.

6. On the Set up a PIN page, in the New PIN and Confirm PIN text boxes, type **1234** and then click **OK**.

7. Take a screen shot showing the Accounts page by pressing **Alt+PrtScr** and then paste it into your Lab02_worksheet file in the page provided by pressing **Ctrl+V**.

8. Log out of Windows 10.

9. Start the login as John Smith, but instead of providing a password, click **Sign-in Options**.

Question 5	*What are the two options can you use to log in with?*

10. In the PIN text box, type **1234**.

Question 6	*Which is more secure, passwords or PINs? Explain your answer.*

11. Click the **Start** button and then click **Settings**.

12. Click **Accounts**.

13. Click **Sign-in options**.

14. To delete a PIN, in the PIN section, click **Remove**.

15. When you are prompted to confirm that you want to remove your PIN, click the **Remove** button. You might need to scroll down to see the Remove button.

16. In the First, verify your account password dialog box, in the Password text box, type **Pa$$w0rd** and then click **OK**.

17. In the Picture password section, click the **Add** button.

18. On the Create a picture password page, in the text box, type **Pa$$Word** and then click **OK**.

19. On the Welcome to picture password page, click **Choose Picture**.

20. In the Open dialog box, navigate to **C:\ProgramData\Microsoft\Windows NT\MSScan** folder and then click the **WelcomeScan** picture. Click **Open**. If you don't see the C:\ProgramData folder, in the File name, text box, type **C:\ProgramData** and then press **Enter** to get you started. The ProgramData folder is a hidden folder.

21. Click **Use this Picture**.

22. Draw three gestures on your picture, as shown on Figure 2-3. Be patient when drawing the gesture three times. Simply make sure the start and end points are the same each time.

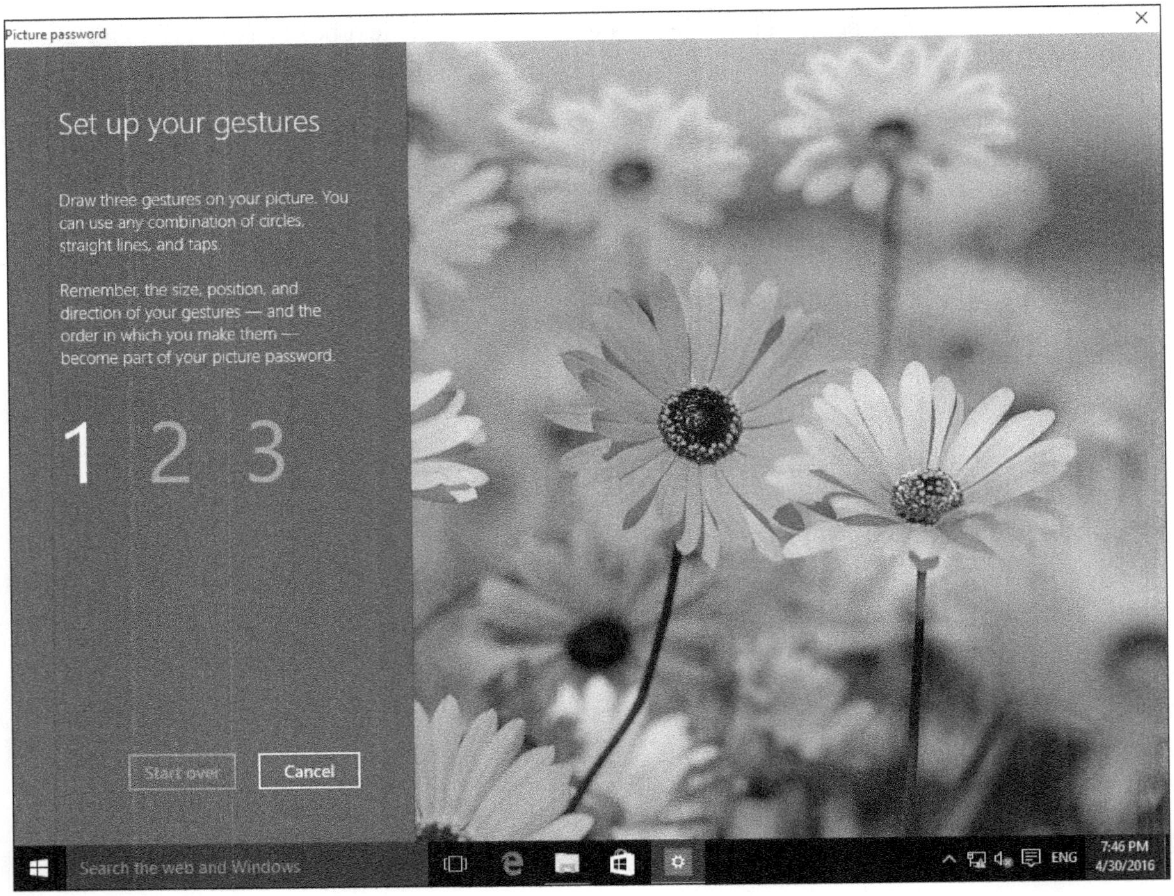

Figure 2-3
Defining gestures

23. Take a screen shot of the Congratulations page by pressing **Alt+PrtScr** and then paste it into your Lab02_worksheet file in the page provided by pressing **Ctrl+V**.
24. Click **Finish**.
25. Log out of Windows 10.
26. Log in with the user account using the picture password.
27. Click the **Start** button, and click **Settings**. When the Settings page opens, click **Accounts**.
28. On the Accounts page, click **Sign-in options**.
29. In the Picture password section, click the **Remove** button.
30. Close the Settings window.

Remain logged in to LON-CL1 for the next exercise.

Exercise 2.3	Creating and Managing Domain User Accounts
Overview	In this exercise, you will use Active Directory Users and Computers to create a domain account. You will then give new domain account access to a computer running Windows 10.
Mindset	A domain is a collection of user and computer accounts that are grouped together to enable centralized management and to apply security. The user and computer accounts are stored in an Active Directory database that is stored on domain controllers. The domain-based accounts provide access to resources on multiple systems.
Completion time	25 minutes

1. Log in to **LON-DC1** as **adatum\administrator** with the password of **Pa$$w0rd**.
2. On **LON-DC1**, in Server Manager, click **Tools > Active Directory Users and Computers**.
3. In Active Directory Users and Computers console, expand the **Adatum.com** node and then click the **Users** node, as shown in Figure 2-4.

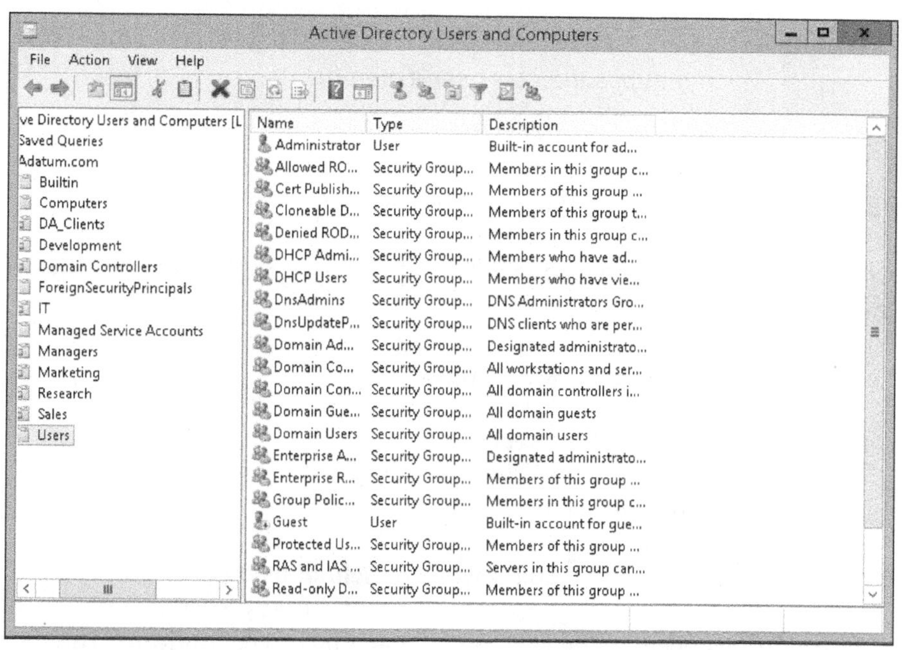

Figure 2-4
Managing users with Active Directory Users and Computers

4. Right-click the **Users** node and choose **New > User**.
5. In the New Object – User dialog box, type the following informaiton and then click **Next**:

   First name: **Tay**

   Last name: **Inham**

   Full name: **Tay Inham**

   User logon name: **TInham**
6. In the Password and Confirm password text boxes, type **Pa$$w0rd** and then click **Next**.
7. Take a screen shot showing the new object to be created by pressing **Alt+PrtScr** and then paste it into your Lab02_worksheet file in the page provided by pressing **Ctrl+V**.
8. Click **Finish**.
9. Right-click the new user that you just created and choose **Properties**.
10. In the Tay Inham Properties dialog box, click the **Member Of** tab.

Question 7	*Which group is the new user a member of?*

11. Click **OK** to close the Tay Inham Properties dialog box.
12. On **LON-CL1**, if you are not logged in as JSmith, login as **LON-CL1\JSmith** with the password of **Pa$$w0rd**.
13. Click the **Start** button and then click **Settings.**
14. In the Settings window opens, click **Accounts**.
15. On the Accounts page, click **Other users**.
16. On the Other users page, click the **Add a work or school user** option.
17. On the Account info is open, in the User account text box, type **adatum\TInham**. For the Account type, select **Administrator** and then click **Add**.
18. Take a screen shot of the Other users page by pressing **Alt+PrtScr** and then paste it into your Lab02_worksheet file in the page provided by pressing **Ctrl+V**.
19. Close the Settings window.
20. Log off **LON-CL1**.

21. On **LON-CL1**, press **Ctrl+Alt+Del**. When the logon screen appears, click **Other user**. Then log in as **adatum\TInham** with the password of **Pa$$w0rd**.
22. When you are prompted to change the password, click **OK**.
23. In the New password and Confirm password text boxes, type **Password01** and then press **Enter**.
24. When the password has been changed, click **OK**.
25. Click **Sign in**.
26. Right-click the **Start** button and choose **Computer Management**.
27. Expand the **Local Users and Groups** node and then click **Groups**.
28. Double-click the **Administrators** group.

Question 8	*Which groups and users are part of the Administrators group?*

29. Close the Administrators Properties dialog box by clicking **OK**.

Leave LON-CL1 open for the next exercise.

Exercise 2.4	Using Credential Manager
Overview	In this exercise, you will use Credential manager to manage the credentials for users when they access servers and websites.
Mindset	Credential Manager allows you to store credentials (such as user names and passwords) that are used to log on to websites or other computers on a network. By storing your credentials, Windows can automatically log you on to websites or other computers. Credentials are saved on your computer, in special folders that are called vaults.
Completion time	10 minutes

1. On **LON-CL1**, right-click the **Start** button and choose **Control Panel**.
2. In the Control Panel, click **User Accounts > Credential Manager**. The Credential Manager control panel applet appears, as shown in Figure 2-5.

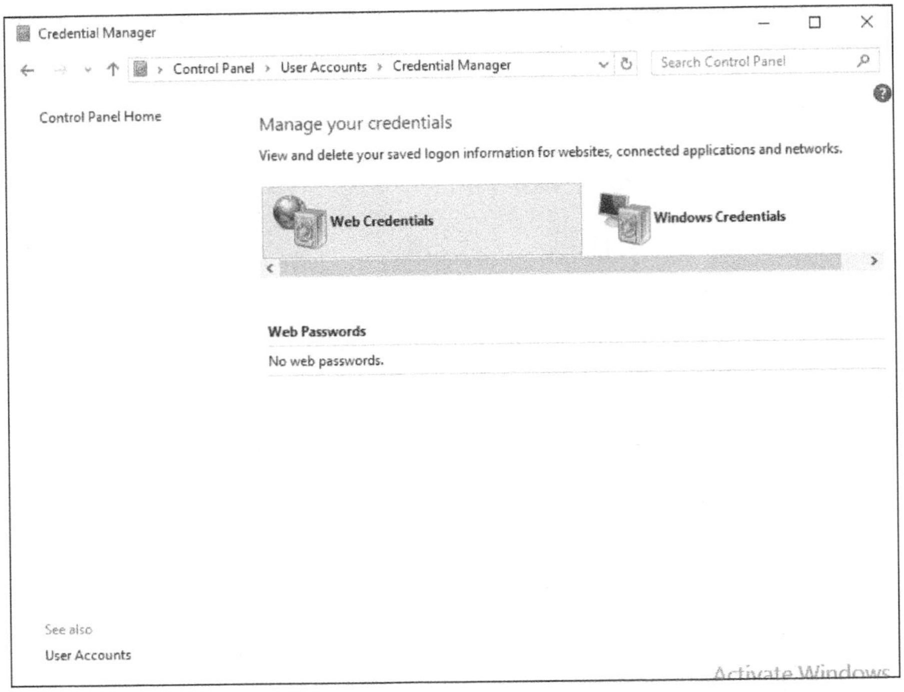

Figure 2-5
Managing stored credentials

3. Click **Windows Credentials** and then click **Add a Windows credential**. The Add a Windows Credential dialog box appears.

4. In the Internet or network address text box, type **\\RemotePC**.

5. In the User name text box, type **Administrator**.

6. In the Password text box, type **Pa$$w0rd** and then click **OK**. The credential appears in the Windows Credentials list. Now any time that you access \\RemotePC, you will use the username administrator with the password of Pa$$w0rd.

7. Take a screen shot of the Windows Credentials control panel showing the new credential you entered by pressing **Ctrl+PrtScr** and then paste the resulting image into the Lab02_worksheet file in the page provided by pressing **Ctrl+V**.

Question 9	*How would you move your saved credentials from one computer to another?*

Exercise 2.5	Creating and Supporting HomeGroups
Overview	In this exercise, you will create and support a HomeGroup on a computer running Windows 10.
Mindset	A HomeGroup is a group of computers on a home network that can share files and printers. To protect your HomeGroup, you can use a password. Similar to share permissions, other users cannot change the files that you share unless you give them permission to do so.
Completion time	15 minutes

1. Log on to **LON-CL4** as **Admin** with the password of **Pa$$w0rd**.
2. On **LON-CL4**, right-click the **Start** button and choose **Control Panel**.
3. In the Control Panel, click **Network and Internet > Network and Sharing Center**.
4. In the Network and Sharing Center control panel, click the **HomeGroup** link at the bottom of the screen. The HomeGroup page opens, as shown in Figure 2-6.

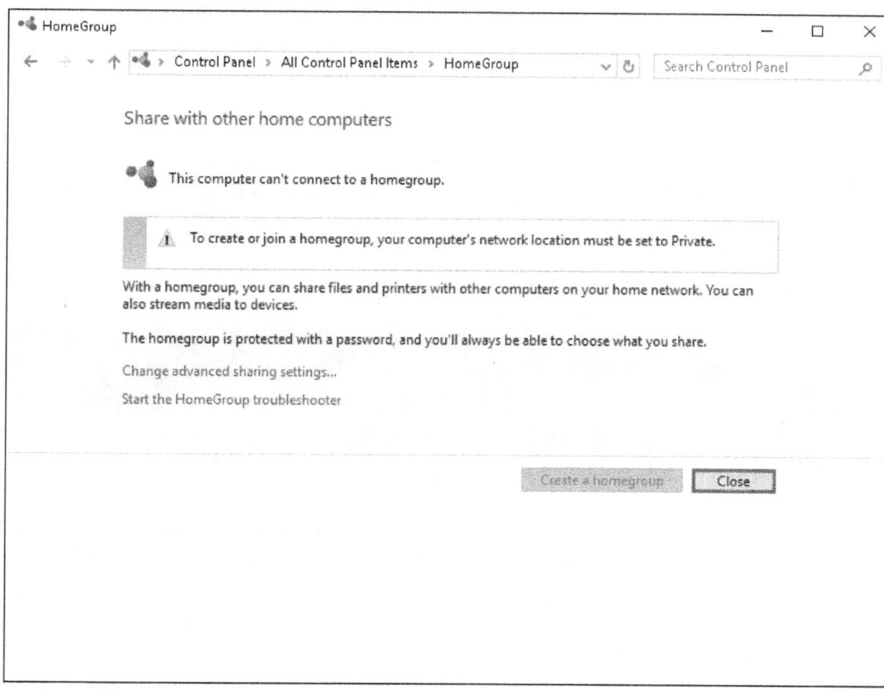

Figure 2-6
Managing HomeGroups

Question 10	*Why is the Create a homegroup button greyed out?*

5. Click **Start the HomeGroup troubleshooter**.
6. When the troubleshooter opens, click **Next**.
7. When you are prompted to troubleshoot network problems, click **Skip this step**.
8. When a message prompts you to change the network location to Private, click **Apply this fix**.
9. When the problem is fixed, click **Close**.
10. Click **Create a homegroup** button.
11. In the Create a HomeGroup wizard, click **Next**.

Question 11	*By default, which library or folder is shared?*

12. Click **Next**.

Question 12	*What is the password for adding other computers to your homegroup?*

13. Click **Finish**.
14. Take a screen shot of the HomeGroup page by pressing **Ctrl+PrtScr** and then paste the resulting image into the Lab02_worksheet file in the page provided by pressing **Ctrl+V**.

Lab Challenge	Managing Account Policies
Overview	In this exercise, you will define a domain-level password policy, including maximum password length and password history.
Mindset	At the domain level, you can define only account policies, which include password policy, account lockout policy, and Kerberos policy. Because most organizations have only one domain, you can set only one.
Completion time	15 minutes

1. Log on to **LON-DC1** as **adatum\administrator** with the password of **Pa$$w0rd**.
2. On **LON-DC1**, using **Server Manager**, click **Tools > Group Policy Management**. The Group Policy Management console opens.

3. Expand the **Forest: Adatum.com** node, expand the **Domains** node, and then click the **Adatum.com** node.

4. Right-click **Default Domain Policy** and choose **Edit**. The Group Policy Management Editor opens.

5. In the left window pane, expand the **Computer Configuration** node, expand the **Policies** node, and then expand the **Windows Settings** folder. Then expand the **Security Settings** node. In the Security Settings node, expand **Account Policies** and then select **Password Policy**, as shown in Figure 2-7.

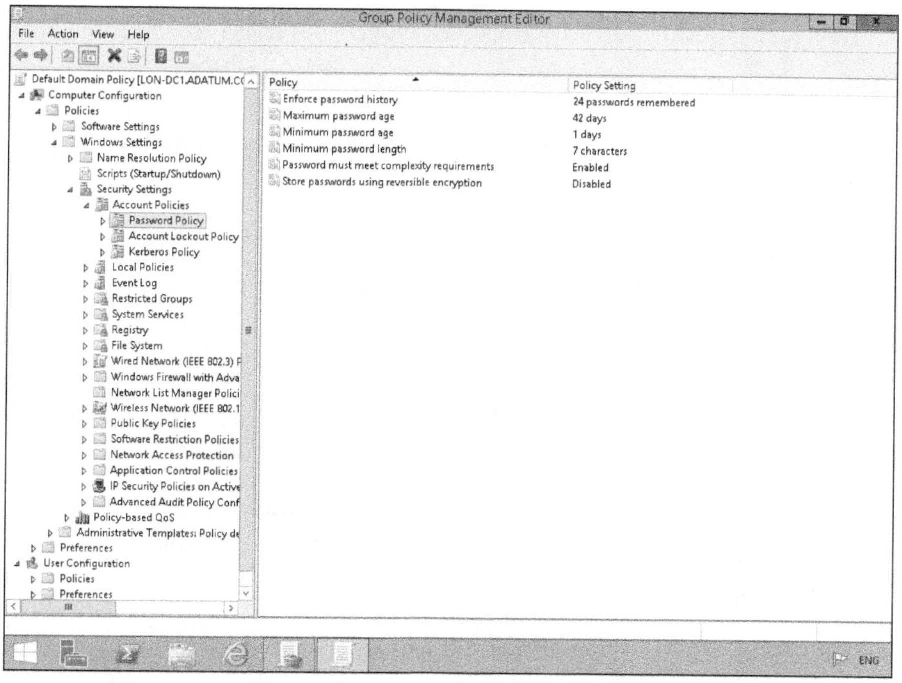

Figure 2-7
Managing GPOs

Question 13	*What is the maximum password age?*

Question 14	*What is the minimum password length?*

Question 15	*How does enforce password history and minimum password age work together to keep a network environment secure?*

6. Double-click the **Minimum password length**. In the Minimum password length Properties dialog box, change the 7 value to **8 characters**. Click **OK** to close the Minimum password length Properties dialog box.

7. Take a screen shot of the Group Policy Management Editor window by pressing **Alt+Prt Scr** and then paste it into your Lab02 worksheet file in the page provided by pressing **Ctrl+V**.

8. Using the Default Domain Policy Group Policy Management Editor console, under Account Policies, click **Account Lockout Policy**.

Question 16	*How are the account lockout settings currently set?*

9. Double-click **Account lockout duration**. In the Account lockout duration Properties dialog box, click to enable the **Define this policy setting**.

Question 17	*What is the default value for the Account lockout duration?*

10. Click **OK** to close the Account lockout duration Properties dialog box. In the Suggested Value Changes dialog box, look at the suggested settings and then click **OK**.

Question 18	*How many invalid logon attempts can be made that will cause an account to be locked?*

11. Take a screen shot of the Account Lockout Policy window by pressing **Alt+Prt Scr** and then paste it into your Lab02_worksheet file in the page provided by pressing **Ctrl+V**.

12. Close the Group Policy Management Editor window for the Default Domain Policy and then close the Group Policy Management console.

End of lab.

LAB 3
MIGRATING AND CONFIGURING USER DATA

THIS LAB CONTAINS THE FOLLOWING EXERCISES AND ACTIVITIES:

Exercise 3.1	Configuring and Managing User Profiles
Exercise 3.2	Configuring Folder Locations
Exercise 3.3	Installing the User State Migration Tool
Exercise 3.4	Migrating User Profiles
Lab Challenge	Creating a Roaming User Profile

BEFORE YOU BEGIN

The lab environment consists of student workstations connected to a local area network, along with a server that functions as the domain controller for a domain called adatum.com. The computers required for this lab are listed in Table 3-1.

Table 3-1
Computers required for Lab 3

Computer	Operating System	Computer Name
Server (VM 1)	Windows Server 2012 R2	LON-DC1
Client (VM 2)	Windows 10	LON-CL1
Client (VM 3)	Windows 10	LON-CL4

In addition to the computers, you will also require the software listed in Table 3-2 to complete Lab 3.

Table 3-2
Software required for Lab 3

Software	Location
Lab 3 student worksheet	Lab03_worksheet.docx (provided by instructor)

Working with Lab Worksheets

Each lab in this manual requires that you answer questions, shoot screen shots, and perform other activities that you will document in a worksheet named for the lab, such as Lab03_worksheet.docx. You will find these worksheets on the book companion site. It is recommended that you use a USB flash drive to store your worksheets, so you can submit them to your instructor for review. As you perform the exercises in each lab, open the appropriate worksheet file, fill in the required information, and then save the file to your flash drive.

SCENARIO

After completing this lab, you will be able to:

- Configure and manage local user profiles
- Configure folder locations
- Install the User State Migration Tool
- Migrate a user profile
- Create a roaming user profile

Estimated lab time: 135 minutes

Exercise 3.1	Configuring and Managing User Profiles
Overview	In this exercise, you will create a new local user and then move the profile to the C:\Profiles folder.
Mindset	A roaming user profile is a copy of a local user profile that is stored on a shared server drive, making it accessible from anywhere on the network.
Completion time	30 minutes

1. Log in to **LON-CL1** as **adatum\administrator** with the password of **Pa$$w0rd**.
2. On **LON-CL1**, right-click the **Start** button and choose **Computer Management**.
3. In the Computer Management console, expand the **Local Users and Group** node and then click **Users**, as shown in Figure 3-1.

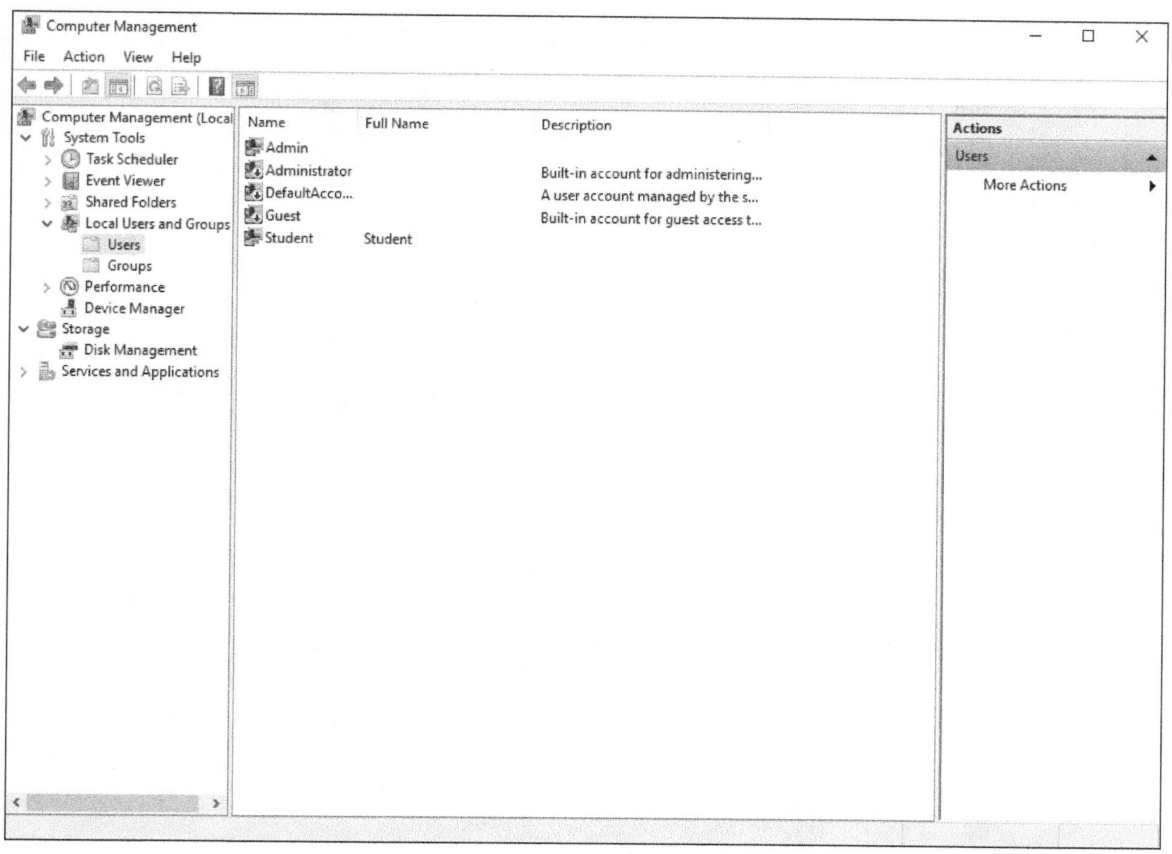

Figure 3-1
Showing local users

4. Right-click the **Users** node and choose **New User**.

5. In the New User dialog box, type the following information:

   User name: **TWayne**

   Full name: **Tony Wayne**

   Password and Confirm password text boxes: **Pa$$w0rd**

6. Deselect the **User must change password at next logon** option and then click **Create**.
7. Close the New User dialog box by clicking **Close**.
8. Log off **LON-CL1**.
9. Log on to **LON-CL1** as **LON-CL1\TWayne** with the password of **Pa$$w0rd**. It will take a couple minutes to create a new profile for Tony Wayne.
10. Open File Explorer by clicking the **File Explorer** icon on the taskbar.
11. When File Explorer opens, click **This PC** and then double-click **Local Disk (C:)**.
12. Double-click the **Users** folder and then double-click the **TWayne** folder.
13. Take a screen shot of the TWayne folder by pressing **Alt+PrtScr** and then paste it into your Lab03_worksheet file in the page provided by pressing **Ctrl+V**.
14. Log off **LON-CL1**.
15. Log on to **LON-CL1** as **adatum\administrator** with the password of **Pa$$w0rd**.
16. On **LON-CL1**, open File Explorer by clicking the **File Explorer** icon on the taskbar.
17. When File Explorer opens, click **This PC** and then double-click **Local Disk (C:)**.
18. Right-click the white part of the **Local Disk (C:)** window and choose **New > Folder**. For the name, type **Profiles**. Press **Enter**.
19. Right-click the **Start** button and choose **Computer Management**.
20. In the Computer Management console, expand the **Local Users and Groups** node and then click the **Users** node.
21. Double-click the **TWayne** account.
22. In the TWayne Prooperties dialog box, click the **Profile** tab.
23. In the User profile section, in the Profile path text box, type **C:\Profiles\%USERNAME%** and then click **Apply**.

Question 1	*What did %USERNAME% change to?*

24. Close the TWayne Properties dialog box by clicking **OK**.
25. Log off **LON-CL1**.
26. Log on as **LON-CL1\TWayne** with the password of **Pa$$w0rd**.
27. Open File Explorer by clicking the **File Explorer** icon on the taskbar.
28. When File Explorer opens, click **This PC** and then double-click **Local Disk (C:)**. Double-click the **Profiles** folder.
29. Take a screen shot of the Profiles folder by pressing **Alt+PrtScr** and then paste it into your Lab03_worksheet file in the page provided by pressing **Ctrl+V**.
30. Double-click the **TWayne.V5** folder.
31. Log off **LON-CL1**.

Question 2	*Which folders are in the TWayne.V5 folder?*

32. Log on as **LON-CL1\TWayne** with the password of **Pa$$w0rd**.
33. To open File Explorer, click the **File Explorer** button on the taskbar.
34. When File Explorer opens, click **This PC** and then double-click **Local Disk (C:)**. Double-click the **Profiles** folder. Double-click the **TWayne.V5** folder.
35. Take a screen shot of the Profiles folder by pressing **Alt+PrtScr** and then paste it into your Lab03_worksheet file in the page provided by pressing **Ctrl+V**.

Remained logged in as TWayne for the next exercise.

Exercise 3.2	Configuring Folder Locations
Overview	In this exercise, you will change the location of the Music library.
Mindset	You can change the location of your personal folders, such as My Documents, My Music, or My Pictures, by specifying a different folder location. Therefore, if one or more of these personal folders grows or the primary drive reaches its capacity, you can move the location to another drive or to a shared network folder.
Completion time	10 minutes

1. On **LON-CL1**, using File Explorer, create a **C:\Music** folder.
2. Right-click the **Music** library and choose **Properties**, as shown in Figure 3-2. (Do *not* right-click the Music folder that you just created.)

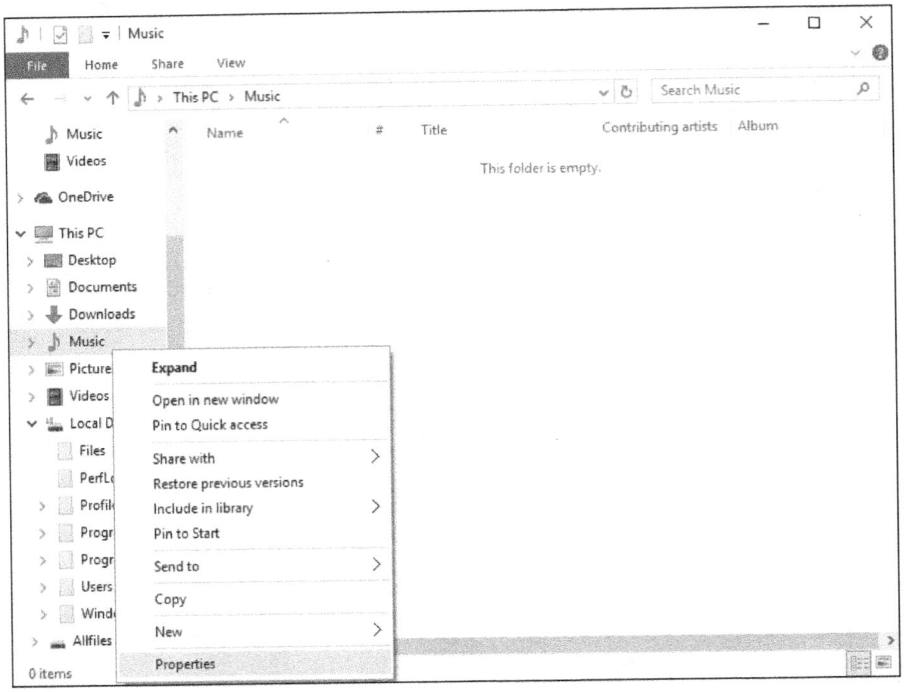

Figure 3-2
Selecting the Properties of the Music folder

3. Click the **Location** tab.
4. Click the **Move** button.
5. In the Select a Destination dialog box, in the Folder text box, type **C:\Music** and then click **Select Folder**.
6. Close the Music Properties dialog box by clicking **OK**.
7. When you are prompted to confirm that you want to move all of the files from the old location to the new location, click **Yes**.
8. In File Explorer, click the **Local Disk (C:)** drive.
9. Take a screen shot of File Explorer showing the Music folder by pressing **Alt+PrtScr** and then paste it into your Lab03_worksheet file in the page provided by pressing **Ctrl+V**.
10. Right-click the **Music** folder and choose **Properties**.
11. In the Music Properties dialog box, click the **Location** tab.
12. Click the **Restore Default** button.

Question 3	*What is the default location?*

13. Click **OK**. When you are prompted to create the Music folder, click **Yes**. When you are prompted to move all of the files from the old location to the new location, click **Yes**.

14. Close **File Explorer**.

15. Log off **LON-CL1**.

Exercise 3.3	Installing the User State Migration Tool
Overview	In this exercise, you will install the User State Migration Tool, which is part of the Windows Assessment and Deployming Kit.
Mindset	One of the most time-consuming tasks you will perform as an administrator is moving user files and settings between computers and operating systems. The User State Migration Tool (USMT) eases this burden. The USMT 10 tool is part of the Windows Assessment and Deployment Kit for Windows 10.
Completion time	10 minutes

1. Log in to **LON-DC1** as **adatum\administrator** with the password of **Pa$$w0rd**.

2. On **LON-DC1**, open File Explorer by clicking the **File Explorer** icon on the taskbar.

3. In File Explorer, navigate to the **C:\Software** folder and then find the adksetup.exe fiel (as shown in Figure 3-3). Double-click **adksetup.exe**.

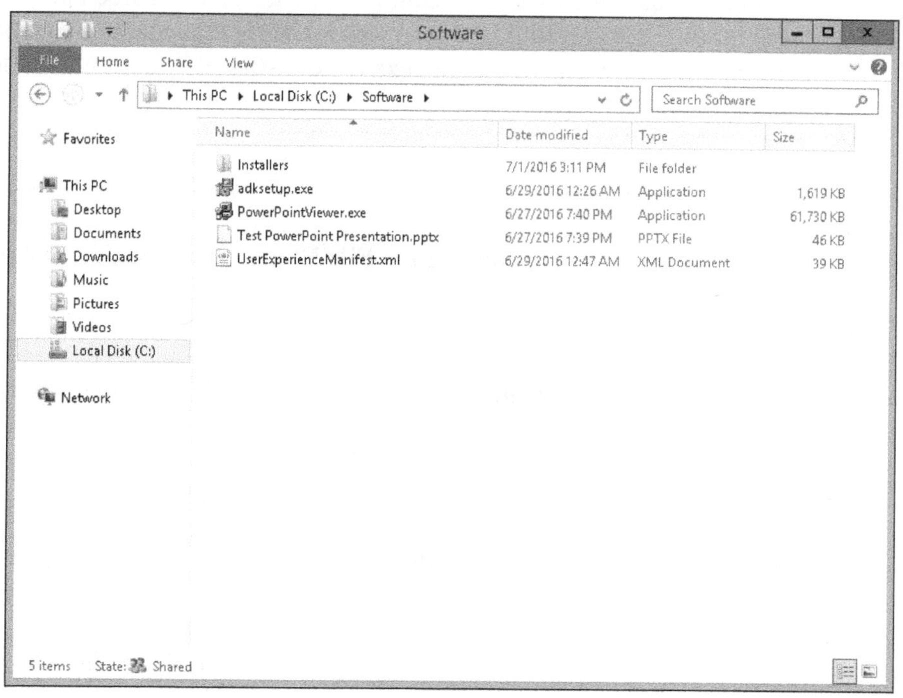

Figure 3-3
Accessing the ADK software folder

4. In the Windows Assessment and Deployment Kit – Windows 10 window, on the Specify Location page, click **Next**.

5. On the Windows Kits Privacy page, click **Next**.

6. On the License Agreement page, click **Accept**.

7. On the Select the features you want to install option, deslect all options except the User State Migration Tool (USMT) and then click **Install**.

8. When USMT is installed, take a screen shot of Welcome screen by pressing **Alt+PrtScr** and then paste it into your Lab03_worksheet file in the page provided by pressing **Ctrl+V**.

9. Click **Close**.

Remain logged on to LON-DC1 for the next exercise.

Exercise 3.4	Migrating User Profiles
Overview	In this exercise, you will create a new account and profile. You will then use the User State Migration Tool to backup the user data for the new account. You will then delete a profile, and restore the profile from the backup.
Mindset	The User State Migration Tool (USMT) is a command-line tool that migrates user data from a previous installation of Windows to a new installation of Windows. The ScanState.exe scans the source computer, collects the files and settings, and creates a store that contains the user's files and settings. The LoadState.exe restores the files and settings on the destination computer.
Completion time	60 minutes

1. On **LON-DC1**, open File Explorer by clicking the **File Explorer** icon on the taskbar.

2. Double-click **Local Disk (C:)**.

3. To create a folder called Migration, right-click the empty white space of the **Local Disk (C:)** and choose **New > Folder**. Type **Migration** and press **Enter**.

4. Using the same method as the last step, create a folder called **C:\Data**.

5. Right-click the **Migration** folder and choose **Properties**.

6. Click the **Sharing** tab, as shown in Figure 3-4.

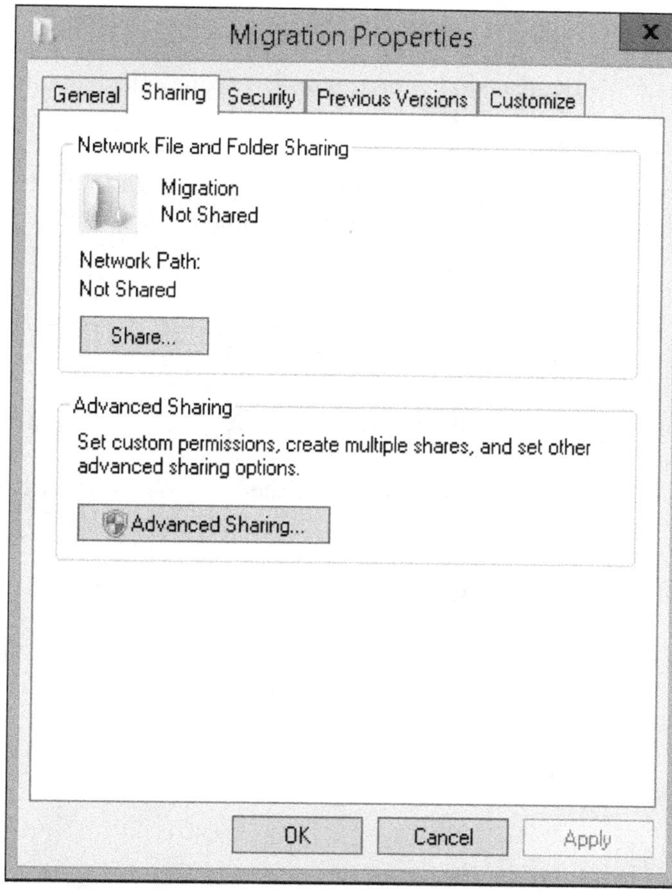

Figure 3-4
Configuring sharing of the Migration folder

7. Click the **Advanced Sharing** button.
8. In the Advanced Sharing dialog box, click the **Share this folder**.
9. Click **Permissions.**
10. In the Permissions for Migration dialog box, with Everyone selected, click to select **Allow Full Control** and then click **OK**.
11. Close the Advanced Sharing dialog box by clicking **OK**.
12. Close the Migration Properties dialog box by clicking **Close**.
13. Right-click the **Data** folder and choose **Properties**.
14. In the Data Properties dialog box, click the **Sharing** tab.
15. Click the **Advanced Sharing** button.
16. In the Advanced Sharing dialog box, click **Share this folder**.

17. Click **Permissions**.

18. In the Permissions for Migration dialog box, with Everyone selected, click to select **Allow Full Control**.

19. Take a screen shot of showing the share permissions of the Data folder by pressing **Alt+PrtScr** and then paste it into your Lab03_worksheet file in the page provided by pressing **Ctrl+V**.

20. Close the Permissions for Data folder by clicking **OK**.

21. Close the Advanced Sharing dialog box by clicking **OK**.

22. Close the Data Properties dialog box by clicking **Close**.

23. Using Server Manager, click the **Tools** menu and then choose **Active Directory Users and Computers**.

24. Right-click the **Users** organizational unit and choose **New > User**.

25. In the New Object – user dialog box, type the following and then click **Next:**

    First name: **Jim**

    Last name: **Austin**

    Full name: **Jim Austin**

    User logon name: **JAustin**

26. In the Password text box and the Confirm password text box, type **Pa$$w0rd**.

27. Click to select **Password never expires**. In the Active Directory Domain Services dialog box, click **OK** and then click **Next**.

28. When the wizard finishes, click **Finish**.

29. On **LON-CL4**, log on as **LON-CL4\Admin** with the password of **Pa$$w0rd**.

30. Right-click the **Start** button and choose **System**.

31. On the System page, on the Computer name, domain, and workgroup settings page, click **Change settings**.

32. In the System Properties dialog box, click the **Change** button.

33. In the Computer Name/Domain Changes dialog box, click to select **Domain**. Then in the Domain text box, type **adatum** and click **OK**.

34. In the Windows Security dialog box, log in as **administrator** with the password of **Pa$$w0rd** and then click **OK**.

35. When the Welcome to the adatum domain message appears, click **OK**.

36. When a message indicates that you must restart your computer to apply these changes, click **OK**.
37. Back on the System Properties dialog box, click **Close**.
38. When a message indicates that you must restart your computer to apply these changes, click **Restart Now**.
39. When LON-CL4 finishes rebooting, log in as **adatum\JAustin** with the password of **Pa$$w0rd**.
40. Right-click the **Desktop** and choose **New > Text Document**. Name the document **Lab3**.
41. Log off **LON-CL4**.
42. On **LON-CL4**, log on using the **Adatum\Administrator** account and the **Pa$$w0rd** password.
43. Open **File Explorer** and click **This PC**.
44. Click the Computer tab, as shown in Figure 3-5, and then click **Map network drive**.

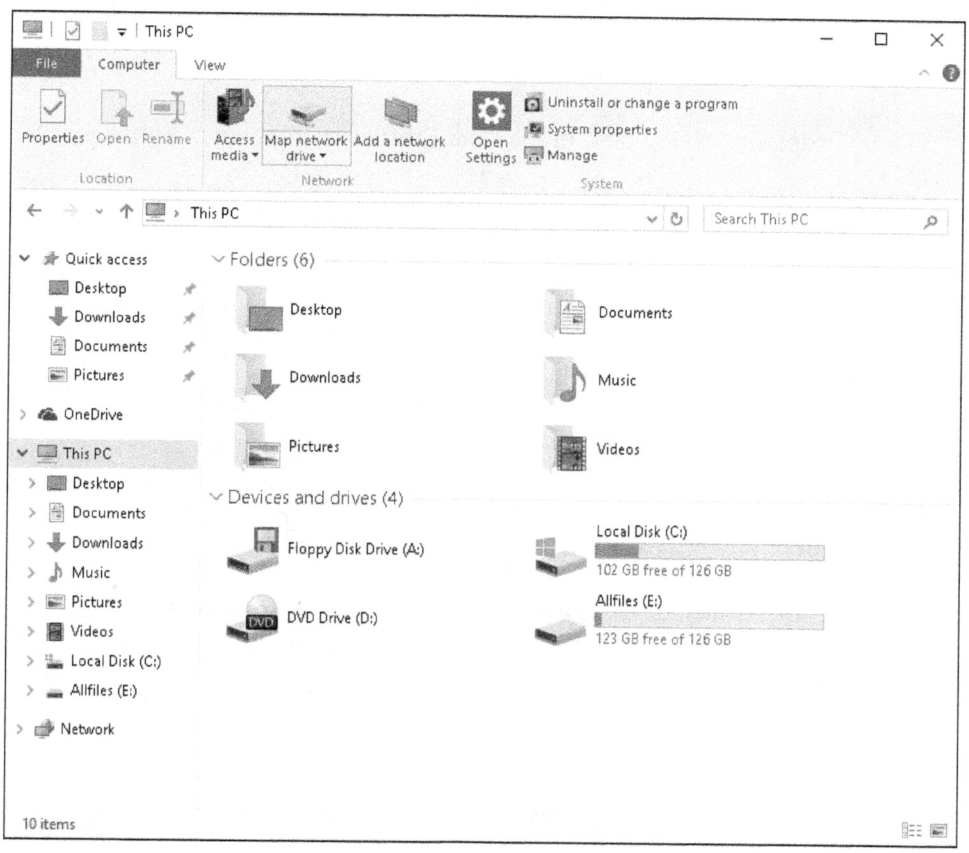

Figure 3-5
Mapping drives in Windows 10

45. In the Map Network Drive window, for the Drive, select **M:**. Then in the Folder text box, type **\\LON-DC1\C$\Program Files (x86)\Windows Kits\10\Assessment and Deployment Kit**. Click **Finish**.

46. Right-click the **Start** button and choose **Command Prompt (Admin)**.

47. In the Administrator: Command Prompt window, type **m:** and then press **Enter**. Then from the M drive, type **CD User State Migration Tool\amd64** and press **Enter**.

48. At the command prompt, execute the following command:

```
scanstate /ue:*\* /ui:adatum\JAustin \\LON-DC1\data
/i:migapp.xml /i:miguser.xml /o /vsc /efs:copyraw /c
```

Question 4	*What does the efs:copyraw option do?*

49. When the migration is finished, take a screen shot of the command prompt window by pressing **Alt+Prt Scr** and then paste it into your Lab03_worksheet file in the page provided by pressing **Ctrl+V**.

50. Right-click the **Start** button and choose **System**.

51. In the System window, click **Advanced system settings**.

52. In the System Properties dialog box, in the User Profiles section, click **Settings**.

53. In the User Profiles dialog box, click **Adatum\JAustin** and then click **Delete**. When you are prompted to confirm this action, click **Yes**.

54. Click **OK** to close the User Profiles dialog box.

55. Click **OK** to close the System Properties dialog box.

56. Return to the command prompt and execute following command:

```
Loadstate /ui:adatum\jaustin \\LON-DC1\data
/i:migapp.xml /i:miguser.xml
```

57. When the migration is finished, take a screen shot of the command prompt window by pressing **Alt+Prt Scr** and then paste it into your Lab03_worksheet file in the page provided by pressing **Ctrl+V**.

58. Log off **LON-CL4**.

59. On **LON-CL4**, log on using the **adatum\JAustin** account and the **Pa$$w0rd** password.

60. Verify that the Lab4 document is located on the Desktop.

61. Log off **LON-CL4**.

62. Log off **LON-DC1**.

Lab Challenge	Creating a Roaming User Profile
Overview	In this exercise, you will create a shared folder and create a roaming user profile.
Mindset	A roaming user profile is simply a copy of a local user profile that is stored on a network share (to which the user has appropriate permissions), so that the user can access it from any computer on the network. No matter which computer a user logs on from, she always receives the files and desktop settings from the profile stored on the server.
Completion time	25 minutes

1. Log on to **LON-DC1** as **adatum\administrator** with the password of **Pa$$w0rd**.
2. On **LON-DC1**, open File Explorer by clicking the **File Explorer** icon on the taskbar.
3. Double-click **Local Disk (C:)**.
4. To create a folder named Roaming, right-click the empty white space of the **Local Disk (C:)** and choose **New > Folder**. Type **Roaming** and then press **Enter**.
5. Right-click the **Roaming** folder and choose **Properties**.
6. In the Roaming Properties dialog box, click the **Sharing** tab.
7. Click the **Advanced Sharing** button.
8. In the Advanced Sharing dialog box, click the **Share this folder**.
9. Click **Permissions**.
10. In the Permissions for Roaming dialog box, with Everyone selected, click to select **Allow Full Control** and then click **OK**.
11. Close the Advanced Sharing dialog box by clicking **OK**.
12. Close the Roaming Properties dialog box by clicking **Close**.
13. On **LON-DC1**, using Server Manager, click **Tools > Active Directory Users and Computers**. If Server Manager is not open, click the Server Manager icon on the taskbar (the first icon next to the Start button).
14. When Active Directory Users and Computers opens, click the **Users** organizational unit, as shown in Figure 3-6.

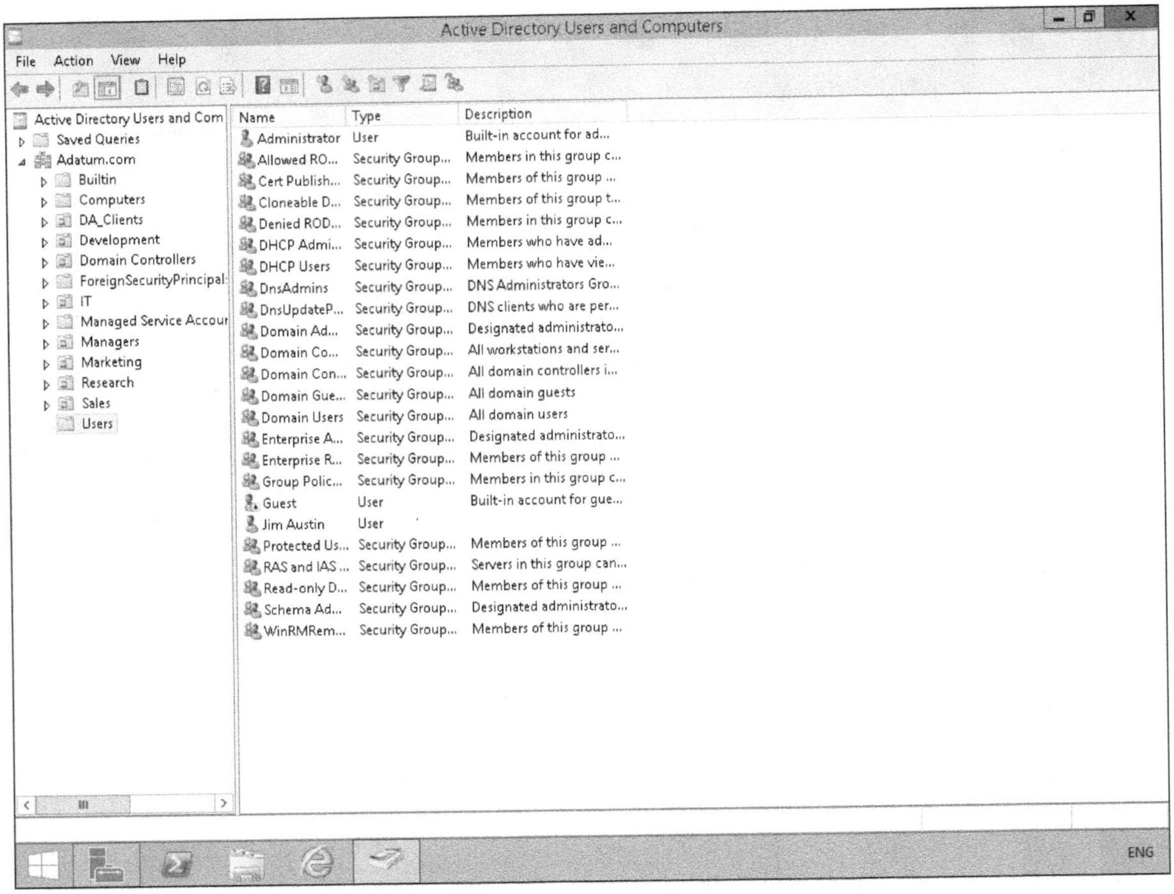

Figure 3-6
Opening the Users organizational unit

15. Right-click the **Users** organizational unit and choose **New > User**.

16. In the New Object – User wizard, type the following and then click **Next**.

    First Name: **Tony**

    Last Name: **Wayne**

    User logon name: **TWayne**

17. In the Password and Confirm password text boxes, type **Pa$$w0rd**.

18. Deselect the **User must change password at next logon** option and then click **Next**.

19. Close the New Object – User wizard by clicking **Finish**.

20. Double-click the **Tony Wayne** user account.

21. In the Tony Wayne Properties dialog box, click the **Profile** tab.

22. In the Profile path text box, type **\\LON-DC1\Roaming\%USERNAME%** and then click **OK**.

23. Double-click **Tony Wayne** user account and then click the **Profile** tab.

24. Take a screen shot of the user profile by pressing **Alt+Prt Scr** and then paste it into your Lab03_worksheet file in the page provided by pressing **Ctrl+V**.

25. Close the Tony Wayne Properteis dialog box by clicking **OK**.

26. On **LON-CL1**, log in as **adatum\TWayne** with the password of **Pa$$w0rd**.

27. On **LON-DC1**, using File Explorer, navigate to the **C:\Roaming** folder.

Question 5	*Which version is the roaming profile and which OS would this version be used for?*

28. Log out of **LON-CL1** and **LON-DC1**.

End of lab.

LAB 4
CONFIGURING HYPER-V

THIS LAB CONTAINS THE FOLLOWING EXERCISES AND ACTIVITIES:

Exercise 4.1 Installing and Configuring Hyper-V

Exercise 4.2 Creating and Managing Virtual Machines

Exercise 4.3 Creating and Managing Virtual Switches

Exercise 4.4 Creating and Managing Virtual Disks

Lab Challenge Creating and Managing Checkpoints

BEFORE YOU BEGIN

The lab environment consists of student workstations connected to a local area network, along with a server that functions as the domain controller for a domain called adatum.com. The computers required for this lab are listed in Table 4-1.

Table 4-1
Computers required for Lab 4

Computer	*Operating System*	*Computer Name*
Server (VM 1)	Windows Server 2012 R2	LON-DC1
Client (VM 3)	Windows 10	LON-CL1

In addition to the computers, you will also require the software listed in Table 4-2 to complete Lab 4.

Table 4-2
Software required for Lab 4

Software	*Location*
Lab 4 student worksheet	Lab04_worksheet.docx (provided by instructor)

Working with Lab Worksheets

Each lab in this manual requires that you answer questions, shoot screen shots, and perform other activities that you will document in a worksheet named for the lab, such as Lab04_worksheet.docx. You will find these worksheets on the book companion site. It is recommended that you use a USB flash drive to store your worksheets, so you can submit them to your instructor for review. As you perform the exercises in each lab, open the appropriate worksheet file, fill in the required information, and then save the file to your flash drive.

SCENARIO

After completing this lab, you will be able to:

- Install and configure Hyper-V
- Create and manage a virtual machine
- Create and manage a virtual switch
- Create and manage a virtual disks
- Create and manage a checkpoints

Estimated lab time: 70 minutes

Exercise 4.1	Installing and Configuring Hyper-V
Overview	In this exercise, you will install and configure the Windows 10 Hyper-V feature using DISM.
Mindset	Client Hyper-V enables you to create and manage virtual machines (VMs) using a virtual switch. These VMs can be used to test your applications for compatibility with new operating systems, allow you to run applications written for older versions of Windows, or isolate an application.
Completion time	10 minutes

1. Log in to **LON-CL1** as **adatum\administrator** with the password of **Pa$$w0rd**.
2. On **LON-CL1**, right-click the **Start** button and choose **Command Prompt (Admin)**.
3. Execute the following two commands.

```
Dism /online /enable-feature /featurename:Microsoft-
Hyper-V /All
```

NOTE	*On a physical computer running Windows 10, you can install Hyper-V using the Programs and Features. On a Hyper-V machine, you cannot run Hyper-V using the Program Features and you cannot run virtual machines. In other words, you can not run a Hyper-V virtual machine on another Hyper-V machine. However, you can install Hyper-V using DISM, and you can create and manage virtual machines.*

4. When you are prompted to reboot, press the **y** key.
5. After the reboot, log in to **LON-CL1** as **adatum\administrator** with the password of **Pa$$w0rd**.
6. Right-click the **Start** button and choose **Programs and Features**.
7. Click **Turn Windows features on or off**.

Question 1	*Where else can you find the Programs and Features?*

8. In the Windows Features dialog box, expand the **Hyper-V** node.
9. Take a screen shot of the Windows Features showing the Hyper-V is installed by pressing **Alt+PrtScr** and then paste it into your Lab04_worksheet file in the page provided by pressing **Ctrl+V**.
10. To close the Turn Windows features on or off dialog box, click OK. PR
11. Close the **Control Panel**.

Leave LON-CL1 logged in for the next exercise.

Exercise 4.2	Creating and Managing Virtual Machines
Overview	In this exercise, you will create and manage a virtual machine.
Mindset	A virtual machine (VM) is a self-contained, isolated unit that can be easily moved from one physical computer to another, runs its own operating system, and includes its own virtual hardware configuration. After you have installed Hyper-V, you can use the Hyper-V Manager console to create and manage VMs.
Completion time	20 minutes

1. On **LON-CL1**, right-click the **Start** button and choose **Control Panel**.
2. In the Search Control Panel text box, type **Administrative Tools**. Then from the search results, click **Administrative Tools**.
3. Double-click **Hyper-V Manager**. Hyper-V Manager opens, as shown in Figure 4-1.

Figure 4-1
The Hyper-V Manager console

4. Right-click **LON-CL1** and choose **New > Virtual Machine**.
5. In the New Virtual Machine Wizard, on the Before You Begin page, click **Next**.
6. On the Specify Name and Location page, in the Name text box, type **VM1**.

Question 2	*What is the default location of the virtual machines?*

7. Click **Next**.

8. On the Specify Generation page, Generation 1 is already selected. Click **Next**.

9. On the Assign Memory page, answer the following question.

Question 3	*What is the default startup memory?*

10. In the Startup memory box, type **2048**. Click **Next**.

11. Normally, you would select a virtual switch. However, because a virtual switch is not configured yet, on the Configuring Networking page, click **Next**.

12. On the Connect Virtual Hard Disk page, change the size to **20** GB. Click **Next**.

13. On the Installation Options page, for our lab environment, click **Next**.

14. On the Summary page, click **Finish**.

15. Take a screen shot of Hyper-V Manager showing the new VM by pressing **Alt+PrtScr** and then paste it into your Lab04_worksheet file in the page provided by pressing **Ctrl+V**.

16. Right-click **VM1** and choose **Settings**.

17. Under Hardware, click **Memory**.

18. Change the RAM to **1024** MB.

19. Under Hardware, click **Processor**.

20. Change the number of virtual processors from 1 to **2**.

21. Take a screen shot of Hyper-V Manager showing the Processor setting by pressing **Alt+PrtScr** and then paste it into your Lab04_worksheet file in the page provided by pressing **Ctrl+V**.

22. Close the Settings window by clicking **OK**.

Leave Hyper-V Manager open for the next exercise.

Exercise 4.3	Creating and Managing Virtual Switches
Overview	In this exercise, you will create an internal switch and a private switch. You will then configure a VM to connect to one of the virutal switches.
Mindset	To set up a test network that includes multiple systems, you need to configure a virtual switch using the Virtual Switch Manager. This enables your VMs to communicate with each other and access your physical network for Internet access.
Completion time	10 minutes

1. On **LON-CL1**, using Hyper-V Manager, under Actions, click **Virtual Switch Manager**. The Virtual Switch Manager dialog box opens, as shown in Figure 4-2.

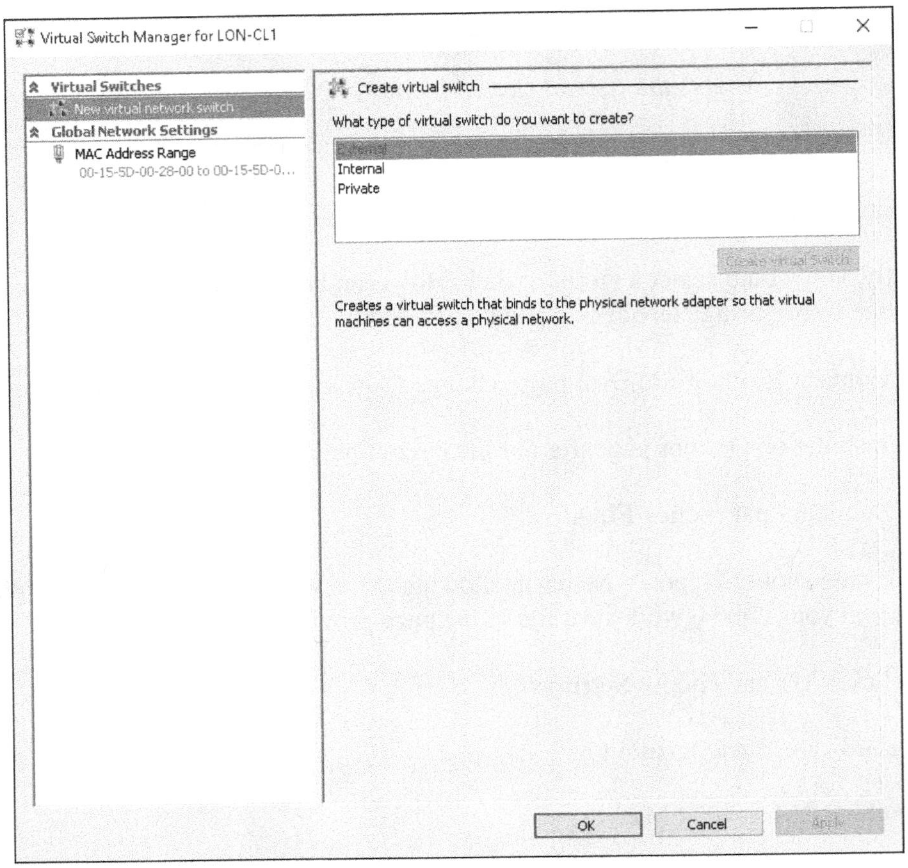

Figure 4-2
Managing virtual switches

2. In the What type type of virtual switch do you want to create? box, select **Private** and then click the **Create Virtual Switch** button.

3. In the Name text box, type **Private Switch** and then click **Apply**.

Question 4	*Which machines can use a private switch?*

4. Take a screen shot of Virtual Switch Manager by pressing **Alt+PrtScr** and then paste it into your Lab04_worksheet file in the page provided by pressing **Ctrl+V**.

5. Click **New virtual network switch**.

6. In the What do you want to connect this virtual switch to? section, click **Internal network** and then click **Create Virtual Switch**.

7. In the Name text box, type **Internal Switch**. Click **Apply**.

8. Take a screen shot of Virtual Switch Manager by pressing **Alt+PrtScr** and then paste it into your Lab04_worksheet file in the page provided by pressing **Ctrl+V**.

9. Click **OK** to close the Virtual Switch Manager.

10. On Hyper-V Manager, using Hyper-V Manager, right-click **VM1** and choose **Settings**.

11. In the Settings dialog box, click the **Network Adapter** vertical tab, as shown in Figure 4-3.

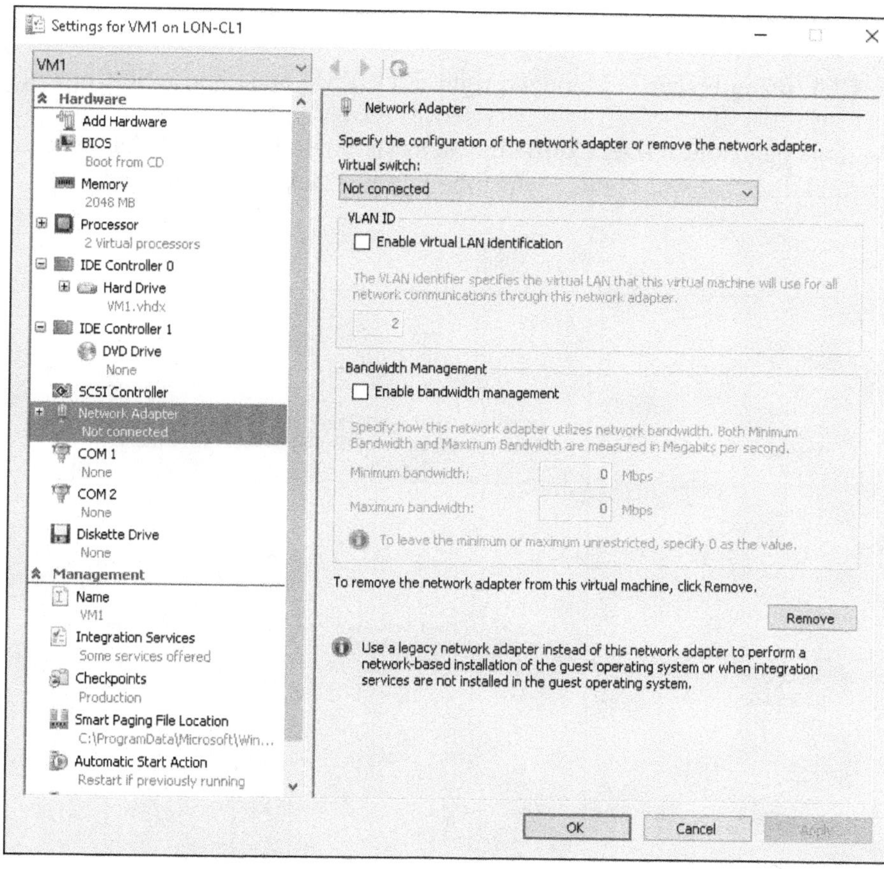

Figure 4-3
Managing network adapters

12. On the Network Adapter page, for the Virtual switch, select **Private switch**.

13. Take a screen shot of Settings page by pressing **Alt+PrtScr** and then paste it into your Lab04_worksheet file in the page provided by pressing **Ctrl+V**.

14. Click **OK** to close the Settings page.

Leave Hyper-V Manager open for the next exercise.

Exercise 4.4	Creating and Managing Virtual Disks
Overview	In this exercise, you will create a second virtual disk on VM1. You will then expand the new disk.
Mindset	A virtual disk is a file that represents a physical disk drive to a guest operating system running on a virtual machine. The user can install a new operating system onto the virtual disk without repartitioning the physical disk or rebooting the host machine.
Completion time	20 minutes

1. On **LON-CL1**, using Hyper-V Manager, right-click **VM1** and choose **Settings**.
2. On the Settings page, click **IDE Controller 0**, as shown in Figure 4-4. As you can see, it already has one virtual disk that was created when the virtual machine was created.

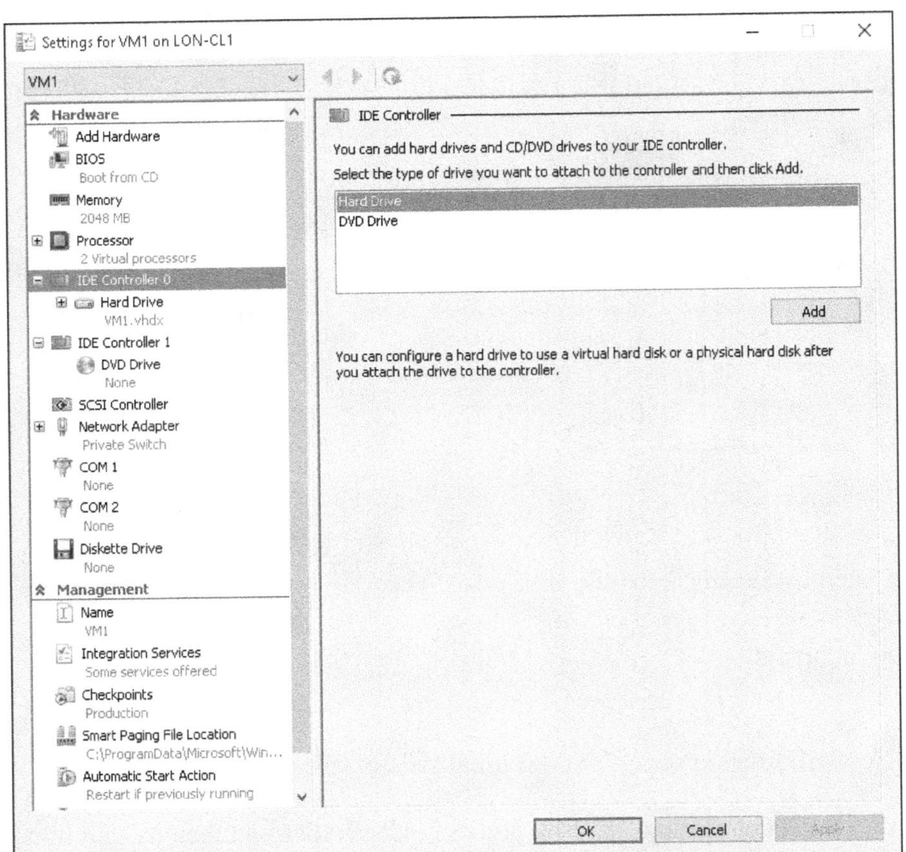

Figure 4-4
Managing virtual disks

3. On the IDE Controller page, select **Hard Drive** and then click **Add**. The Hard Drive page opens.

4. With the Virtual hard disk option selected, click the **New** button.

5. In the New Virtual Hard Disk Wizard, on the Before You Begin page, click **Next**.

6. On the Choose Disk Format page, VHDX is already selected. Answer the following question and then click **Next**.

Question 5	*What is the size limit of VHD?*

7. On the Choose Disk Type page, answer the following question and then click **Next**.

Question 6	*Which virtual disk type will consume the most space?*

8. On the Specify Name and Location page, in the Name text box, type **HD1**.

Question 7	*What is the location of the virtual hard disk file?*

9. Click **Next**.

10. On the Create a New Blank Virtual Hard Disk page, specify the size of the disk, such as **10** GB. Click **Next**.

11. Take a screen shot of New Virtual Hard Disk Wizard page by pressing **Alt+PrtScr** and then paste it into your Lab04_ worksheet file in the page provided by pressing **Ctrl+V**.

12. Click **Finish**.

13. Click **OK** to close the Settings dialog box.

14. Right-click **VM1** and choose **Settings**.

15. Under IDE Controller 0, click the second **Hard Drive (HD1.vhdx)**. Then click the **Edit** button.

16. In the Edit Virtual hard Disk Wizard, click **Next**.

17. On the Choose Action page, select the **Expand** option and then click **Next**.

18. On the Configure Disk page, for the New Size, type **15** GB and click **Next**.
19. Take a screen shot of Edit Virtual Hard Disk Wizard page by pressing **Alt+PrtScr** and then paste it into your Lab04_worksheet file in the page provided by pressing **Ctrl+V**.
20. Click **Finish**.
21. Click **OK** to close the Settings window.

Leave Hyper-V Manager open for the next exercise.

Lab Challenge	Creating and Managing Checkpoints
Overview	In this challenge, you will create multiple checkpoints. You will then delete a checkpoint and roll back to a checkpoint.
Mindset	In Hyper-V, a checkpoint is a captured image of the state, data, and hardware configuration of a VM at a particular moment in time.
Completion time	10 minutes

1. On **LON-CL1**, using Hyper-V Manager, click **VM1**.
2. Right-click **VM1** and choose **Checkpoint**.
3. Right-click **VM1** and choose **Checkpoint** a second time.
4. Take a screen shot showing the checkpoints by pressing **Alt+PrtScr** and then paste it into your Lab04_worksheet file in the page provided by pressing **Ctrl+V**.
5. Right-click the second checkpoint and choose **Delete Checkpoint**. When you are prompted to confirm, click **Delete**.
6. Right-click the first checkpoint and choose **Apply**. When you are prompted to confirm, click **Apply**.
7. Right-click the first checkpoint and choose **Delete Checkpoint**. When you are prompted to confirm, click **Delete**.

Question 8	*How long should you keep a snapshot?*

End of lab.

LAB 5
SUPPORTING MOBILITY OPTIONS

THIS LAB CONTAINS THE FOLLOWING EXERCISES AND ACTIVITIES:

Exercise 5.1 Configuring Power Settings

Lab Challenge Using Powercfg.exe

BEFORE YOU BEGIN

The lab environment consists of student workstations connected to a local area network, along with a server that functions as the domain controller for a domain called adatum.com. The computers required for this lab are listed in Table 5-1.

Table 5-1
Computers required for Lab 5

Computer	*Operating System*	*Computer Name*
Server (VM 1)	Windows Server 2012	LON-DC1
Client (VM 3)	Windows 10	LON-CL1

In addition to the computers, you will also require the software listed in Table 5-2 to complete Lab 5.

Table 5-2
Software required for Lab 5

Software	*Location*
Lab 5 student worksheet	Lab05_worksheet.docx (provided by instructor)

Working with Lab Worksheets

Each lab in this manual requires that you answer questions, shoot screen shots, and perform other activities that you will document in a worksheet named for the lab, such as Lab05_worksheet.docx. You will find these worksheets on the book companion site. It is recommended that you use a USB flash drive to store your worksheets, so you can submit them to your instructor for review. As you perform the exercises in each lab, open the appropriate worksheet, fill in the required information, and then save the file to your flash drive.

SCENARIO

After completing this lab, you will be able to:

- Configure power settings
- Create and manage power plans
- Use Powercfg.exe to export and import power plans

Estimated lab time: 30 minutes

Exercise 5.1	Configuring Power Settings
Overview	In this exercise, you will configure basic power settings. You will then create and manage a power plan.
Mindset	Power management is the balancing of power consumption with performance. Windows 10 includes extensive power management capabilities, including supporting the Advanced Configuration and Power Interface (ACPI), which can be configured using power plans. The power plans can be configured using the Control Panel Power Options, using Group Policy, or via the command prompt.
Completion time	20 minutes

1. Log in to **LON-CL1** as **adatum\administrator** with the password of **Pa$$w0rd**.
2. On **LON-CL1**, right-click the **Start** button and choose **Control Panel**.
3. Click **Hardware and Sound > Power Options**. The Power Options page opens as shown in Figure 5-1.

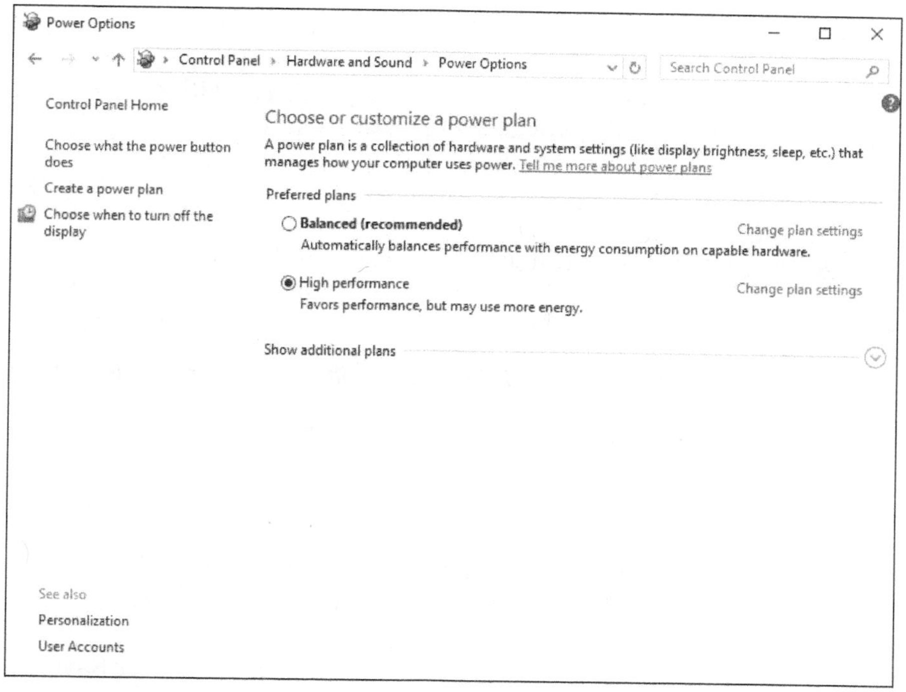

Figure 5-1
Managing Power Options

4. Click the **Choose what the power button does** option.

Question 1	*By default, what happens when the power button is pressed?*

5. Click the **Back** (left arrow) button.

Question 2	*Which power plan is the system using?*

6. Click the down arrow next to **Show additional plans.**

Question 3	*Which power plan was hidden?*

7. Click the **Create a power plan** option.

8. In the Create a Power Plan Wizard, Balanced (recommended) is already selected. In the Plan name text box, type **MyPowerPlan** and then click **Next**.

9. On the Change Settings for the Plan page, click the **Create** button.

10. Take a screen shot of the Power Options page by pressing **Alt+PrtScr** and then paste it into your Lab05_worksheet file in the page provided by pressing **Ctrl+V**.

11. Next to MyPowerPlan, click **Change plan settings**.

12. Click **Change advanced power settings**. The Power Options dialog box opens.

Question 4	*When does is the hard disk turned off (when it's not being used)?*

13. Change the Setting (Minutes) to **30**.

14. Take a screen shot of the Power Options dialog box by pressing **Alt+PrtScr** and then paste it into your Lab05_worksheet file in the page provided by pressing **Ctrl+V**.

15. Expand the **Wireless Adapter Settings** node and then expand the **Power Savings Mode** node.

Question 5	*Which power saving mode for wireless adapters is the system set to?*

16. Click **OK**.

17. Close the Edit Plan Settings window.

Leave LON-CL1 logged on for the next exercise.

Lab Challenge	Using Powercfg.exe
Overview	In this challenge, you will use the Powercfg.exe to export a power plan and then import the power plan.
Mindset	Powercfg.exe is the command-line program to manage Windows 10 power options. Powercfg is the most comprehensive power management interface, enabling you to configure settings that are not available from Control Panel or in Group Policy. For example, you can export entire power management plans to file and import them on another computer.
Completion time	10 minutes

1. On **LON-CL1**, right-click the **Start** button and choose **Command Prompt** (Admin).
2. In the command prompt, execute the following command:

```
powercfg.exe -list
```

Question 6	*Which power plan is current being used?*

Question 7	*What is the GUID for the current power plan?*

3. Using the GUID that you wrote down in Question 7, export a plan to the powerplan.pow file by executing the following command:

```
powercfg.exe -export powerplan.pow <GUID>
```

4. After you copy the files to another system, you can import the plan on another system by executing the following command:

```
powercfg.exe -import powerplan.pow
```

5. Take a screen shot of the Command Prompt window by pressing **Alt+PrtScr** and then paste it into your Lab05_worksheet file in the page provided by pressing **Ctrl+V**.

End of lab.

LAB 6
SUPPORTING AND MANAGING DEVICES WITH MICROSOFT INTUNE

THIS LAB CONTAINS THE FOLLOWING EXERCISES AND ACTIVITIES:

Exercise 6.1	Managing Microsoft Intune Users and Devices
Exercise 6.2	Managing Microsoft Intune Groups
Exercise 6.3	Managing Microsoft Intune Policies
Exercise 6.4	Configuring Microsoft Intune Monitoring and Alerts
Lab Challenge	Running Microsoft Intune Reports

BEFORE YOU BEGIN

The lab environment consists of student workstations connected to a local area network, along with a server that functions as the domain controller for a domain called adatum.com. The computers required for this lab are listed in Table 6-1.

Table 6-1
Computers required for Lab 6

Computer	Operating System	Computer Name
Client	Windows 10	A machine running Windows 10 that is connected to the Internet.

In addition to the computers, you will also require the software listed in Table 6-2 to complete Lab 6.

Table 6-2
Software required for Lab 6

Software	Location
Lab 6 student worksheet	Lab06_worksheet.docx (provided by instructor)

Working with Lab Worksheets

Each lab in this manual requires that you answer questions, shoot screen shots, and perform other activities that you will document in a worksheet named for the lab, such as Lab06_worksheet.docx. You will find these worksheets on the book companion site. It is recommended that you use a USB flash drive to store your worksheets, so you can submit them to your instructor for review. As you perform the exercises in each lab, open the appropriate worksheet file, fill in the required information, and then save the file to your flash drive.

SCENARIO

After completing this lab, you will be able to:

- Manage Microsoft Intune Users and Devices
- Manage Microsoft Intune Groups
- Manage Microsoft Intune Policies
- Configure Microsoft Intune Monitoring and Alerts
- Run Microsoft Intune Reports

Estimated lab time: 65 minutes

NOTE	*If you are using the MOAC Labs Online system, you will not be able to perform this exercise. Instead, you need to use a computer running Windows 10 with access to the Internet. If your classroom has a dedicated Windows Server 2012 R2 or Windows Server 2016, you can use a virtual machine running Windows 10.*

Exercise 6.1	Managing Microsoft Intune Users and Devices
Overview	In this exercise, you will create a user in the Office 365 Admin Center. You will then add a device to Microsoft Intune by installing the Microsoft Intune client that is downloaded from the Microsoft Intune console.
Mindset	To perform an administrator deployment, you basically download the client software and manually install it on the target computers. You can automate the process by using Group Policy if you need to install it on a large number of computers.
Completion time	25 minutes

1. Log on to a computer running Windows 10 that is connected to the Internet.

2. Open **Internet Explorer** and go to the **Microsoft Intune Account Portal** (http://portal.office.com). The Admin center preview page opens, similar to what is shown in Figure 6-1.

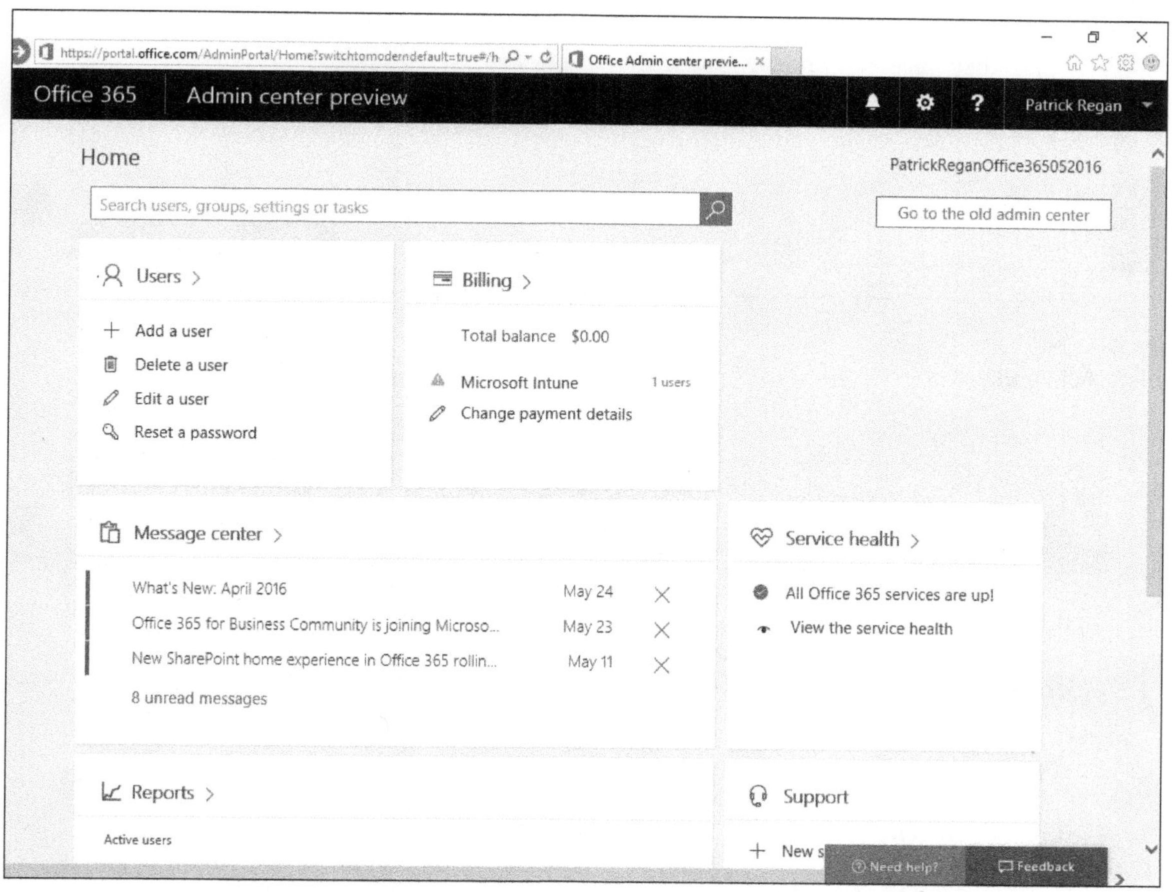

Figure 6-1
The Microsoft Intune Admin Center

3. In the left pane, click the **Users** icon (the icon under the Home icon) shown in Figure 6-2 and then click **Active users**.

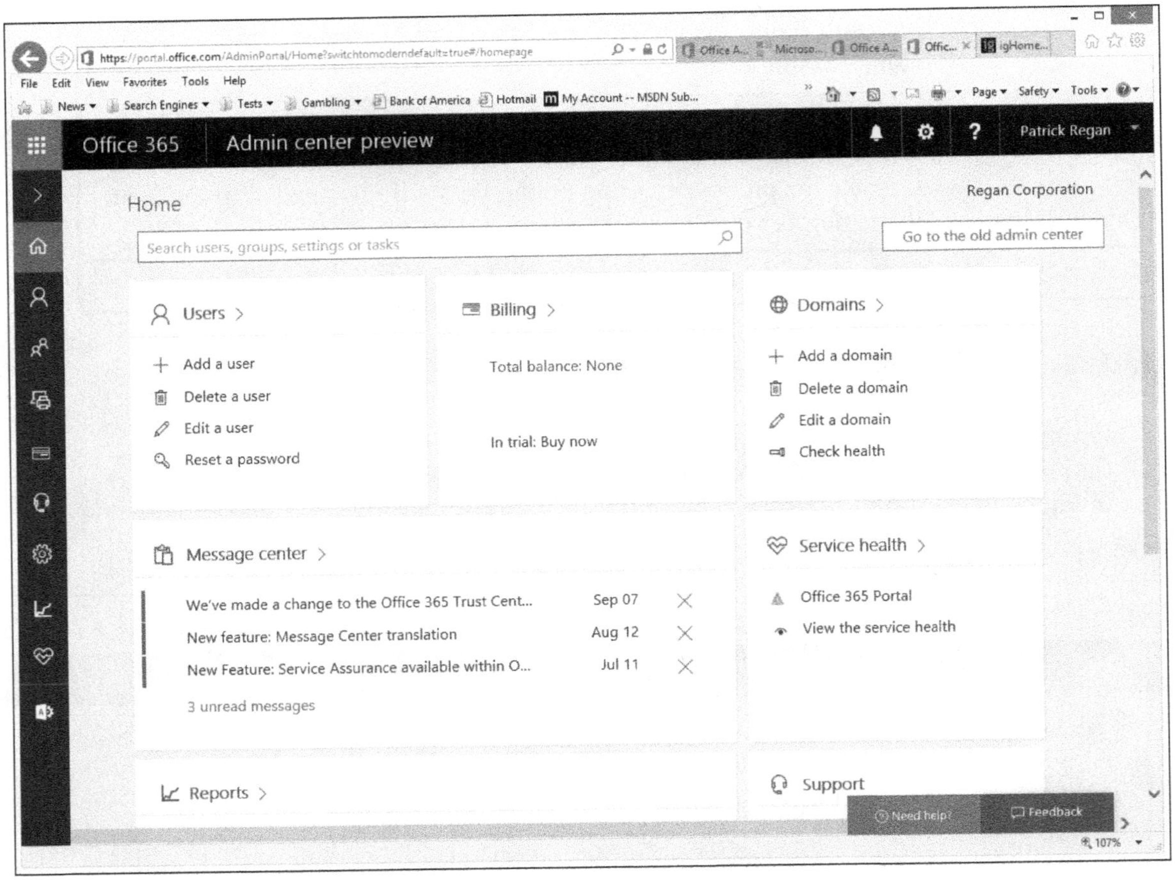

Figure 6-2
Selecting Active users

Question 1	*Which user accounts are shown and what is the status of those accounts?*

4. At the top of the page, click **Add a user**.

5. On the New User page, type the following:

   First name: **Alex**

   Last name: **DeWitt**

   Display name: **Alex DeWitt**

   User name: **ADeWitt**

6. Click **Contact information** and then type the following:

   Job Title: **Sales Manager**

   Department: **Sales**

   Office phone: **123-456-1234**

7. Click **Password**.

Question 2	*What are the default settings for the password?*

8. Click **Roles**.

Question 3	*What role is assigned to the user?*

9. Select **Global administrator**.

Question 4	*Which features and tasks of the admin center can be performed by the global administrator?*

10. Click **Product licenses**.

Question 5	*How many licenses do you have available?*

11. Click the **Add** button.

Question 6	*Which password was assigned to Alex Dewitt?*

12. Take a screen shot of the User was added page by pressing **Alt+PrtScr** and then paste it into your Lab06_worksheet file in the page provided by pressing **Ctrl+V**.

13. Click the **Send email and close** button. If the new user does not show in the Active users page, refresh the web page.

14. Click the **Admin centers** icon and then click **Intune**, as shown in Figure 6-3.

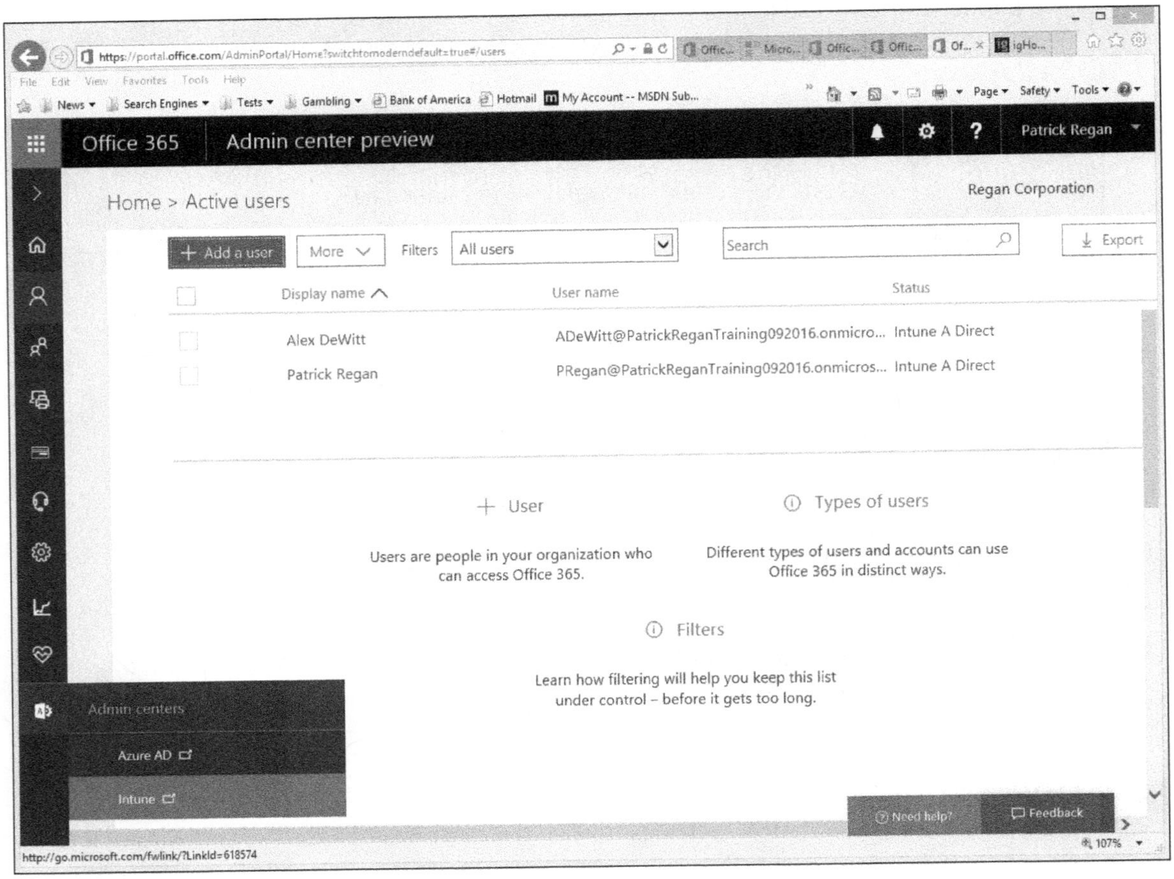

Figure 6-3
Viewing Active users

15. In the Microsoft Intune console's left pane, click **Admin**.

16. Click **Client Software Download**.

17. On the Client Software Download page, click **Download Client Software**.

18. From the Windows Internet Explorer box, click **Save as**.

19. In the Save As box, click **Desktop** and then click **Save**. This places a file named Microsoft_Intune_Setup.zip on your desktop.

20. Minimize the Microsoft Intune console, right-click the **Microsoft_Intune_Setup.zip** file, and choose **Extract All**.

21. In the Select a Destination and Extract Files page, click **Extract**.

22. Double-click the **Microsoft_Intune_Setup** folder. When the Microsoft_Intune_Setup window opens, you will see two files in the Microsoft_Intune_Setup folder: Microsoft_Intune_Setup.exe and MicrosoftIntune.accountcert. These files must be kept together at all times. The MicrosoftIntune.accountcert is used by the setup program.

23. Double-click **Microsoft_Intune_Setup.exe**.

24. In the Microsoft Intune Setup Wizard, click **Next.** If you are prompted to confirm that you want to allow this app to install software on your PC, click **Yes**.

25. When the client is installed, click **Finish**. Microsoft Intune continues to update and install software on the computer. You can use the computer while the process continues in the background.

26. Back on the Microsoft Intune console, click the **GROUPS** workspace. Then click **All Devices**.

27. Take a screen shot of the All Devices page by pressing **Alt+PrtScr** and then paste it into your Lab06_worksheet file in the page provided by pressing **Ctrl+V**.

Leave Internet Explorer open for the next exercise.

Exercise 6.2	Managing Microsoft Intune Groups
Overview	In this exercise, you will create a group and add the new computer to the group.
Mindset	To simplify the process of deploying Microsoft Intune policies, software packages, and software updates, consider using Microsoft Intune Groups. Microsoft Intune Groups, which are used to quickly organize and manage your computers and users, are created and managed in the Groups workspace.
Completion time	10 minutes

1. On the Windows 10 computer that is connected to the Internet, using the Internet Explorer/Microsoft Intune console, you should already be in the GROUPS workspace. Click **Overview** (see Figure 6-4).

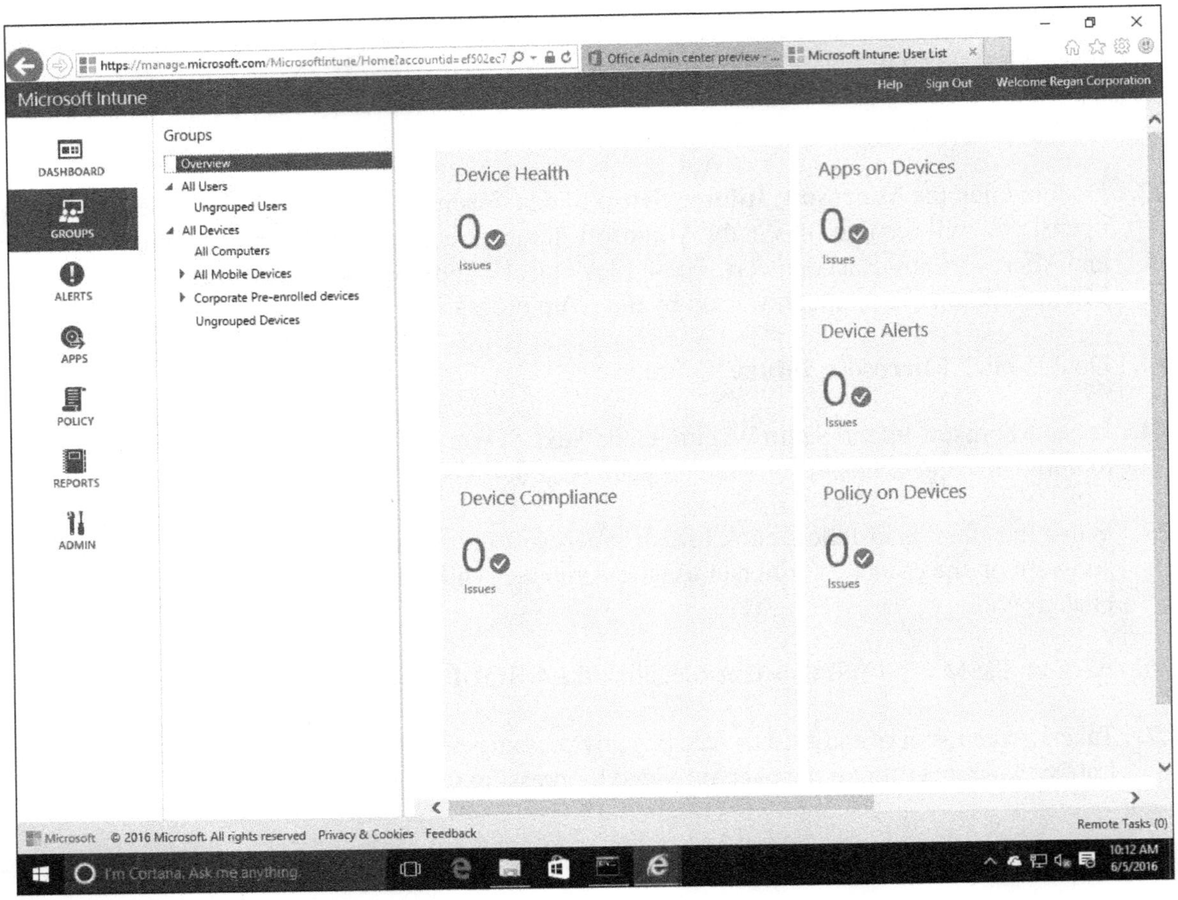

Figure 6-4
Viewing the Groups Overview page

2. Click the **All Devices** node.
3. Right-click the **All Devices** node and choose **Create Group**.
4. In the Group name field, type **My Test Group**.
5. In the Description field, type **Computers used to test deployments of new updates**.
6. Under the Select a parent group, click **All Devices**.

Question 7	*Which group will already have all of your computers running Windows 7, 8/8.1, and Windows 10?*

7. Click **Next**.
8. On the Define Membership Criteria page, for the Device type, select **Computer**. Then click **Next**.
9. On the Define Direct Membership screen, for the Include specific members section, click **Browse**. Be careful to select the Browse button that is just to the right of the **Include specific members** field. If you select the one on the far right, you will exclude specific members.
10. Choose the Windows 10 computer on which you installed the Microsoft Intune client software in the earlier exercise and then click **Add**. Your Windows 10 computer should appear in the Include specific members column. Click **OK** to continue.
11. On the Define Direct Membership page, click **Next**.
12. Review the General, Criteria Membership and Direct Membership on the Summary page. Then take a screen shot of Create Group page by pressing **Alt+PrtScr** and then paste it into your Lab06_worksheet file in the page provided by pressing **Ctrl+V**.
13. Click **Finish**.
14. Under Groups, click **My Test Group** and then click **Devices**. The computer should appear as a member of the group.

Leave Internet Explorer open for the next exercise.

Exercise 6.3	Managing Microsoft Intune Policies
Overview	In this exercise, you will create a general configuration policy and then deploy the policy to the group you created in the last exercise.
Mindset	Microsoft Intune provides policies to help control the security settings on mobile devices, computer updates, Endpoint Protection, firewall settings, and the end-user experience.. These policies apply to domain-joined computers in any domain and to non-domain-joined computers.
Completion time	10 minutes

1. On the Windows 10 computer that is connected to the Internet, using the Internet Explorer/Microsoft Intune console, click the **Policy** workspace, as shown in Figure 6-5.

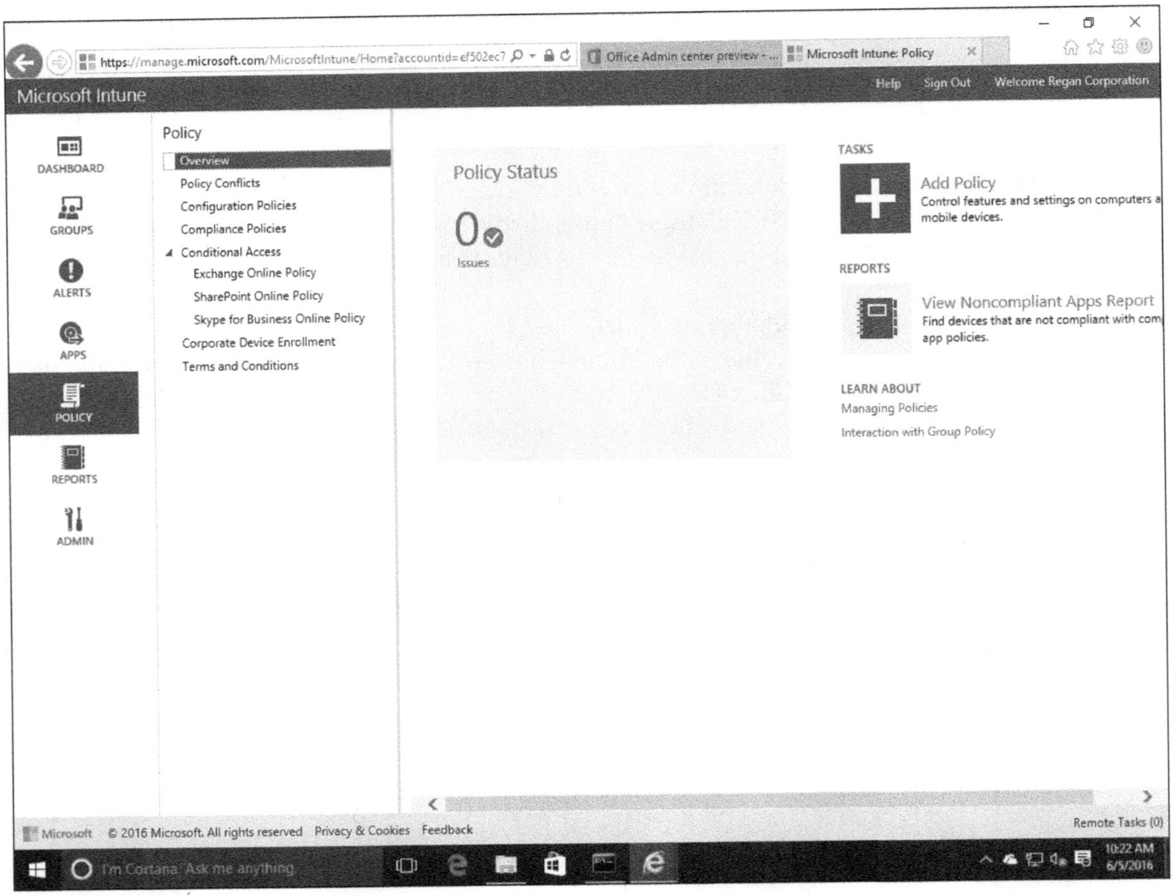

Figure 6-5
Viewing policies

2. Under Tasks, click **Add Policy**.

Question 8	*Which policy allows you to configure Endpoint Protection Services?*

3. In the Create a New Policy dialog box, expand the **Windows** node and then click **General Configuration (Windows 10 Desktop and Moble and later)**. Click **Create Policy**.

4. On the Create Policy page, in the Name text box, type **Test Policy.**

5. Under Security, select **Minimum password length type is not configured**. Then set the Minimum password length to **8**.

6. Scroll down to the Hardware section and then select the **Allow camera is not configured**. Change the value from Yes to **No**.

7. Click **Save Policy**.

8. When you are prompted to confirm that you want to deploy this policy now, click **Yes**.

9. On the **Select the groups to which you want to deploy this policy** page, click **My Test Group**, and then click **Add**. Then click **OK**.

10. Take a screen shot of the Policies page by pressing **Alt+PrtScr** and then paste it into your Lab06_worksheet file in the page provided by pressing **Ctrl+V**.

Leave Internet Explorer open for the next exercise.

Exercise 6.4	Configuring Microsoft Intune Monitoring and Alerts
Overview	In this exercise, you will look to see whether you have any current alerts and then set up Microsoft Intune to send you alerts to your email account when they happen.
Mindset	Computers configured with the Microsoft Intune agent can be tracked both on and off the corporate network. As computers are configured with the Microsoft Intune agent, they start to report back to Microsoft Intune. Because Microsoft Intune is cloud-based, users do not have to be attached to your corporate network to receive updates, patches, or to receive help removing malware.
Completion time	10 minutes

1. On the Windows 10 computer that is connected to the Internet, using Internet Explorer/Microsoft Intune console, click the **Alerts** workspace, as shown in Figure 6-6.

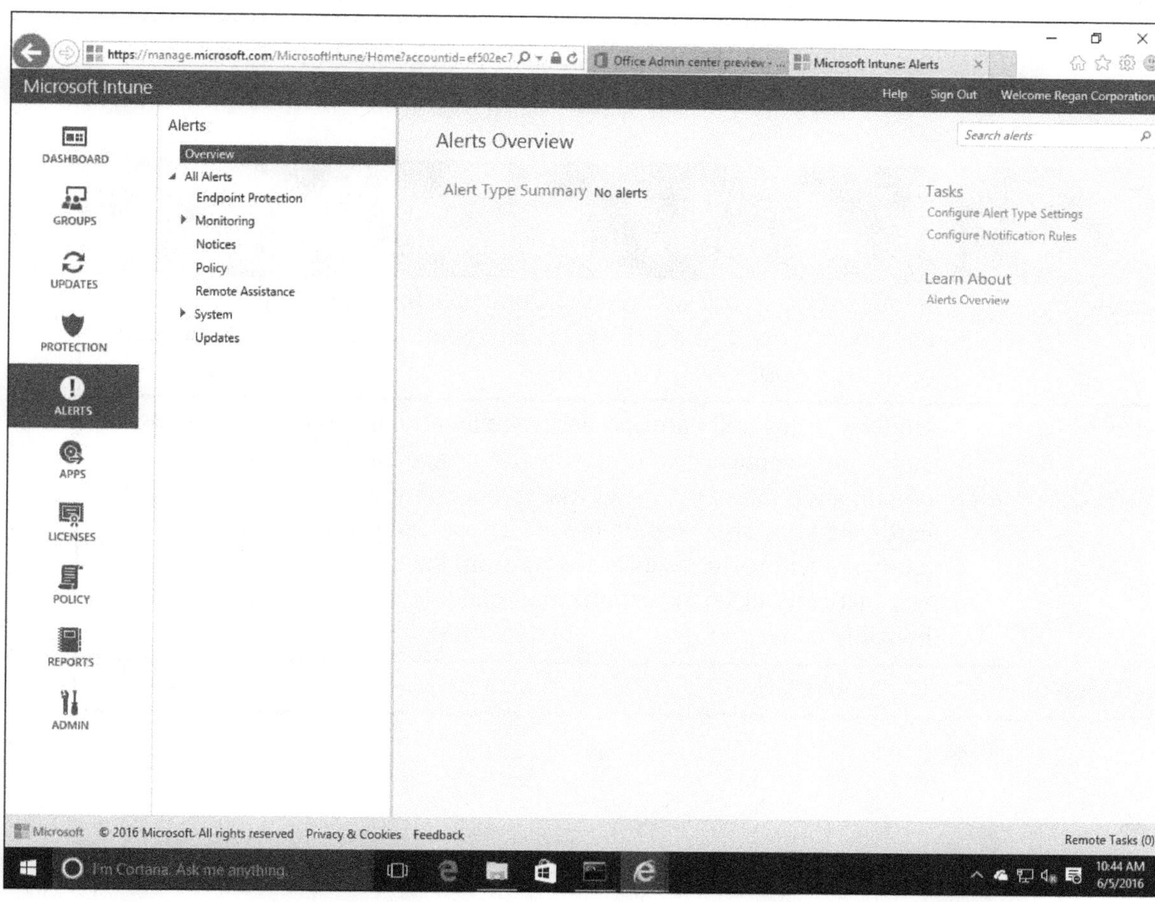

Figure 6-6
Viewing alerts

Question 9	*Do you have any alerts?*

2. On the Alerts Overview page, under Tasks, click **Configure Alert Type Settings**.

Question 10	*Which type of alert is the Client Software Deployment Failure set to?*

3. Scroll down, right-click the **NTFS – File System Corrupt message** alert type, and choose **Enable**.
4. Click the **Recipients** node.
5. In the Recipients pane, click **Add**.
6. In the Add Notification Recipient window, in the Email address and Confirm email address text boxes, type your Office 365 address. It should be <FirstInitial><LastName>@<FirstName><Last Name>Office365<Month> <Year>.onmicrosoft.com. Then click **OK**.
7. Take a screenshot of the Review the Recipients page by pressing **Alt+PrtScr** and then paste it into your Lab06_worksheet file in the page provided by pressing **Ctrl+V**.

Leave Internet Explorer open for the next exercise.

Lab Challenge	Running Microsoft Intune Reports
Overview	In this exercise, you will run the Computer Inventory Reports. When the report is open, you will export the report to your desktop and then open the report.
Mindset	Understanding software and hardware assets can aid in the planning and deployment process of new software and hardware across your organization. Managing your assets means knowing the software and hardware your organization uses. Microsoft Intune also collects hardware and software information from the agent. This happens automatically or on a customizable schedule; the process is entirely invisible to the end user.
Completion time	10 minutes

1. On the Windows 10 computer that is connected to the Internet, using Internet Explorer/Microsoft Intune console, click the **REPORTS** workspace, as shown in Figure 6-7.

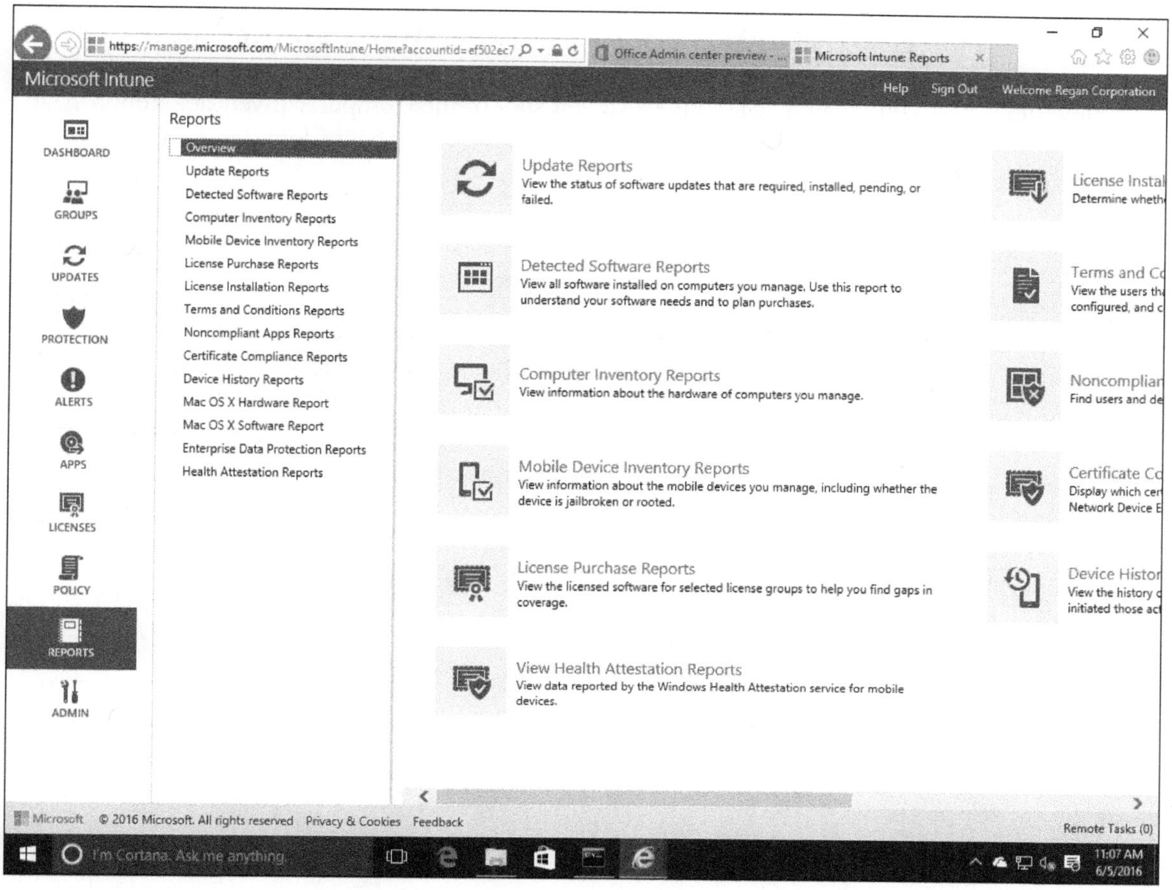

Figure 6-7
Managing Microsoft Intune reports

2. In the left pane, click **Computer Inventory Reports**.
3. Under Select operating systems, click **Edit**.
4. Select **Include only the following**, choose **Windows 10**, and then click **OK**.
5. Click **View Report**.
6. Move your mouse over the icon in the upper-right corner and then click **Export (black icon with right arrow)**.
7. On the Select the Export Format for Your Data Page, click the down arrow and then choose **.html**. Click **Export**.

8. Choose **Desktop** as the location to save your file to and then type **MyWin10InvRpt**. Click **Save**.
9. When the report is exported, click **Close**.
10. To open the file, go to your desktop and double-click the **MyWin10InvRpt** file.
11. View the report you created. Then take a screen shot of the Computer Inventory Report page by pressing **Alt+PrtScr** and then paste it into your Lab06_worksheet file in the page provided by pressing **Ctrl+V**.
12. Close the report.

Question 11	*You just added several computers a few minutes ago to Microsoft Intune and you ran the software report, but the report didn't report any software. What is the problem?*

End of lab.

LAB 7 DEPLOYING SOFTWARE UPDATES BY USING MICROSOFT INTUNE

THIS LAB CONTAINS THE FOLLOWING EXERCISES AND ACTIVITIES:

Exercise 7.1 Identifying, Approving, and Declining Updates Using Microsoft Intune

Exercise 7.2 Deploying Automatic Updates in Microsoft Intune

Lab Challenge Deploying Third-Party Updates with Microsoft Intune

BEFORE YOU BEGIN

The lab environment consists of student workstations connected to a local area network, along with a server that functions as the domain controller for a domain called adatum.com. The computers required for this lab are listed in Table 7-1.

Table 7-1
Computers required for Lab 7

Computer	*Operating System*	*Computer Name*
Client	Windows 10	A machine running Windows 10 that is connected to the Internet.

In addition to the computers, you will also require the software listed in Table 7-2 to complete Lab 7.

Table 7-2
Software required for Lab 7

Software	***Location***
Lab 7 student worksheet	Lab07_worksheet.docx (provided by instructor)

Working with Lab Worksheets

Each lab in this manual requires that you answer questions, shoot screen shots, and perform other activities that you will document in a worksheet named for the lab, such as Lab07_worksheet.docx. You will find these worksheets on the book companion site. It is recommended that you use a USB flash drive to store your worksheets, so you can submit them to your instructor for review. As you perform the exercises in each lab, open the appropriate worksheet file, fill in the required information, and then save the file to your flash drive.

SCENARIO

After completing this lab, you will be able to:

- Identify, approve and decline updates using Microsoft Intune
- Configure automatic updates using Microsoft Intune
- Deploy third-party updates with Microsoft Intune

Estimated lab time: 55 minutes

NOTE	*If you are using the MOAC Labs Online system, you will not be able to perform this exercise. Instead, you need to use a computer running Windows 10 with access to the Internet. If your classroom has a dedicated Windows Server 2012 R2 or Windows Server 2016, you can use a virtual machine running Windows 10.*

Exercise 7.1	Identifying, Approving, and Declining Updates Using Microsoft Intune
Overview	In this exercise, you will view and filter the various updates available in Microsoft Intune. You will then approve and decline updates.
Mindset	Because updates can cause problems with Windows or other applications, you might want to review and manage certain updates closely before approving and deploying them. In these situations, perform a manual update from the Updates workspace.
Completion time	15 minutes

1. Log in to a computer running Windows 10 that is connected to the Internet.

2. Launch Internet Explorer and then go to the **Microsoft Intune Account Portal (http://portal.office.com)**. Log in with your Intune account.

3. Click the **Admin centers** workspace (last workspace) and then click **Intune**.

4. Click the Updates workspace and then click **All Updates**, as shown in Figure 7-1.

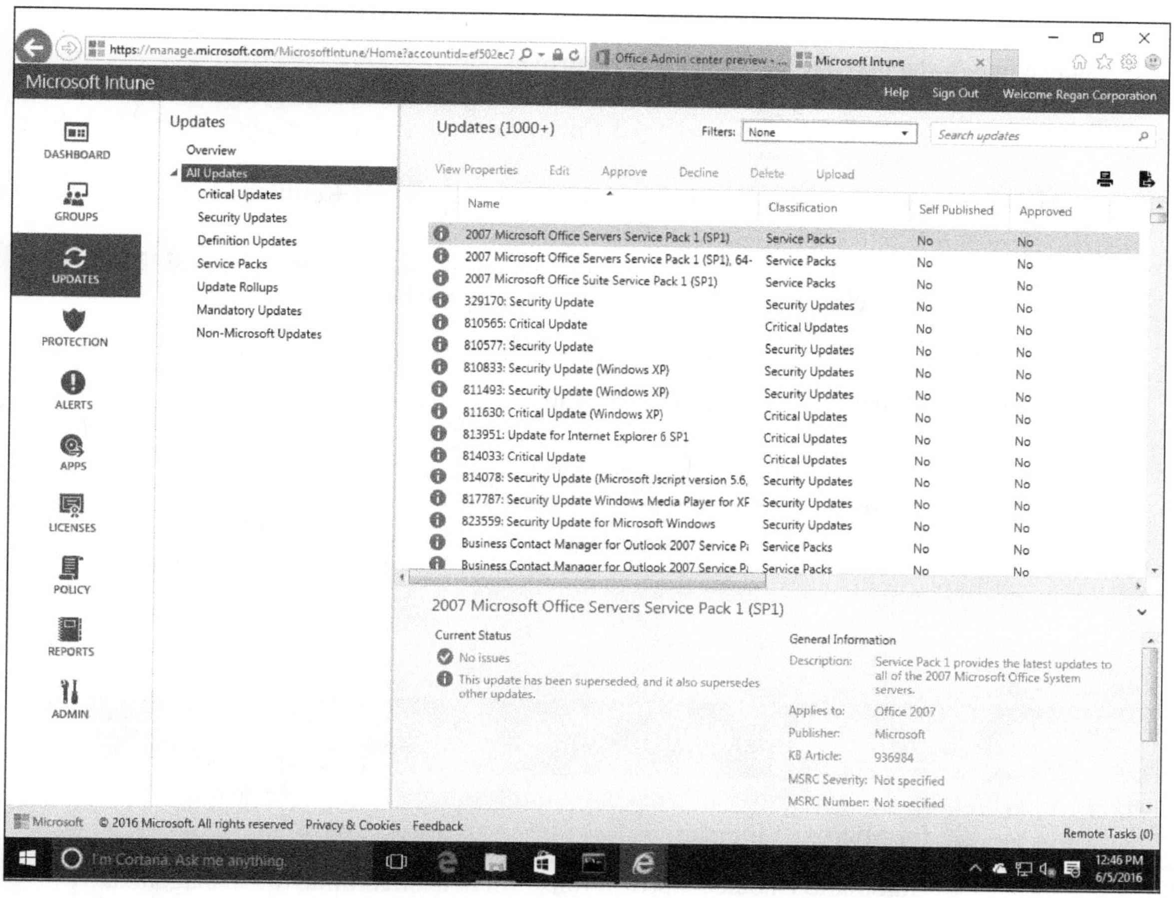

Figure 7-1
Viewing all updates

5. At the top of the page, from the **Filters** drop-down menu, select **New updates to approve**.

6. From the **Filters** drop-down menu, select the **None** filter.

7. In the Search updates text box, type "**Windows 10**" (with the quotes) and press **Enter**.

8. Select the first update.

Question 1	*What is the KB article associated with the update?*

9. Look at the bottom pane to view information about the update.
10. From the **Filters** drop-down menu, select **Superseded**.
11. Choose one of the updates and then click **Approve**.
12. On the Select Groups page, choose the **All Computers** group and then click **Add**. Click **Next**.
13. On the Deployment Action page, for the approval column, select **Required Install**. Click **Finish**.
14. Take a screen shot of the Updates page by pressing **Alt+PrtScr** and then paste it into your Lab07_worksheet file in the page provided by pressing **Ctrl+V**.
15. To decline an update, right-click the same update you approved before and choose **Decline**. When you are prompted to confirm, click **Decline**.
16. Take a screen shot of the Updates page by pressing **Alt+PrtScr** and then paste it into your Lab07_worksheet file in the page provided by pressing **Ctrl+V**.

Leave Internet Explorer open for the next exercise.

Exercise 7.2	Configuring Automatic Updates in Microsoft Intune
Overview	In this exercise, you will configure Automatic Update Approval rules for Microsoft Intune.
Mindset	Automatic Update Approval rules can help streamline the management of your computers. When you create a rule, Microsoft Intune automatically approves the installation of all critical and security updates as soon as Microsoft releases them. This ensures your clients are updated as soon as possible.
Completion time	15 minutes

1. On the Windows 10 computer that is connected to the Internet, using Enternet Explorer/ Microsoft Intune console, you should already be in the UPDATES workspace. Under tasks, click **Configure Updates**. The Service Settings: Updates page opens, as shown in Figure 7-2.

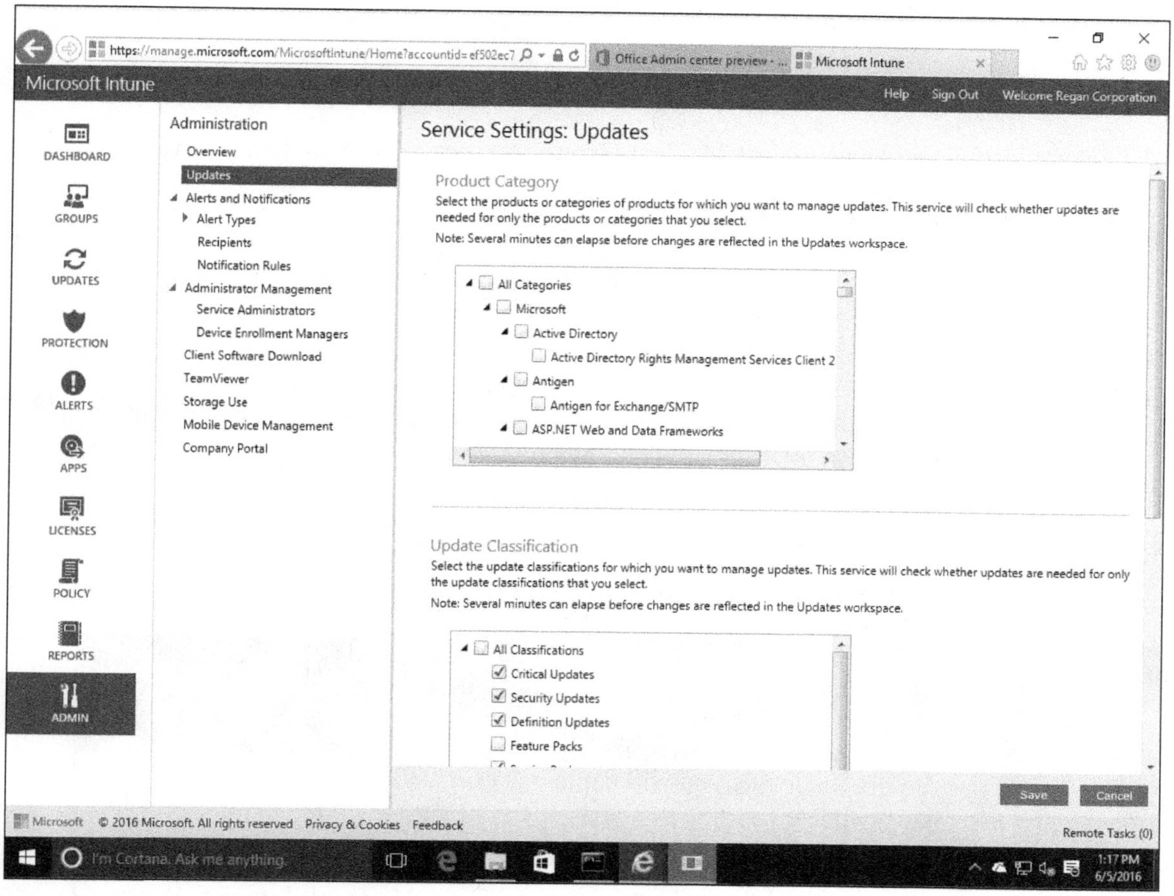

Figure 7-2
Managing updates

Question 2	*Under Product Category, scroll down to Microsoft Office. Which versions are already selected?*

2. Scroll down and view the versions of Windows that are selected.

Question 3	*In the Update Classification settings, which classifications are selected?*

3. Scroll down until you see the Automatic Approval Rules section. Then click **New**.

4. In the Create Automatic Approval Rule window, on the General page, in the Name text box, type **ApprovalRule**. Click **Next**.

5. On the Product Categories page, select **Windows 10** and **Office 2016**. Click **Next**.

6. On the Update Classifications page, select **All Classifications** and then click **Next**.

7. On the Deployment page, select **My Test Group** and then click **Add**. Click **Next**.

8. On the Summary page, click **Finish**.

9. Back on on the Service Settings: Updates page, click **Run Selected**.

10. Click **Save**.

11. Take a screen shot of the Updates page by pressing **Alt+PrtScr** and then paste it into your Lab07_worksheet file in the page provided by pressing **Ctrl+V**.

Leave Internet Explorer open for the next exercise.

Lab Challenge	Deploying Third-Party Updates with Microsoft Intune
Overview	In this challenge, you will deploy an executable file as a third-party update.
Mindset	Unlike System Center Updates Publisher, Microsoft Intune does not use a catalog of updates. However, you can use Microsoft Intune to deploy updates from third-party vendors. You can download an update file (.msi, msp, or exe) from the vendor and use Microsoft Intune to install it just as it would install any other application. Microsoft Intune allows you to add updates to the Microsoft Intune Updates workspace, which allows you to manage third-party updates just as you would with Microsoft updates.
Completion time	25 minutes

1. On the Windows 10 computer that is connected to the Internet, using Enternet Explorer/ Microsoft Intune console, you should already be in the ADMIN workspace. Click **Overview**.

2. Click the **UPDATES** workspace.

3. Under Tasks, click **Add Updates**.

4. In the Application Run – Security dialog box for the Microsoft Intune Software Publisher (as shown in Figure 7-3), click **Run**.

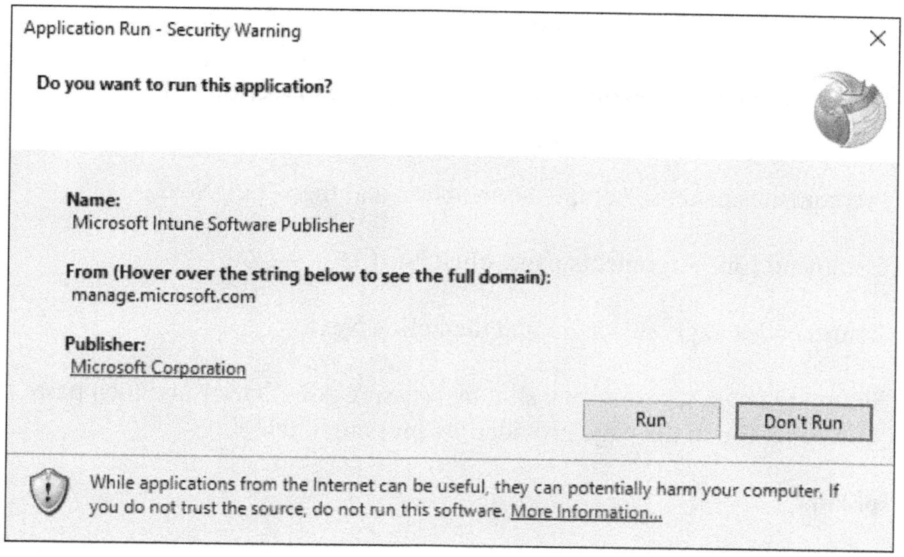

Figure 7-3
Running the application

5. If you are prompted for credentials, log in with your Microsoft Intune credentials.

6. In the Upload Update wizard, on the Before you begin page, click **Next**.

7. On the Update files page, click the **Browse** button and then browse to and select the C:\Software\PowerPointViewer.exe file used in Lab 1. Then click **Open**. Although the PowerPointViewer.exe is a Microsoft file (and not a third-party program), the procedures is still the same.

Question 4	*How big is the setup file?*

8. Click **Next**.

9. On the Update description page, in the Publisher text box, type **Microsoft-Type**.

Question 5	*Which classification is selected?*

10. Click **Next**.

11. On the Requirements page, click **Next**.
12. On the Detection rules page, select the **Use the default detection rules** option and then click **Next**.
13. On the Prerequisites page, select the **None** option and then click **Next**.
14. On the Command Line Arguments page, click **Next**.
15. On the Return codes page, select **No** and then click **Next**.
16. On the Summary page, take a screen shot by pressing **Alt+PrtScr** and then paste it into your Lab07_worksheet file in the page provided by pressing **Ctrl+V**.
17. Click **Upload**.
18. When the upload is complete, click **Close**.
19. Under All Updates, click **Non-Microsoft Updates**.
20. Right-click the **PowerPointViewer.exe** and choose **Approve**.
21. In the PowerPointViewer.exe window, select **My Test Group** and then click **Add**. Click the **Next** button.
22. For the Approval, select **Required Install** and then click **Finish**.
23. Take a screen shot of the Non-Microsoft Updates page by pressing **Alt+PrtScr** and then paste it into your Lab07_worksheet file in the page provided by pressing **Ctrl+V**.
24. Right-click the **PowerPointViewer.exe** file and choose **Delete**. When you are prompted to confirm, click **Yes**.

End of lab.

LAB 8 CONFIGURING IP SETTINGS

THIS LAB CONTAINS THE FOLLOWING EXERCISES AND ACTIVITIES:

Exercise 8.1 Configuring IPv4 Settings

Exercise 8.2 Configuring IPv6 Settings

Exercise 8.3 Configuring Advanced Shared Settings and Network Locations

Lab Challenge Troubleshooting IP Network Problems

BEFORE YOU BEGIN

The lab environment consists of student workstations connected to a local area network, along with a server that functions as the domain controller for a domain called adatum.com. The computers required for this lab are listed in Table 8-1.

Table 8-1
Computers required for Lab 8

Computer	*Operating System*	*Computer Name*
Server (VM 1)	Windows Server 2012 R2	LON-DC1
Client (VM 3)	Windows 10	LON-CL1

In addition to the computers, you will also require the software listed in Table 8-2 to complete Lab 8.

Table 8-2
Software required for Lab 8

Software	*Location*
Lab 8 student worksheet	Lab08_worksheet.docx (provided by instructor)

Working with Lab Worksheets

Each lab in this manual requires that you answer questions, shoot screen shots, and perform other activities that you will document in a worksheet named for the lab, such as Lab08_worksheet.docx. You will find these worksheets on the book companion site. It is recommended that you use a USB flash drive to store your worksheets, so you can submit them to your instructor for review. As you perform the exercises in each lab, open the appropriate worksheet file, fill in the required information, and save the file to your flash drive.

SCENARIO

After completing this lab, you will be able to:

- Configure IPv4 settings
- Configuring IPv6 settings
- Configure advanced shared settings and network locations
- Troubleshoot IP network problems

Estimated lab time: 50 minutes

Exercise 8.1	Configuring IPv4 Settings
Overview	In this exercise, you will configure IPv4 settings, including enabling a DHCP address and manually configuring IPv4 settings.
Mindset	Network settings can be configured manually or you can configure them automatically by using DHCP. Using manual settings can introduce configuration issues that can affect communications. Using a centralized approach to IP address management requires you to have a solid understanding of DHCP.
Completion time	20 minutes

1. Log in to **LON-CL1** as **adatum\administrator** with the password of **Pa$$w0rd**.
2. On **LON-CL1**, right-click the **Network Status** icon and choose **Open Network and Sharing Center**. The Network and Sharing Center opens, as shown in Figure 8-1.

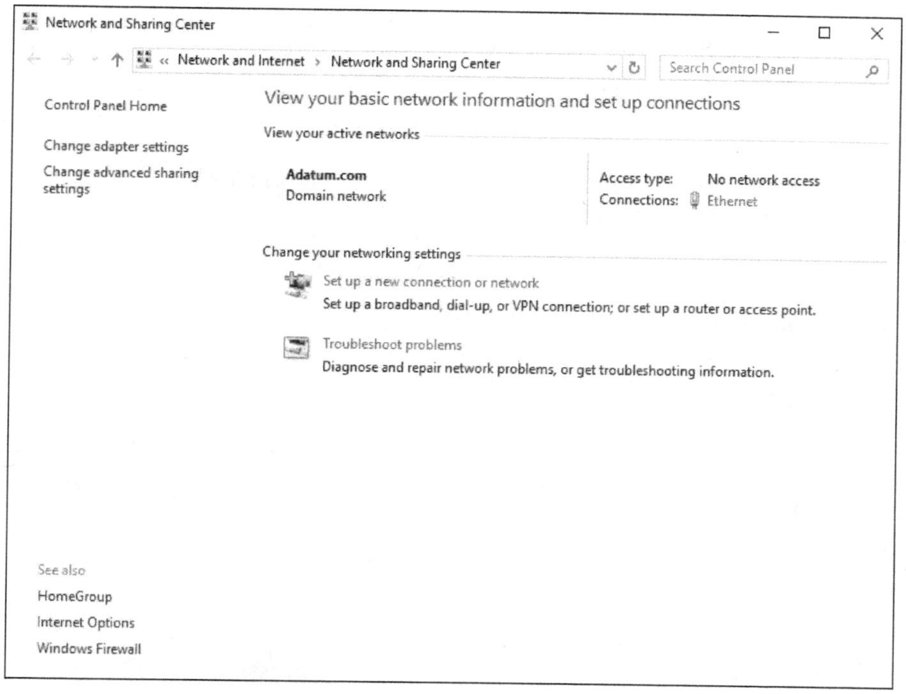

Figure 8-1
The Network and Sharing Center

3. On the Network and Sharing Center page, click **Change adapter settings**.
4. Double-click the **Ethernet** connection.
5. In the Ethernet Status dialog box, click **Properties**.
6. In the Ethernet Properties dialog box, scroll down and double-click **Internet Protocol Version 4 (TCP/IPv4)**.

Question 1	*What is the current IP address configuration for the Ethernet adapter Ethernet connection?*

7. Select the **Obtain an IP address automatically** option. Then select the **Obtain DNS server address automatically** option. Click **OK**.
8. Close the Ethernet Properties dialog box by clicking **OK**.
9. Close the Ethernet Status dialog box by clicking **Close**.
10. Right-click the **Start** button and choose **Command Prompt (Admin)**.

11. At the command prompt, execute the following command:

```
ipconfig
```

Question 2	*What is the current IP address configuration for Ethernet adapter Ethernet connection?*

12. At the command prompt, execute the following command:

```
ipconfig /all
```

Question 3	*How do you know that this address for Ethernet adapter Ethernet was assigned by a DHCP server?*

13. Take a screen shot of the Command Prompt window by pressing **Alt+PrtScr** and then paste it into your Lab08_worksheet file in the page provided by pressing **Ctrl+V**.

Question 4	*Which addresses could be assigned to the Default gateway that would indicate a local router?*

14. Go back to the **Network and Sharing Center** window and double-click **Ethernet**.
15. In the Ethernet Status dialog box, click the **Properties** button.
16. Double-click **Internet Protocol Version 4 (TCP/IPv4)**.
17. In the Internet Protocol Version 4 (TCP/IPv4) Properties dialog box, select **Use the following IP address**.
18. Specify the following information:

    IP address: **172.16.0.40**

    Subnet mask: **255.255.0.0**

    Default gateway: **172.16.0.1**

19. Select the **Use the following DNS server addresses** option and specify the following:

    Preferred DNS server: **172.16.0.10**

20. Close the Internet Protocol Version 4 (TCP/IPv4) Properties dialog box by clicking **OK**.

21. Close the Ethernet Properties dialog box by clicking **OK**.

22. Close the Ethernet Status dialog box by clicking **Close**.

23. Go back to the command prompt window and execute the following command:

```
ipconfig
```

24. Take a screen shot of the Command Prompt window by pressing **Alt+PrtScr** and then paste it into your Lab08_worksheet file in the page provided by pressing **Ctrl+V**.

Leave the Command prompt and Network and Sharing Center open for the next exercise.

Exercise 8.2	Configuring IPv6 Settings
Overview	In this exercise, you will configure IPv6 settings.
Mindset	To overcome the problem of running out of public IPv4 addresses as well as a few issues, IPv6 was developed as the next-generation Internet Protocol version. Because IPv6 uses 128 bits, the addresses are usually divided into groups of 16 bits, written as 4 hex digits.
Completion time	10 minutes

1. On **LON-CL1**, using Network and Sharing Center, click **Ethernet**.

2. In the Ethernet Properties dialog box, click the **Details** button.

3. In the Network connections Details dialog box, answer the following question and then click **Close**.

Question 5	*What is the Link-local IPv6 address?*

4. In the Ethernet Status dialog box, click the **Properties** button.

5. Scroll down and double-click **Internet Protocol Version 6 (TCP/IPv6)**, as shown in Figure 8-2.

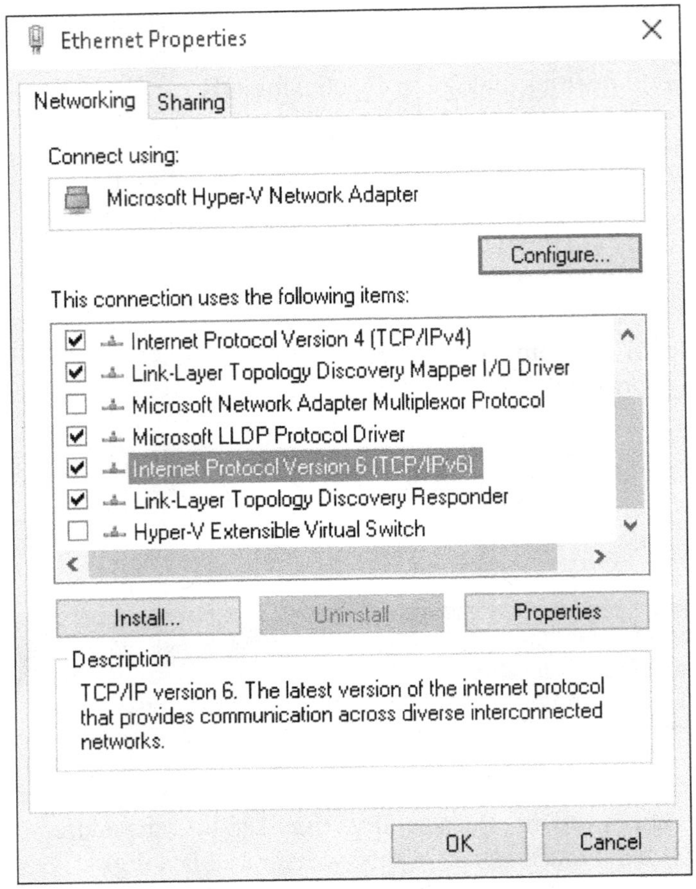

Figure 8-2
Opening Internet Protocol Version 6 (TCP/IPv6) properties

6. Select **Use the following IPv6 address.**

7. Type the following and then click **OK.**

   IPv6 address: **Fe80:0:ac4a:aa04:713A:0:0:CE2B**

   Subnet prefix lenth: **64**

8. Close the Ethernet Properties dialog box by clicking **OK.**

9. Close the Ethernet Status dialog box by clicking **Close.**

10. Go back to the command window and execute the following command:

```
ipconfig
```

11. Take a screen shot of the Command Prompt window by pressing **Alt+PrtScr** and then paste it into your Lab08_worksheet file in the page provided by pressing **Ctrl+V.**

Close the Command Prompt window, but leave the Network and Sharing Center open for the next exercise.

Exercise 8.3	Configuring Advanced Shared Settings and Network Locations
Overview	In this exercise, you will configure the Advanced Shared Settings for Network Locations.
Mindset	Windows 10 has advanced sharing settings that allow you to configure network sharing settings based on your network location. Windows 10 is organized according three sections: Private, Guest, or Public, and All Networks. Each network profile has different defaults that are applied when connecting to and selecting a network connection.
Completion time	10 minutes

1. On **LON-CL1**, using the Network and Sharing Center, answer the following questions:

Question 6	*Which type of network location is being used by the Ethernet connection?*

Question 7	*If you have a second Ethernet adapter, which network location is being used by the adapter?*

2. Click **Change advanced sharing settings**. The Advanced Sharing Settings page is shown (see Figure 8-3).

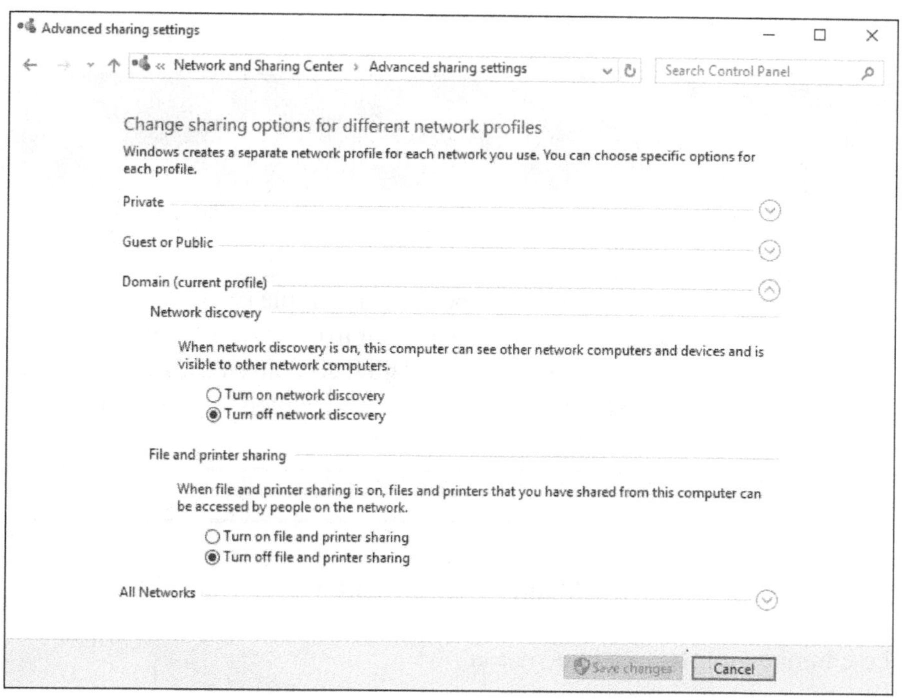

Figure 8-3
Configuring advanced sharing settings

3. Expand the the down arrow next to Domain.

Question 8	*Is network discovery on or off?*

Question 9	*Is file and printer sharing on or off?*

4. Click the Down arrow for All Networks.

Question 10	*Is public folder sharing on or off?*

5. Select the **Turn on sharing so anyone with network access can read and write files in the Public folders** option.

6. Take a screen shot of the Advanced Sharing Settings page by pressing **Alt+PrtScr** and then paste it into your Lab08_worksheet file in the page provided by pressing **Ctrl+V**.

7. Click **Save changes**.

Close the Network and Sharing Center window.

Lab Challenge	Troubleshooting IP Network Problems
Overview	In this challenge, you will use IPConfig, Ping, and NSLookup to troubleshoot IP network problems.
Mindset	Regardless of whether your network is simple or complex, there are several tools that are invaluable when troubleshooting network connectivity problems. No matter how complex your network, you should always follow a troubleshooting methodology that will help you quickly isolate and pinpoint the problem.
Completion time	10 minutes

1. On **LON-CL1**, open the **Network and Sharing Center** again.

2. Click the **Change adapter settings** option.

3. Right-click the **Ethernet 2** adapter and choose **Enable**.
4. Right-click the **Ethernet 2** adapter and choose **Properties**.
5. Double-click **Internet Protocol Version 4 (TCP/IPv4)**.
6. Make sure the **Obtain an IP address automatically** option is selected and then click **OK**.
7. Close the Ethernet 2 Properties dialog box by clicking **OK**.
8. Right-click the **Start** button and choose **Command Prompt (Admin)**.
9. At the command prompt, execute the following command:

```
Ipconfig
```

Question 11	*What is the IP address of the second Ethernet adapter?*

Question 12	*Describe the significance of this address.*

10. To test communications with the domain controller, execute the following command:

```
ping LON-DC1
```

11. Take a screen shot of the Command Prompt window by pressing **Alt+PrtScr** and then paste it into your Lab08_worksheet file in the page provided by pressing **Ctrl+V**.
12. Run the IPConfig command again.

Question 13	*What is the default gateway?*

13. Execute the following command:

```
ping 172.16.0.1
```

Question 14	*If you were not able to ping the default gateway, what problem would this cause with the client?*

14. Execute the following command:

```
Nslookup LON-DC1
```

Question 15	*What is the address of the DNS server that responded with the answer?*

15. Execute the following command:

```
Nslookup 172.16.0.10
```

16. To flush the DNS cache, execute the following command:

```
Ipconfig /flushdns
```

End of lab.

LAB 9 CONFIGURING NETWORK SETTINGS

THIS LAB CONTAINS THE FOLLOWING EXERCISES AND ACTIVITIES:

Exercise 9.1 Configuring Network Adapters

Lab Challenge Configuring Wi-Fi Networking

BEFORE YOU BEGIN

The lab environment consists of student workstations connected to a local area network, along with a server that functions as the domain controller for a domain called adatum.com. The computers required for this lab are listed in Table 9-1.

Table 9-1
Computers required for Lab 9

Computer	*Operating System*	*Computer Name*
Server (VM 1)	Windows Server 2012 R2	LON-DC1
Client (VM 3)	Windows 10	LON-CL1
Client	Windows 10	Client computer with Wi-Fi adapter

In addition to the computers, you will also require the software listed in Table 9-2 to complete Lab 9.

Table 9-2
Software required for Lab 9

Software	*Location*
Lab 9 student worksheet	Lab09_worksheet.docx (provided by instructor)

Working with Lab Worksheets

Each lab in this manual requires that you answer questions, shoot screen shots, and perform other activities that you will document in a worksheet named for the lab, such as Lab09_worksheet.docx. You will find these worksheets on the book companion site. It is recommended that you use a USB flash drive to store your worksheets, so you can submit them to your instructor for review. As you perform the exercises in each lab, open the appropriate worksheet file, fill in the required information, and then save the file to your flash drive.

SCENARIO

After completing this lab, you will be able to:

- Configure Network adapters
- Configure Wi-Fi networking

Estimated lab time: 35 minutes

Exercise 9.1	Configuring Network Adapters
Overview	In this exercise, you will configure advanced settings of network adapters.
Mindset	Network adapters are manufactured many vendors, all of which have different capabilities. To get the most out of network adapters, you need to configure the network adapter properties to specify speed settings, MAC address, performance, and power consumption settings.
Completion time	10 minutes

1. Log in to **LON-CL1** as **adatum\administrator** with the password of **Pa$$w0rd**.
2. On **LON-CL1**, right-click the **Network Status** icon and choose **Open Network and Sharing Center**.
3. In the Network and Sharing Center, click the **Ethernet** connection.
4. In the Ethernet Status dialog box, click the **Properties** button.
5. In the Ethernet Properties dialog box, click the **Configure** button.
6. In the Microsoft Hyper-V Network Adapter Properties dialog box (as shown in Figure 9-1), click the **Advanced** tab.

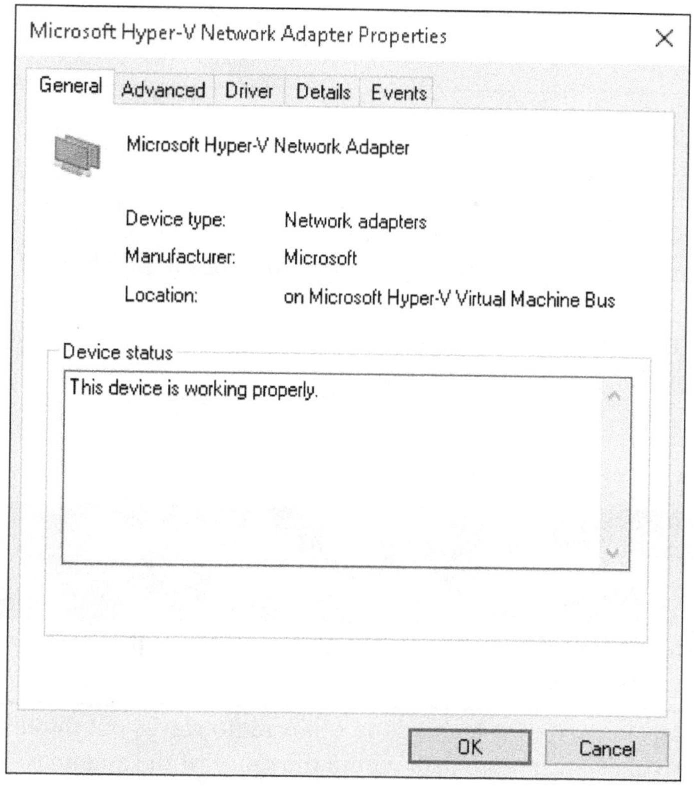

Figure 9-1
The Microsoft Hyper-V Network Adapter Properties dialog box

7. Click the **Receive Buffer Size** property.

Question 1	*What is the Receive Buffer Size set to?*

8. Change the Receive Buffer Size to **4MB**.

9. Take a screen shot of the Microsoft Hyper-V Network Adapter Properties window by pressing **Alt+PrtScr** and then paste it into your Lab09_worksheet file in the page provided by pressing **Ctrl+V**.

10. Click the **Send Buffer Size** property.

Question 2	*What is the Send Buffer Size set to?*

11. Click the **IPSec Offload** property.

Question 3	*What is the IPSec Offload set to?*

12. Close the Microsoft Hyper-V Network Adapter Properties dialog box by clicking **OK**.
13. Close the Ethernet Status dialog box by clicking **Close**.

Log off LON-CL1.

Lab Challenge	Configuring Wi-Fi Networking
Overview	In this exercise, you will configure Wi-Fi on a physical computer running Windows 10.
Mindset	Because wireless technology sends radio waves out into the open, anyone can capture data within the range of the antennas. Therefore, you need to implement encryption and other security measures to prevent data from being read over wireless technology.
Completion time	25 minutes

NOTE	*To perform this exercise, you will need to use a physical laptop or desktop with a wireless network card running Windows 10.*

1. Turn on the workstation and log on using the **adatum\Administrator** account and the **Pa$$w0rd** password (or any other credentials provided by your instructor).
2. Right-click the **Start** button and choose **Control Panel**. The Control Panel window appears.
3. Click **Network and Internet > Network and Sharing Center**. The Network and Sharing Center control panel appears.
4. Click **Change adapter settings**.
5. If the Wireless Network Connection is disabled, right-click the connection and choose **Enable**.

Question 4	*When a laptop has a built-in wireless adapter or the wireless adapter is physically installed on a computer and it does not appear in Network Connections, what is most likely the problem?*

6. Right-click the **Wireless Network Connection** and choose **Properties**.

Question 5	*Which type of wireless network adapter do you have?*

7. Right-click **Wireless Network Connection** and choose **Connect/Disconnect**.

Question 6	*Which wireless connections are being broadcasted as available?*

Question 7	*When you are using a laptop computer and you are expecting to see a wireless connection being broadcast but none are being displayed, what should you check first?*

NOTE	*Some OEM mobile computers might also have hot keys or software components that allow you to turn on or off the wireless radio.*

8. Click **Open Network and Sharing Center**.
9. Click **Manage wireless networks**.
10. Click the **Add** button.
11. When you are prompted to confirm that you want to add a network, click the **Manually create a network profile** option.
12. For the **Network name**, type **Adatum01** (or other name provided by your instructor). For the Security type select **WPA2-Personal**. Type **Pa$$w0rd** for the security key.

Question 8	*By default, which Encryption Type is used for WPA2?*

13. Deselect the **Start this connection automatically** and then select **Connect even if the network is not broadcasting**. Click the **Next** button.
14. Click the **Close** button.
15. Go back to the **Manage Wireless Networks**. You should notice the Adatum connection is there.

16. Go back to the **Network Connections** and then right-click **Wireless Network Connection** and choose **Connect/Disconnect**.

17. Click **Adatum01** and click **Connect**.

18. Take a screen shot of the Network and Sharing Center showing you are connected to a wireless network by pressing **Alt+PrtScr** and then paste it into your Lab09_worksheet file in the page provided by pressing **Ctrl+V**.

19. Open a command prompt and execute the ipconfig command.

20. Run a command to ping the default gateway.

21. Back at the **Network Connections**, right-click **Wireless Network Connection** and choose **Status**.

Question 9	*What is the SSID?* *What is the speed?* *What is the signal quality?*

22. Click the **Details** button. Notice the IPv4 address is the same address displayed when you executed the ipconfig command.

23. Click **Close** to close the **Wireless Network Connection Status** dialog box.

24. Notice the Wireless connection icon in the taskbar. Click the wireless connection icon. Then move the mouse pointer to **Adatum01**, but don't click on it.

Question 10	*What is the Radio Type?*

25. Click **Adatum01** and then click **Disconnect**.

End of lab.

LAB 10
CONFIGURING AND MAINTAINING NETWORK SECURITY

THIS LAB CONTAINS THE FOLLOWING EXERCISES AND ACTIVITIES:

Exercise 10.1 Configuring Windows Firewall

Exercise 10.2 Configuring Connection Security Rules (IPsec)

Lab Challenge Creating an Authentication Exception Rule

BEFORE YOU BEGIN

The lab environment consists of student workstations connected to a local area network, along with a server that functions as the domain controller for a domain called adatum.com. The computers required for this lab are listed in Table 10-1.

Table 10-1
Computers required for Lab 10

Computer	*Operating System*	*Computer Name*
Server (VM 1)	Windows Server 2012 R2	LON-DC1
Client (VM 2)	Windows 10	LON-CL1
Client (VM 3)	Windows 10	LON-CL4

In addition to the computers, you will also require the software listed in Table 10-2 to complete Lab 10.

Table 10-2
Software required for Lab 10

Software	*Location*
Lab 10 student worksheet	Lab10_worksheet.docx (provided by instructor)

Working with Lab Worksheets

Each lab in this manual requires that you answer questions, shoot screen shots, and perform other activities that you will document in a worksheet named for the lab, such as Lab10_worksheet.docx. You will find these worksheets on the book companion site. It is recommended that you use a USB flash drive to store your worksheets, so you can submit them to your instructor for review. As you perform the exercises in each lab, open the appropriate worksheet file, fill in the required information, and then save the file to your flash drive.

SCENARIO

After completing this lab, you will be able to:

- Configure Windows Firewall
- Configure Connection Security Rules (IPsec)
- Create an Authentication Exception Rule

Estimated lab time: 60 minutes

Exercise 10.1	Configuring Windows Firewall
Overview	In this exercise, you will create a Windows Firewall outbound rule.
Mindset	By default, Windows Firewall allows only certain packets to pass to and from the computer. If you have packets that need to be sent from your computer without being blocked by the Windows Firewall, you need to know how to adjust the firewall.
Completion time	10 minutes

1. Log in to **LON-CL1** as **adatum\administrator** with the password of **Pa$$w0rd**.
2. On **LON-CL1**, right-click the **Start** button and choose **Control Panel**.

3. In the Control Panel, click **System and Security** and then click **Windows Firewall**.

Question 1	*You just installed a new application but users cannot connect to the application remotely. Which feature should be checked to ensure it's not preventing users from accessing a remote application?*

4. On the Windows Firewall page (see Figure 10-1), in the left pane, click **Advanced settings**.

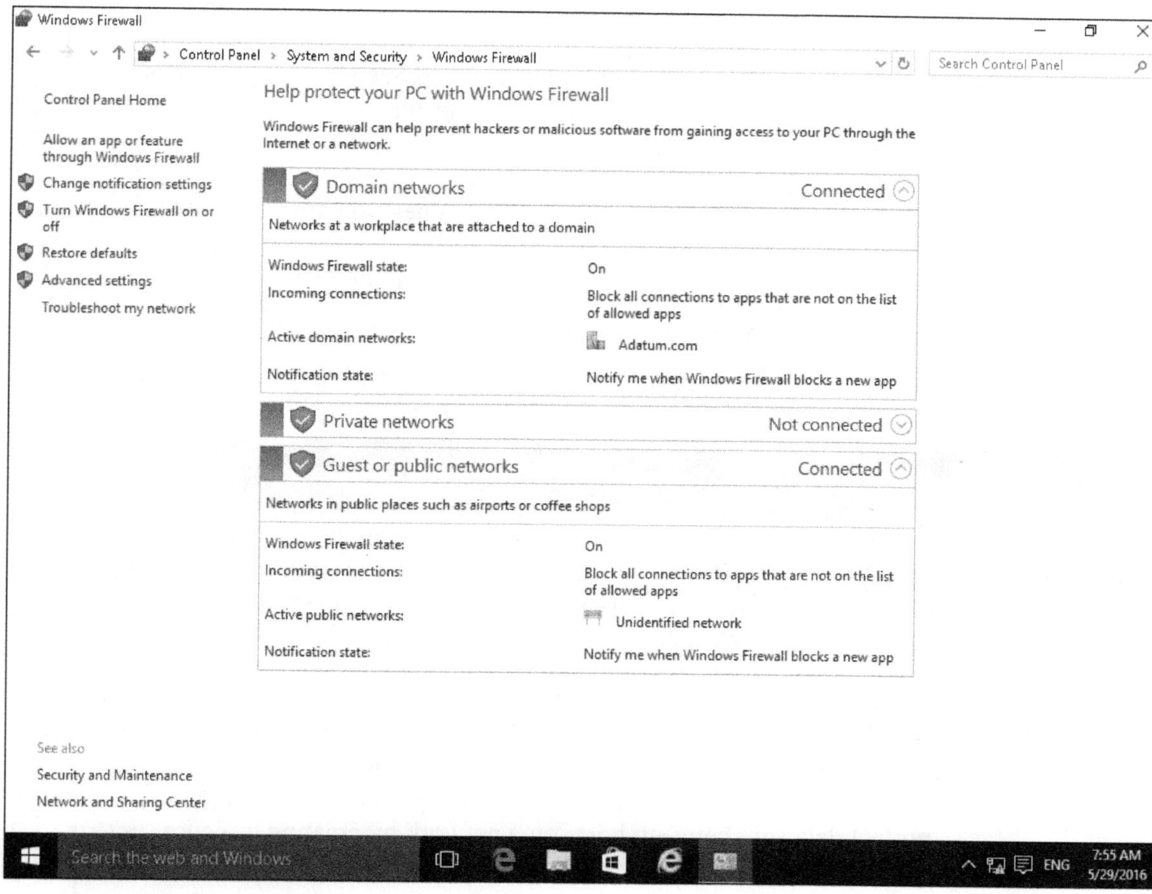

Figure 10-1
The Windows Firewall page

5. Click, and then right-click, **Outbound Rules.** Choose **New Rule**.

6. Select **Program** and then click **Next**.

7. Click **Browse** and then navigate to the location of your installation of Internet Explorer. This can usually be found at C:\Program Files\Internet Explorer\iexplore.exe. Click **iexplore.exe** and then click **Open**.

8. On the New Outbound Rule Wizard page, click **Next**.
9. Select **Block the connection** and then click **Next**.
10. Select **Domain, Private, and Public** and then click **Next**.
11. For the name of the profile, type **IE Restriction**; for the description, type **Restricts IE from connecting to the Internet**.
12. Click **Finish**.
13. Close the Control Panel Windows Firewall window.
14. Take a screen shot of the Windows Firewall with Advanced Security window by pressing **Alt+Prt Scr** and then paste it into your Lab10_worksheet file in the page provided by pressing **Ctrl+V**.
15. Right-click the **IE Restriction** rule and choose **Delete**. When you are prompted to confirm, click **Yes**.

Leave Windows Firewall with Advanced security logged in for the next exercise.

Exercise 10.2	Configuring Connection Security Rules (IPsec)
Overview	In this exercise, on LON-CL4, you will create an inbound rule that allows ICMPv4 packets through the firewall that will accept the packet only if it is secure. You will then create connection security rules betweewn LON-CL1 and LON-CL4 that will provide security between the two machines.
Mindset	IP security (IPsec) is a suite of protocols that provides a mechanism for data integrity, authentication, and privacy for the Internet Protocol by providing message authentication and/or encryption. It can be used to protect data sent between hosts on a network by creating a secure electronic tunnel between two hosts. It can also be used for remote access/VPN connections.
Completion time	40 minutes

1. Log on to LON-CL4 as **LON-CL4\Admin** with the password of **Pa$$w0rd**.
2. On **LON-CL4**, using **Windows Firewall with Advanced Security** (as shown in Figure 10-2), click, and then right-click, **Inbound Rules**. Click **New Rule**.

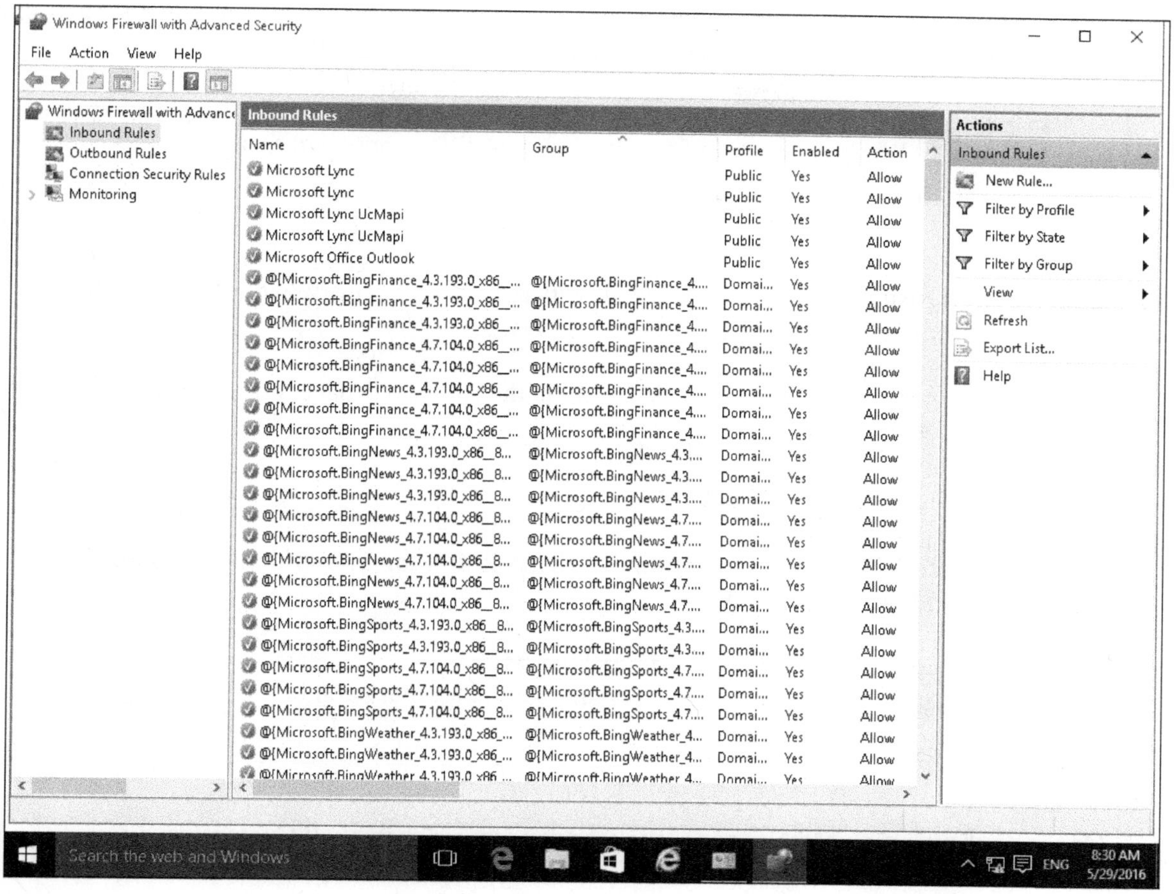

Figure 10-2
The Inbound Rules page

3. In the New Inbound Rule Wizard dialog box, on the Rule Type page, click **Custom** and then click **Next**.

4. On the Program page, click **Next**.

5. On the Protocols and Ports page, in the Protocol type list, select **ICMPv4** and then click **Next**.

6. On the Scope page, click **Next**.

7. On the Action page, click **Allow the connection if it is secure** and then click **Next**.

8. On the Users page, click **Next**.

9. On the Computers page, click **Next**.

10. On the Profile page, click **Next**.

11. On the Name page, in the Name box, type **ICMPv4 Allowed** and then click **Finish**.

12. Take a screen shot of the Inbound Rules window by pressing **Alt+Prt Scr** and then paste it into your Lab10_worksheet file in the page provided by pressing **Ctrl+V**.

Question 2	*Which program is used to configure IPSec between two computers?*

13. On **LON-CL1**, using the Windows Firewall with Advanced Security window, click, and then right-click, **Connection Security Rules**. Click **New Rule**.

14. In the New Connection Security Rule Wizard, on the Rule Type page, click **Server-to-Server** and then click **Next**.

15. On the Endpoints page, click **Next**.

16. On the Requirements page, click **Require authentication for inbound and outbound connections** and then click **Next**.

Question 3	*When using IPsec, how can you ensure that each computer uses its own private key pair?*

17. On the Authentication Method page, click **Advanced** and then click **Customize**.

18. In the Customize Advanced Authentication Methods dialog box, under First authentication, click **Add**.

19. In the Add First Authentication Method dialog box, click **Preshared Key**, type **secret**, and then click **OK**.

20. In the Customize Advanced Authentication Methods dialog box, click **OK**.

21. On the Authentication Method page, click **Next**.

22. On the Profile page, click **Next**.

23. On the Name page, in the Name box, type **Client to Client** and then click **Finish**.

24. Take a screen shot of the Connection Security Rules window by pressing **Alt+Prt Scr** and then paste it into your Lab10_worksheet file in the page provided by pressing **Ctrl+V**.

25. On **LON-CL4**, using Windows Firewall with Advanced Security, click, and then right-click, **Connection Security Rules**. Click **New Rule**.

26. In the New Connection Security Rule Wizard, on the Rule Type page, click **Server-to-Server** and then click **Next**.

27. On the Endpoints page, click **Next**.

28. On the Requirements page, click **Require authentication for inbound and outbound connections** and then click **Next**.

29. On the Authentication Method page, click **Advanced** and then click **Customize**.

30. In the Customize Advanced Authentication Methods dialog box, under First authentication, click **Add**.

31. In the Add First Authentication Method dialog box, click **Preshared Key**, type **secret**, and then click **OK**.

32. In the Customize Advanced Authentication Methods dialog box, click **OK**.

33. On the Authentication Method page, click **Next**.

34. On the Profile page, click **Next**.

35. On the Name page, in the Name box, type **Client to Client** and then click **Finish**.

36. Close the Windows Firewall window.

37. Take a screen shot of the Connection Security Rules window by pressing **Alt+Prt Scr** and then paste it into your Lab10_worksheet file in the page provided by pressing **Ctrl+V**.

38. On **LON-CL1**, right-click the **Start** button and choose **Command Prompt (Admin)**.

39. At the command prompt, type **ping 172.16.0.43** and press **Enter**. 172.16.0.43 is the IP address of LON-CL4.

40. Switch to Windows Firewall with Advanced Security. Expand **Monitoring**, expand **Security Associations**, and then click **Main Mode**.

41. In the right-pane, double-click the listed item. View the information in **Main Mode**.

42. Take a screen shot of the Main Mode window by pressing **Alt+Prt Scr** and then paste it into your Lab10_worksheet file in the page provided by pressing **Ctrl+V**.

43. Click **OK**.

44. Click **Quick Mode**.

45. Take a screen shot of the Quick Mode window by pressing **Alt+PrtScr** and then paste it into your Lab10_worksheet file in the page provided by pressing **Ctrl+V**.

46. In the right-pane, double-click the listed item. View the information in **Quick Mode** and then click **OK**.

47. On **LON-CL1**, click the **Connection Security Rules** node under Windows Firewall with Advanced Security. Do not click the Connection Security Rules under Monitoring.

48. Right-click the **Client to Client** security rule and choose **Delete**. When you are prompted to confirm, click **Yes**.

49. On **LON-CL4**, click **Connection Security Rules** node under Windows Firewall with Advanced Security. Do not click the Connection Security Rules under Monitoring.

50. Right-click the **Client to Client** security rule and choose **Delete**. When you are prompted to confirm, click **Yes**.

51. Click the **Inbound Rules** node.

52. Right-click the **ICMPv4 Allowed rule** and choose **Delete**. When you are prompted to confirm, click **Yes**.

Leave LON-CL4 logged in for the next exercise.

Lab Challenge	Creating an Authentication Exception Rule
Overview	In this challenge, you will create an authentication exception rule.
Mindset	Inbound firewall rules specify computers and users that are authorized to access the local computer over the network. However, with Windows Firewall with Advanced Security, you can create an authentication exemption that designates computers that do not require authentication, such as those computers that are in an isolated domain.
Completion time	10 minutes

1. On **LON-CL4**, in the Windows Firewall with Advanced Security console, click **Connection Security Rules**, right-click it, and then choose **New Rule**.

2. In the New Connection Security Rule Wizard, on the Rule Type page, click **Authentication exemption** and then click **Next**.

3. On the Exempt Computers page, create a new exemption and then click **Add**.

4. In the IP Address dialog box, to add a single IP address, click **This IP address or subnet**, type **172.16.0.40** in the text box, and then click **OK**.

Question 4	*If you wanted to apply an exception for the current subnet, what would you type?*

5. Click **Next**.

6. On the Profile page, click **Next**.

7. On the Name page, type **Authentication Exemption** and then click **Finish**.

8. Take a screen shot of the Connection Security Rules window by pressing **Alt+PrtScr** and then paste it into your Lab10_worksheet file in the page provided by pressing **Ctrl+V**.

9. Right-click **Authentication Exception** and choose **Delete**. When you are prompted to confirm, click **Yes**.

End of lab.

LAB 11
SUPPORTING DATA STORAGE

THIS LAB CONTAINS THE FOLLOWING EXERCISES AND ACTIVITIES:

Exercise 11.1 Creating a Simple Volume

Exercise 11.2 Creating a Storage Pool and a Storage Space

Exercise 11.3 Installing and Configuring BranchCache on a File Server

Exercise 11.4 Creating a DFS Namespace

Lab Challenge Using OneDrive to Manage Files/Folders

BEFORE YOU BEGIN

The lab environment consists of student workstations connected to a local area network, along with a server that functions as the domain controller for a domain called adatum.com. The computers required for this lab are listed in Table 11-1.

Table 11-1
Computers required for Lab 11

Computer	*Operating System*	*Computer Name*
Server (VM 1)	Windows Server 2012 R2	LON-DC1
Server (VM 2)	Windows Server 2012 R2	LON-SRV1
Server (VM 3)	Windows Server 2012 R2	LON-SRV2
Client (VM 4)	Windows 10	LON-CL1

In addition to the computers, you will also require the software listed in Table 11-2 to complete Lab 11.

Table 11-2
Software required for Lab 11

Software	*Location*
Lab 11 student worksheet	Lab11_worksheet.docx (provided by instructor)

Working with Lab Worksheets

Each lab in this manual requires that you answer questions, shoot screen shots, and perform other activities that you will document in a worksheet named for the lab, such as Lab11_worksheet.docx. You will find these worksheets on the book companion site. It is recommended that you use a USB flash drive to store your worksheets, so you can submit them to your instructor for review. As you perform the exercises in each lab, open the appropriate worksheet file, fill in the required information, and then save the file to your flash drive.

SCENARIO

After completing this lab, you will be able to:

- Create a Simple Volume
- Create a Storage Pool and a Storage Space
- Install and Configure BranchCache on a File Server
- Create a DFS Namespace
- Use OneDrive to Manage Files/Folders

Estimated lab time: 130 minutes

Exercise 11.1	Creating a Simple Volume
Overview	In this exercise, you will first create a simple volume and then you will expand the simple volume.
Mindset	A simple volume is a type of volume that uses free space available on a single disk. Since it only requires a single disk, a simple volume is the quickest and easiest to set up.
Completion time	20 minutes

1. Log in to **LON-CL1** as **adatum\administrator** with the password of **Pa$$w0rd**.

2. On **LON-CL1**, right-click the **Start** button and choose **Disk Management**. Disk Management opens, as shown in Figure 11-1.

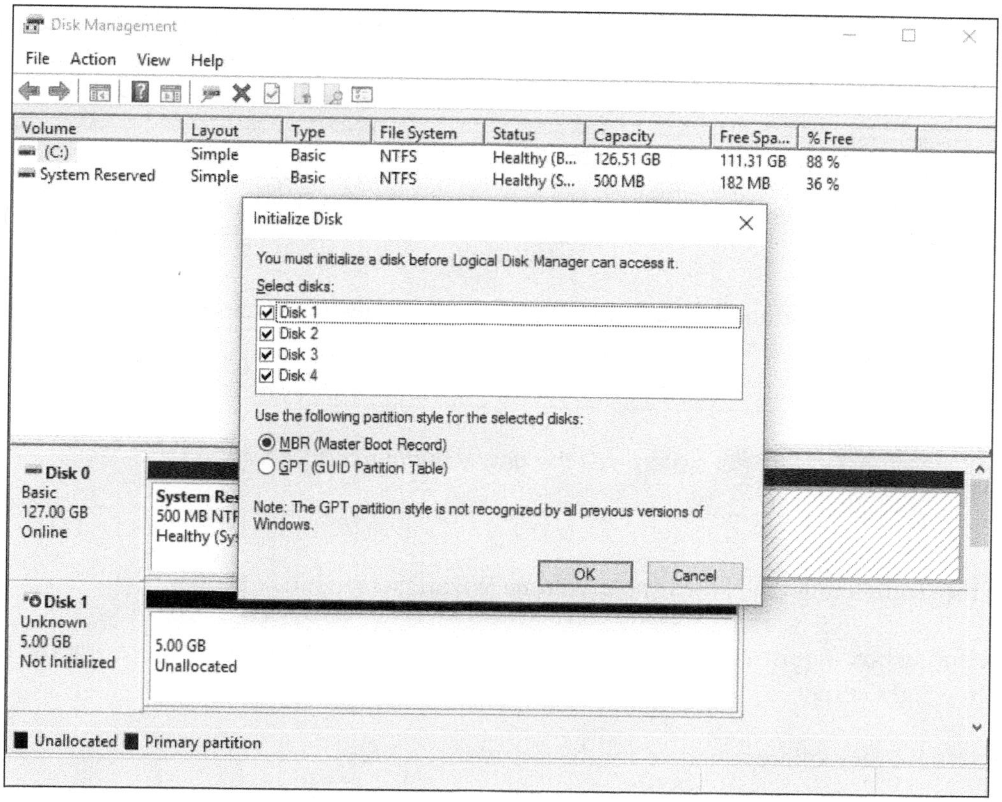

Figure 11-1
Managing Disks with Disk Management

Question 1	*Where else can you find Disk Management?*

3. Close the Intialize Disk dialog box by clicking **Cancel**.

4. Expand Disk Management to fill the entire screen.

Question 2	*How many spare non-initialized disks do you have?*

5. Right-click the 10 GB disk and choose **Initialize Disk**.

6. In the Initialize Disk dialog box, click **OK**.

7. Right-click the 10 GB Unallocated disk and choose **New Simple Volume**.

8. In the New Simple Volume Wizard, on the Welcome screen, click **Next**.

9. On the Specify Volume Size page, for the Simple volume size in MB, type **5000** and then click **Next**.

10. On the Assign Drive Letter or Path screen, answer the following question. Then make sure that the assign the drive letter is **F** and then click **Next**.

Question 3	*What drive letter is going to be assigned to the new volume?*

11. On the Format Partition screen, answer the following question. Then in the Volume label text box, type **Data**. Click **Next**.

Question 4	*What file system will the new volume use?*

12. On the Completing the New Simple Volume Wizard screen, click **Finish**.

13. If a dialog box inquires about formatting a drive, close the dialog box by clicking the **X** button in the top right corner.

14. Close the File Explorer window for the E drive.

15. Take a screen shot of Disk Management showing the new volume by pressing **Alt+PrtScr** and then paste it into your Lab11_worksheet file in the page provided by pressing **Ctrl+V**.

16. To expand the new drive, right-click the partition that you just created (F drive) and choose **Extend Volume**.

17. In the Extend Volume Wizard, on the Welcome page, click **Next**.

18. On the Select Disks page, answer the following question and then click **Next**.

Question 5	*How much free disk space is available on Disk 4?*

19. On the Completing the Extend Volume Wizard page, click **Finish**.

20. Take a screen shot of Disk Management showing the new volume by pressing **Alt+PrtScr** and then paste it into your Lab11_worksheet file in the page provided by pressing **Ctrl+V**.

Remain logged in to LON-CL1 for the next exercise.

Exercise 11.2	Creating a Storage Pool and a Storage Space
Overview	In this exercise, you will create a storage pool and then you will create a storage space.
Mindset	To improve the performance and reliability of the disk system used on Windows 10, you can use Storage Pool and Storage Space to use disk space from multiple disks.
Completion time	10 minutes

1. On **LON-CL1**, right-click the **Start** button and choose **Control Panel**.
2. In the Control Panel pane, click **System and Security > Storage Spaces**.
3. On the Manage Storage Spaces page (see Figure 11-2), click **Create a new pool and storage space**.

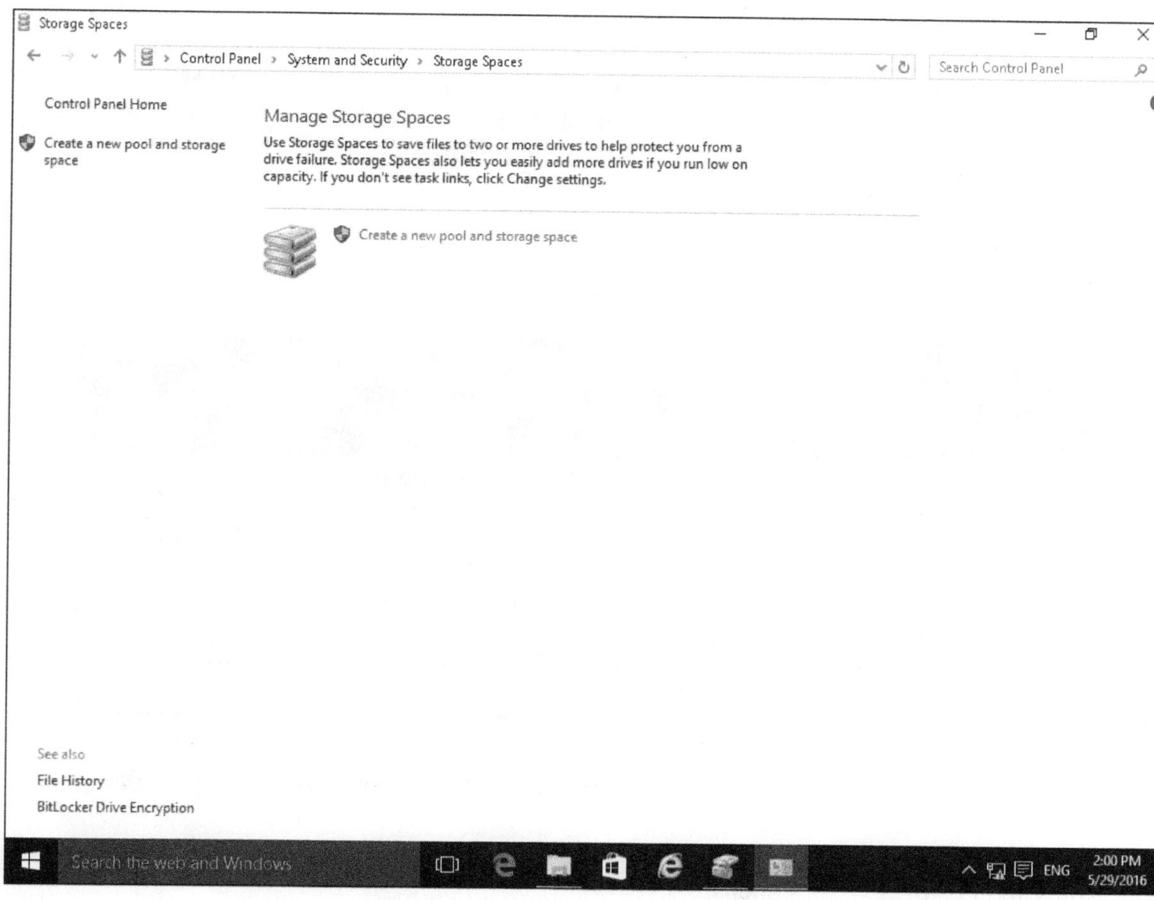

Figure 11-2
The *Manage Storage Spaces* page

4. On the Select drives to create a storage pool page, click **Create pool**.

Question 6	*Which drive letter will be assigned to the Storage space?*

5. Change the drive letter to **G**.

Question 7	*What is the default resiliency type?*

Question 8	*How many disk failures can a two-way mirror have before you lose the data?*

6. Click the **Create storage space** button.
7. Take a screen shot showing the Manage Storage Spaces page by pressing **Alt+PrtScr** and then paste it into your Lab11_worksheet file in the page provided by pressing **Ctrl+V**.

Close any open windows before you begin the next exercise.

Exercise 11.3	Installing and Configuring BranchCache on a File Server
Overview	In this exercise, you will install and configure BranchCache so that it can be used with file shares.
Mindset	BranchCache allows for WAN acceleration functionality by using multiple systems to create a cache infrastructure, which is used to increase performance of web sites and shared folders.
Completion time	40 minutes

1. On **LON-SVR1**, log on using the **adatum\administrator** account and the **Pa$$w0rd** password.
2. On **LON-SVR1**, using Server Manager, click **Manage > Add Roles and Features**. The Add Roles and Features Wizard opens.

3. Click **Next**.

4. On the Select Installation Type page, ensure that **Role-based or feature-based installation** is selected and then click **Next**.

5. On the Select destination server page, click **LON-SVR1.adatum.com** and then click **Next**.

6. On the Select server roles page, under Roles, expand **File and Storage Services** and then expand **File and iSCSI Services**. Click to select **BranchCache for Network Files** and then click **Next**.

7. On the Select features page, select **BranchCache** and then click **Next**.

8. On the Confirm installation selections page, click **Install**. When installation is complete, click **Close**.

9. On **LON-DC1**, log on using the **adatum\administrator** account and the **Pa$$w0rd** password.

10. On **LON-DC1**, using Server Manager, click **Tools > Active Directory Users and Computers**.

11. In the Active Directory Users and Computers console, right-click **Adatum.com** and choose **New > Organizational Unit**.

12. In the New Object – Organization Unit dialog box, in the Name text box, type **Servers** and then click **OK**.

13. Close **Active Directory Users and Computers**.

14. On **LON-DC1**, using Server Manager, click **Tools > Group Policy Management**. The Group Policy Management console opens.

15. Navigate to and right-click the **Servers** OU and then choose **Create a GPO in this domain, and Link it here**.

16. In the New GPO dialog box, in the Name text box, type **BranchCache for Servers**.

17. Click **OK** to close the New GPO dialog box.

18. Expand the **Servers** OU and then right-click the **BranchCache for Servers** GPO and choose **Edit**.

19. In the Group Policy Management Editor window, expand the following path: **Computer Configuration > Policies > Administrative Templates > Network**. Under Network, click **Lanman Server** (see Figure 11-3).

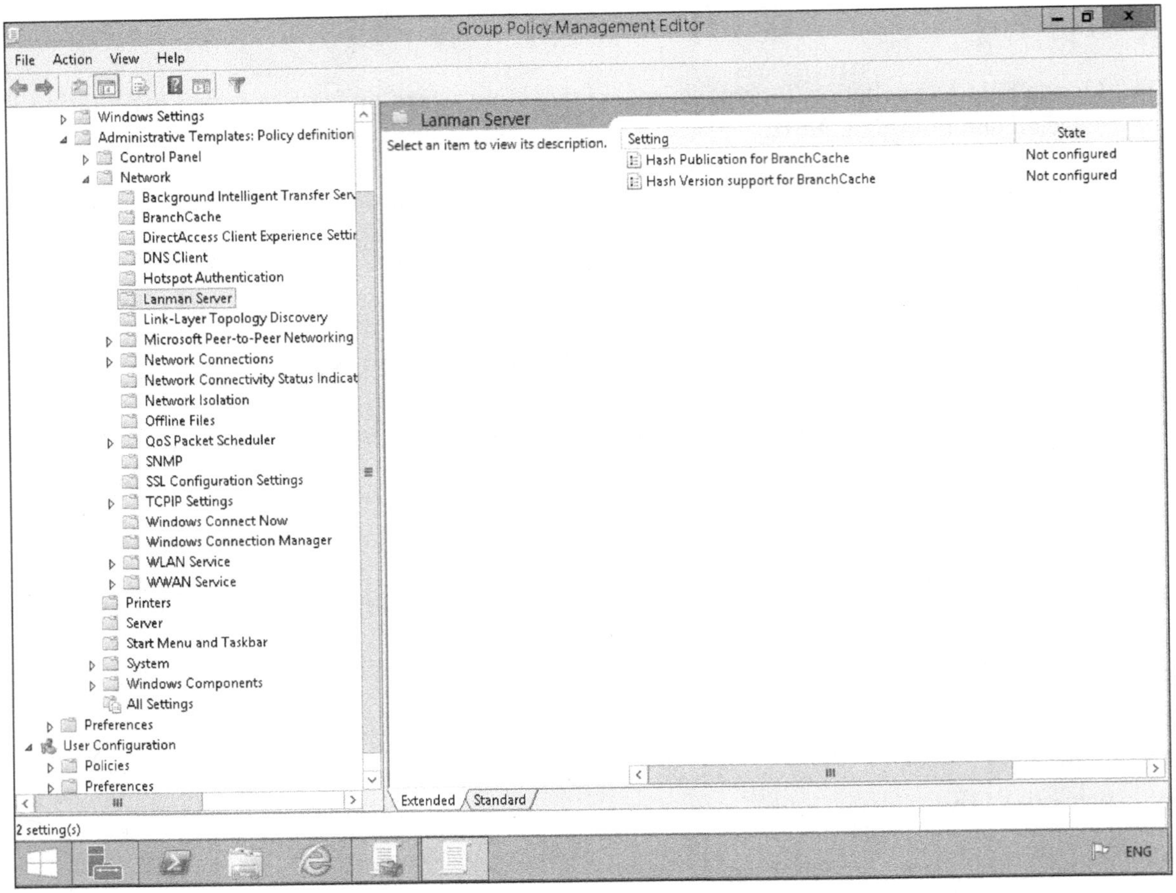

Figure 11-3
The *Lanman Server* node in a GPO

Question 9	*What must all servers in a BranchCache infrastructure have?*

20. Double-click **Hash Publication for BranchCache**. The Hash Publication for BranchCache dialog box opens.
21. In the Hash Publication for BranchCache dialog box, click **Enabled**.
22. In the Options section, **Allow hash publication for all shared folders** is already selected.
23. Take a screen shot of the Hash Publication for BranchCache window by pressing **Alt+PrtScr** and then paste it into your Lab11_worksheet file in the page provided by pressing **Ctrl+V**.
24. Click **OK** to close the Hash Publication for BranchCache window.
25. Close **Group Policy Management Editor**.
26. On **LON-SVR1**, open File Explorer by clicking the **File Explorer** icon on the taskbar.

27. Expand **This PC**, right-click **Local Disk (C:)**, and then choose **New > Folder**. Name the folder **SharedFolder** and then press **Enter**.

28. Right-click the **C:\SharedFolder** and choose **Properties**.

29. Click the **Sharing** tab.

30. Click **Advanced Sharing**.

31. Click **Share this folder** and then click **OK** to close the Advanced Sharing dialog box.

32. Click **Close** to close the SharedFolder Properties dialog box.

33. Close **File Explorer**.

34. On **LON-SVR1**, using Server Manager, click **Tools > Computer Management**.

35. In the Computer Management console, under **System Tools**, expand **Shared Folders** and then click **Shares**.

36. In the Details pane, right-click **SharedFolder** and choose **Properties**. The share's Properties dialog box opens.

37. In the Properties dialog box, on the General tab, click **Offline Settings**. The Offline Settings dialog box opens.

38. Ensure that **Only the files and programs that users specify are available offline** is selected and then click to select **Enable BranchCache**.

39. Take a screen shot of the Offline Settings dialog box by pressing **Alt+PrtScr** and then paste it into your Lab11_worksheet file in the page provided by pressing **Ctrl+V**.

40. Click **OK** twice.

41. Close **Computer Management**.

42. On **LON-DC1**, using Group Policy Management, expand **Group Policy Objects** and then right-click **BranchCache for Servers** and choose **Edit**.

43. In the Group Policy Management Editor window, navigate to the **Computer Configuration > Policies > Administrative Templates > Network** node and then click **BranchCache**.

44. Double-click **Set BranchCache Distributed Cache mode**.

45. In the **Set BranchCache Distributed Cache mode** dialog box, click **Enabled**.

46. Click **OK** to close the Set BranchCache Distributed Cache mode.

47. Close **Group Policy Management Editor**.

48. Close **Group Policy Management**.

49. Using Server Manager, open **Active Directory Users and Computers**.

50. In the Active Directory Users and Computers window, under the Adatum.com domain, click the **Computers** OU.

51. Right-click **LON-SVR1** and choose **Move**.

52. In the Move dialog box, scroll down and click the **Servers** OU and then click **OK**.

53. Close the Active Directory Users and Computers window.

Remain logged in to LON-SVR1 for the next exercise.

Exercise 11.4	Creating a DFS Namespace
Overview	In this exercise, you will install DFS namespace and then create a DFS Namespace that groups \\LON-SVR1\share and \\LON-SVR2\share.
Mindset	DFS Namespace can be used to organize multiple shared folders into a shared folder infrastructure. By accessing the DFS Namespace, users do not worry about which server the shared folders are. Instead, users click and go the specific shared folder.
Completion time	40 minutes

1. On **LON-SVR1**, click the **Server Manager** button on the taskbar to open Server Manager.

2. At the top of Server Manager, select **Manage** and then click **Add Roles and Features**. The Add Roles and Feature Wizard opens.

3. On the Before you begin page, click **Next**.

4. Select Role-based or feature-based installation and then click **Next**.

5. Click Select a server from the server pool, click the name of the server to install **DFS** to, and then click **Next**.

6. Scroll down and expand **File and Storage Services** and then **expand File and iSCSI Services**. Select **File Server, DFS Namespaces,** and **DFS Replication**.

7. When prompted to add features to DFS Namespace, click **Add Features**.

8. When you are back on the Select server roles page, click **Next**.

9. On the Select features page, click **Next**.

10. On the Confirm installation selections, click **Install**.

11. When the installation is complete, click the **Close** button.

12. On **LON-SVR2**, log in as **adatum\administrator** with the password of **Pa$$w0rd**. On the taskbar, click the **Server Manager** tile.

13. At the top of Server Manager, select **Manage** and then click **Add Roles and Features**. The Add Roles and Feature Wizard opens.

14. On the Before you begin page, click **Next**.

15. Select Role-based or feature-based installation and then click **Next**.

16. Click Select a server from the server pool, click the name of the server to install **DFS** to, and then click **Next**.

17. Scroll down and expand **File and Storage Services** and then **expand File and iSCSI Services**. Select **File Server**, **DFS Namespaces**, and **DFS Replication**.

18. When prompted to add features to DFS Namespace, click **Add Features**.

19. When you are back on the Select server roles page, click **Next**.

20. On the Select features page, click **Next**.

21. On the Confirm installation selections, click **Install**.

22. When the installation is complete, click the **Close** button.

23. On **LON-SVR1**, open **File Explorer** and create a folder named **C:\Share**.

24. Right-click the **Share** folder and choose **Properties**. The Properties dialog box opens.

25. Click the **Sharing** tab and then click **Advanced Sharing**.

26. Select the **Share this folder** check box.

27. Click **Permissions**. Click **Allow Full Control** for **Everyone**. To close the Permissions dialog box, click **OK**.

28. Close the Advanced Sharing dialog box by clicking **OK.**

29. Close the Share Properties dialog box by clicking **Close**.

30. On **LON-SVR2**, open **File Explorer** and create a folder named **C:\Share**.

31. Right-click the **Share** folder and choose **Properties**. The Properties dialog box opens.

32. Click the **Sharing** tab and then click **Advanced Sharing**.

33. Select the **Share this folder** check box.

34. Click **Permissions**. Click **Allow Full Control** for **Everyone**. To close the Permissions dialog box, click **OK**.

35. Close Advanced Sharing dialog box by clicking **OK.**

36. Close the Share Properties dialog box by clicking **Close**.

37. On **LON-SVR1**, with Server Manager, click **Tools > DFS Management** to open the DFS Management console, as shown in Figure 11-4.

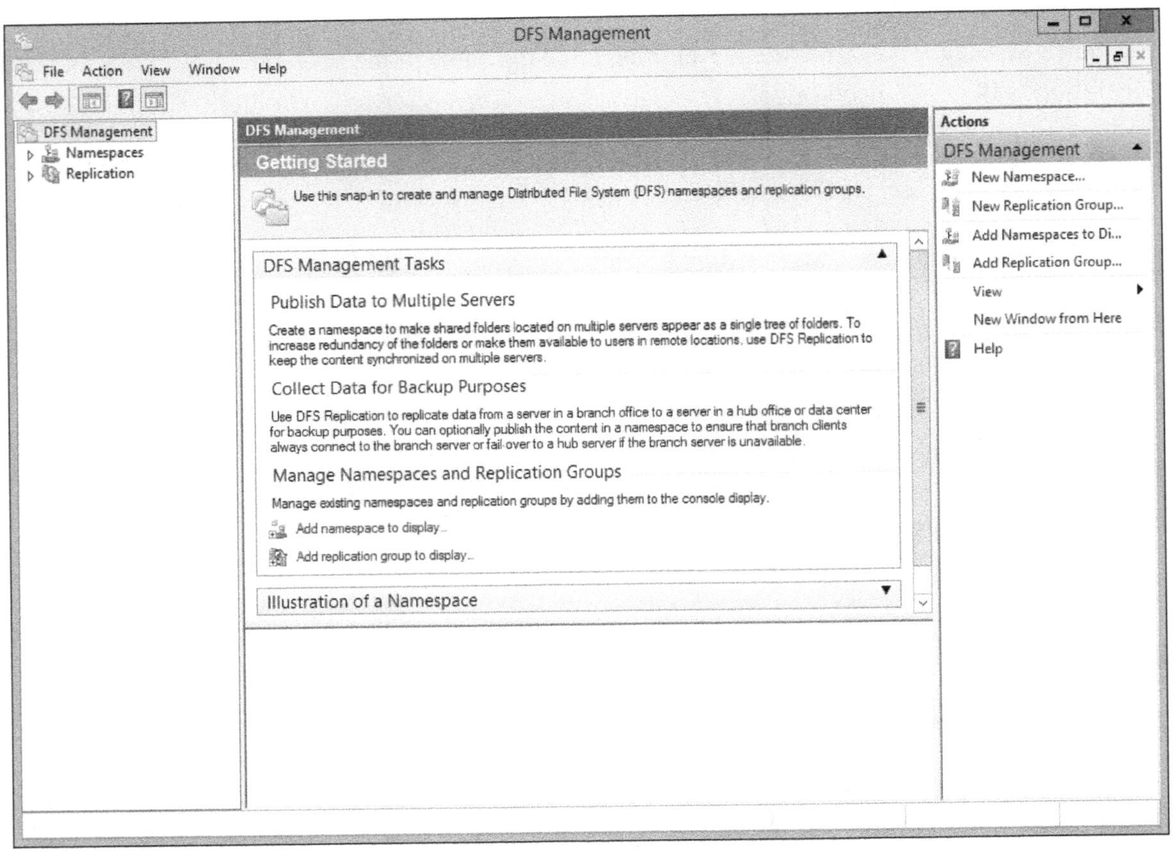

Figure 11-4
The DFS Management console

38. In the left-pane, right-click **Namespaces** and then choose **New Namespace**. The New Namespace Wizard starts.

39. On the Namespace Server page, in the Server text box, type **LON-SVR1** and then click **Next**.

40. On the Namespace Name and Settings page, in the Name text box, type **Shares**.

41. Click **Edit Settings**. The Edit Settings dialog box opens.

42. Click **All users have read and write permissions**. Click **OK** to close the Edit Settings dialog box.

43. On the Namespace Name and Settings page, click **Next**.

44. On the Namespace Type page, with Domain-based namespace already selected and Enable Windows Server 2008 mode selected, click **Next**.

45. Take a screen shot of the New Namespace Wizard box by pressing **Alt+PrtScr** and then paste it into your Lab11_worksheet file in the page provided by pressing **Ctrl+V**.

46. On the Review Settings and Create Namespace page, click **Create**.

47. When the name space is created, click **Close**.

48. On the DFS Management console, in the left pane, expand the Namespaces node and then click **\\Adatum.com\Shares**.

49. Under **Actions**, click **New Folder**. The New Folder dialog box opens.

50. In the Name text box, type **LON Shares**.

51. To specify the shared folder, click **Add**.

52. In the Path to folder target text box, type **\\LON-SVR1\Share** and then click **OK**.

53. Click the **Add** button again.

54. In the Path to folder target text box, type **\\LON-SVR2\Share** and then click **OK**.

55. Close the New Folder dialog box by clicking **OK**.

56. When you are prompted to confirm that you want to create a replication group, click **Yes**.

57. In the Replicate Folder Wizard, on the Replication Group and Replicated Folder name, click **Next**.

58. On the Replication Eligibility page, click **Next**.

59. On the Primary Member page, for the Primary member option, select **LON-SVR1** and then click **Next**.

60. On the Topology Selection page, click **Next**.

61. On the Replication Group Schedule and Bandwidth page, click **Next**.

62. On the Review Settings and Create Replication Group page, click **Create**.

63. On the Confirmation page, take a screen shot by pressing **Alt+PrtScr** and then paste it into your Lab11_worksheet file in the page provided by pressing **Ctrl+V**.

64. Click **Close**. If a Replication Delay dialog box appears, click **OK**.
65. Expand the **\\adatum.com\Shares** node and then click **LON Shares**.
66. Take a screen shot of the LON Shares window by pressing **Alt+PrtScr** and then paste it into your Lab11_worksheet file in the page provided by pressing **Ctrl+V**.
67. Click the **Start** button, type **\\Adatum.com\shares**, and then press **Enter**. When File Explorer opens, you are accessing the DFS namespace shares.

Close all windows and log off LON-SRV1 and LON-SRV2.

Lab Challenge	Using OneDrive to Manage Files/Folders
Overview	In this challenge, you will use OneDrive online to create a folder and a document. You will then download the document to your desktop and delete the document. Finally, you will upload a document from your desktop.
Mindset	OneDrive is a file-hosting service that allows you to store and create files and folders and share them with other users and groups. OneDrive for Business is different from the public version of OneDrive because OneDrive for Business is based on SharePoint. By using SharePoint, OneDrive for Business can be used by team members to store and work on documents with others and it helps ensure that business files for your users are stored in a central location.
Completion time	10 minutes

NOTE	*If you are using the MOAC Labs Online system, you will not be able to perform this exercise. Instead, you need to use a computer running Windows 10 with access to the Internet. If your classroom has a dedicated Windows Server 2012 R2 or Windows Server 2016, you can use a virtual machine running Windows 10.*

1. Log in to a Windows 10 computer that is connected to the Internet.
2. Open Internet Explorer and go to the **http://onedrive.live.com** web page. If you are not automatically logged in, click **Sign In** and sign in with your Office 365 credentials. When you are logged in, you should see a page similar to that which is shown in Figure 11-5.

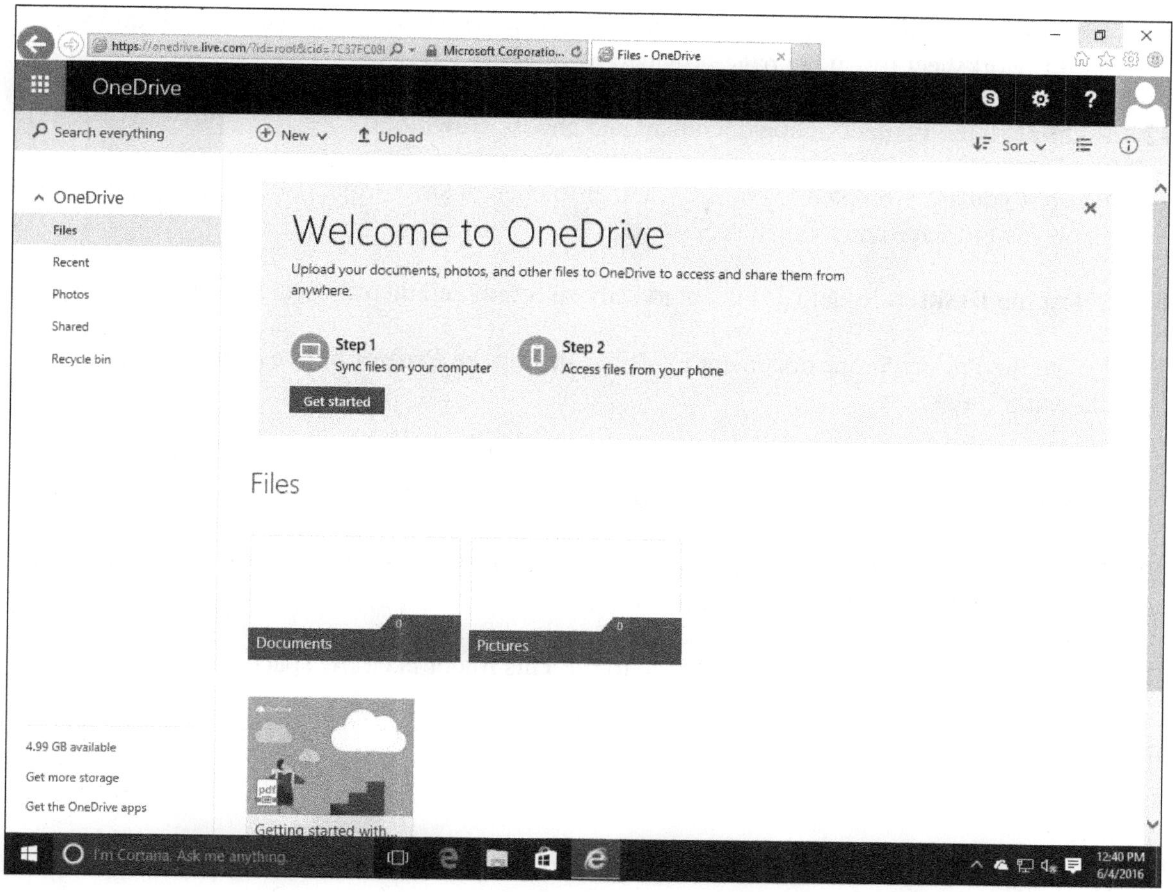

Figure 11-5
Using OneDrive

3. Click the **Documents** folder.
4. From the menu at the top of the page, click **New > Folder**.
5. In the Folder text box, type **Project Files** and then click the **Create** button.
6. Click the **Project Files** folder.
7. From the menu at the top of the page, click **New > Word document**.
8. Type a few words in the document. As you type text, the Word document will be saved frequently.
9. To specify a file name, click Document at the top of the window and then replace that name by typing **Project Scope**.
10. Click the **Project Files** link (located at the upper-left corner, next to Word Online) to return to the main screen.

11. Take a screen shot of the OneDrive page by pressing **Alt+PrtScr** and then paste it into your Lab11_worksheet file in the page provided by pressing **Ctrl+V**.

12. Right-click the **Project Scope** document and choose **Download**.

13. When it you are prompted to choose whether to open or save Project Scope.docx, click the down arrow next to Save and then click **Save as**.

14. Select the **Desktop** folder (if it is not already selected) and then click the **Save** button.

15. Delete the Project Scope document by right-clicking the **Project Scope** document and choosing **Delete**.

16. Take a screen shot of the OneDrive page by pressing **Alt+PrtScr** and then paste it into your Lab11_worksheet file in the page provided by pressing **Ctrl+V**.

17. Minimize the IE window so that it takes up only half of the desktop so you can see the Project Scope document that you saved on the desktop.

18. Drag the **Project Scope.docx** document to the This folder is empty space.

End of lab.

LAB 12 SUPPORTING DATA SECURITY

THIS LAB CONTAINS THE FOLLOWING EXERCISES AND ACTIVITIES:

Exercise 12.1	Managing NTFS and Share Permissions
Exercise 12.2	Encrypting Files with Encrypting File System (EFS)
Exercise 12.3	Encrypting a Volume with BitLocker
Lab Challenge	Using Dynamic Access Control

BEFORE YOU BEGIN

The lab environment consists of student workstations connected to a local area network, along with a server that functions as the domain controller for a domain called adatum.com. The computers required for this lab are listed in Table 12-1.

Table 12-1
Computers required for Lab 12

Computer	*Operating System*	*Computer Name*
Server (VM 1)	Windows Server 2012 R2	LON-DC1
Server (VM 2)	Windows Server 2012 R2	LON-SRV1
Client (VM 3)	Windows 10	LON-CL1

In addition to the computers, you will also require the software listed in Table 12-2 to complete Lab 12.

Table 12-2
Software required for Lab 12

Software	***Location***
Lab 12 student worksheet	Lab12_worksheet.docx (provided by instructor)

Working with Lab Worksheets

Each lab in this manual requires that you answer questions, shoot screen shots, and perform other activities that you will document in a worksheet named for the lab, such as Lab12_worksheet.docx. You will find these worksheets on the book companion site. It is recommended that you use a USB flash drive to store your worksheets, so you can submit them to your instructor for review. As you perform the exercises in each lab, open the appropriate worksheet file, fill in the required information, and then save the file to your flash drive.

SCENARIO

After completing this lab, you will be able to:

- Configure shared folder permissions
- Configure NTFS permissions
- Encrypt files and folders by using EFS
- Encrypt a volume with BitLocker
- Set permissions with Dynamic Access Control (DAC)

Estimated lab time: 105 minutes

Exercise 12.1	Managing NTFS and Share Permissions
Overview	In this exercise, you will create a folder, share the folder, and then configure the NTFS and share permissions.
Mindset	As a Windows administrator, you need to know how to manage files and folders, including how to configure NTFS and share permissions so that users can access the files that they need in order to perform their job while preventing other users from accessing the same files.
Completion time	30 minutes

1. On **LON-DC1**, log on using the **adatum\administrator** account and the **Pa$$w0rd** password.
2. On **LON-DC1**, using Server Manager, click **Tools > Active Directory Users and Computers**.
3. Right-click the **Users** OU and choose **New > User**.
4. In the New Object – User dialog box, type the following and then click **Next**.

   First Name: **Todd**

   Last Name: **Williams**

   User logon name: **TWilliams**
5. For the Password text box and the Confirm password text box, type **Pa$$w0rd**. Click to deselect **User must change password at next logon** and then select **Password never expires**. Click **Next**.
6. Click **Finish**.
7. Close **Active Directory Users and Computers**.
8. On **LON-CL1**, log on using the **adatum\administrator** account and the **Pa$$w0rd** password.
9. On the taskbar, open File Explorer by clicking the **File Explorer** icon.
10. Under This PC, click **Local Disk (C:)**. Then right-click **Local Disk (C:)** and choose **New > Folder**. For the folder name, type **Data** and then press **Enter**.
11. Right-click the **Data** folder and choose **Properties**.
12. Click the **Sharing** tab.
13. Click the **Advanced Sharing** button.
14. Click to select **Share this folder**.
15. To configure the share permissions, click the **Permissions** button.
16. With Everyone already selected, click to select **Allow Full Control**.
17. Click **OK** to close the Permission for Data dialog box.
18. Click **OK** to close the Advanced Sharing dialog box.
19. To manage the NTFS permissions, click the **Security** tab.

Question 1	*Which permissions do Authenticated Users have?*

20. Click the **Advanced** button.

21. In the Advanced Security Settings for Data dialog box (see Figure 12-1), click the **Effective Access** tab.

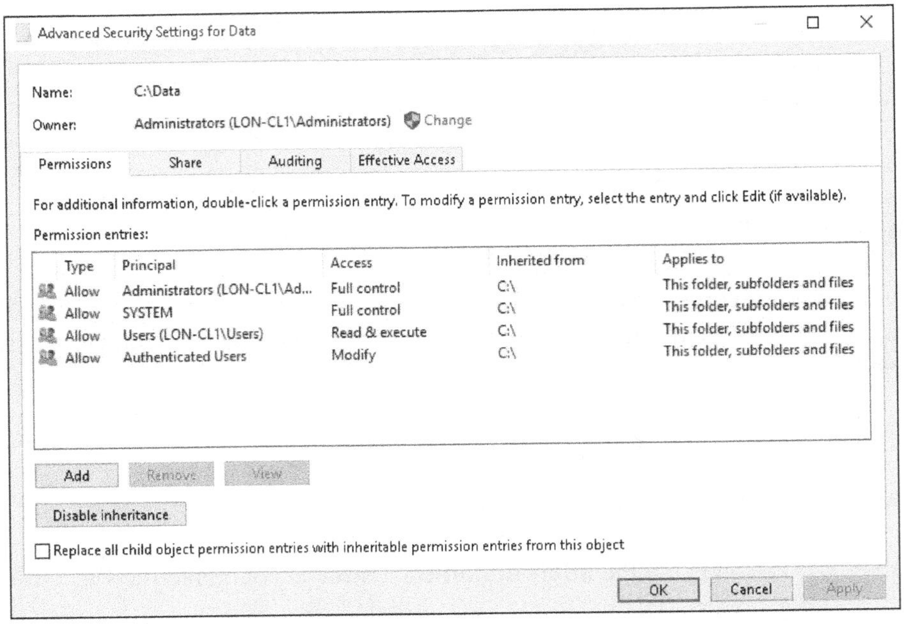

Figure 12-1
The *Advanced Security Settings for Data* dialog box

22. Click **Select a user**.

23. In the Select User, Computer, Service Account, or Group dialog box, in the Enter the object name to select text box, type **TWilliams** and then click **OK**.

24. Click the **View effective access** button.

Question 2	*Which permission does TWilliams not have for the Data folder?*

25. Click **OK** to close the Advanced Security Settings for Data dialog box.

26. Click the **Edit** button.

27. In the Permissions for Data dialog box, click **Add**.

28. In the Select Users, Computers, Service Accounts, or Groups dialog box, in the Enter the object name to select text box, type **TWilliams** and then click **OK**.

29. With **TWilliams** selected, click to select **Allow Full control**.

30. Click **OK** to close the Permissions for Data dialog box.

31. In the Data Properties dialog box, click the **Advanced** button.

32. Click the **Effective Access** tab.

33. Click **Select a user**.

34. In the Select User, Computer, Service Account, or Group dialog box, in the Enter the object name to select text box, type **TWilliams** and then click **OK**.

35. Click the **View effective access** button.

Question 3	*Which permission does TWilliams not have for the Data folder?*

36. Take a screen shot of the Advanced Security Settings for Data dialog box by pressing **Alt+PrtScr** and then paste it into your Lab12_worksheet file in the page provided by pressing **Ctrl+V**.

37. Click **OK** to close the Advanced Security Settings for Data dialog box.

38. Click **Close** to close the Data Properties dialog box.

Close all windows on LON-CL1.

Exercise 12.2	Encrypting Files with Encrypting File System (EFS)
Overview	For files that are extremely sensitive, you can use EFS to encrypt the files. In this exercise, you will encrypt a file using Encrypting File System (EFS), which is a built-in feature of NTFS.
Mindset	Encryption adds an additional level of security. As an example, by using encryption, you can ensure that if a laptop is stolen and the laptop's hard drive is put into another system where the thief or hacker is an administrator, the thief is not able to read the files without using the proper key. If you want to encrypt individual documents, you can use Encrypting File System (EFS).
Completion time	20 minutes

First, you will encrypt files with EFS by performing the following steps:

1. On **LON-CL1**, on the taskbar, open File Explorer by clicking the **File Explorer** icon.

2. Click **This PC** and then double-click **Local Disk (C:)**.

3. Double-click the **Data** folder.
4. Right-click the white space of the **Data** folder and choose **New > Text Document**. For the document name, type **Test** and then press **Enter**.
5. Go back to the **C:** folder. Then right-click the **C:\Data** folder and choose **Properties**. The Properties dialog box opens, as shown in Figure 12-2.

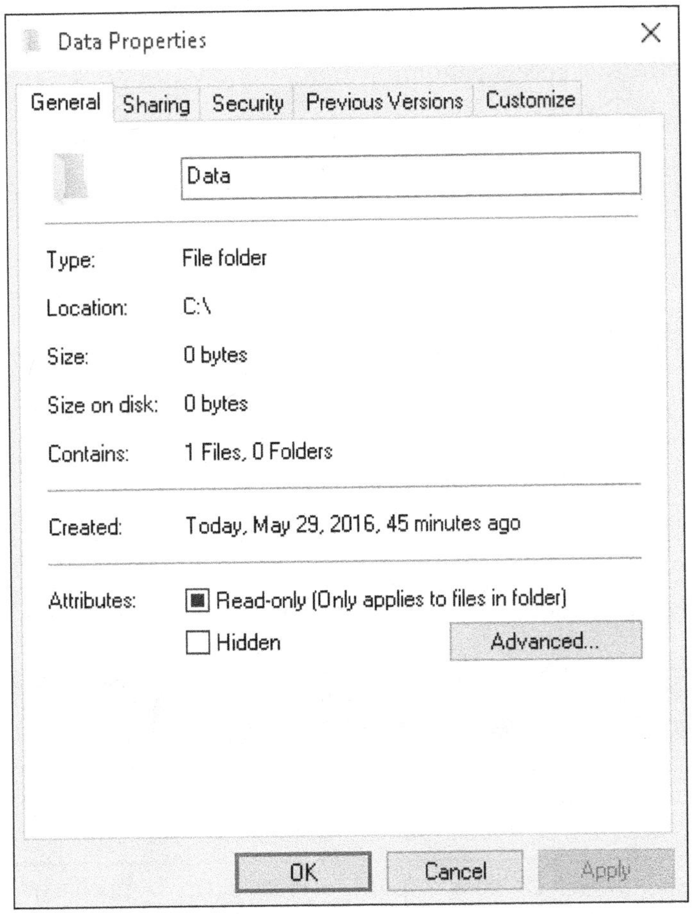

Figure 12-2
The Data folder properties

6. On the **General** tab, click the **Advanced** button. The Advanced Attributes dialog box appears.
7. Click to select **Encrypt contents to secure data** and then click **OK**.
8. Close the Data Properties dialog box by clicking **OK**.
9. When you are prompted to confirm the changes, click **OK**.
10. In File Explorer, click the **View** tab and then click the **Options** button.
11. In the Folder Options dialog box, click the **View** tab.

12. Scroll down and select the **Show encrypted or compressed NTFS files in color** option.

13. Close the Folder Options dialog box by clicking **OK**.

Question 4	*Which color is the C:\Data folder and what does the color indicate?*

Question 5	*Is the test.txt file in the C:\Data folder encrypted?*

14. Take a screen shot of the Data folder window by pressing **Alt+PrtScr** and then paste it into your Lab12_worksheet file in the page provided by pressing **Ctrl+V**.

15. Log off **LON-CL1**.

16. On **LON-CL1**, log in as **adatum\TWilliams** with the password of **Pa$$w0rd**.

17. Open **File Explorer** and navigate to the **C:\Data** folder.

18. Try to open the Test text document.

Question 6	*Although TWilliams had full control permissions to the Data folder, which error message appeared because of the EFS encryption.*

19. Log off **LON-CL1**.

20. On **LON-CL1**, log in as **adatum\administrator** with the password of **Pa$$w0rd**.

21. Open **File Explorer** and navigate to the **C:\Data** folder.

22. Right-click the **C:\Data** folder and choose **Properties**. The Properties dialog box opens.

23. On the **General** tab, click **Advanced**. The Advanced Attributes dialog box appears.

24. Click to deselect the **Encrypt contents to secure data** check box. To close the Advanced Attributes dialog box, click **OK**.

25. Click **OK** to close the Data Properties dialog box.

26. When you are prompted to confirm attribute changes, click **OK**.

Close all Windows on LON-CL1.

Exercise 12.3	Encrypting a Volume with BitLocker
Overview	In this exercise, you will create a new volume and then use BitLocker to encrypt the entire volume.
Mindset	EFS will only encrypt individual files and folders; BitLocker can encrypt an entire volume. In other words, to encrypt an entire drive on a laptop, you can use BitLocker.
Completion time	15 minutes

1. On **LON-CL1**, right-click the **Start menu** and choose **Control Panel**.
2. Click **System and Security > BitLocker Drive Encryption**. The BitLocker Drive Encryption window opens (see Figure 12-3).

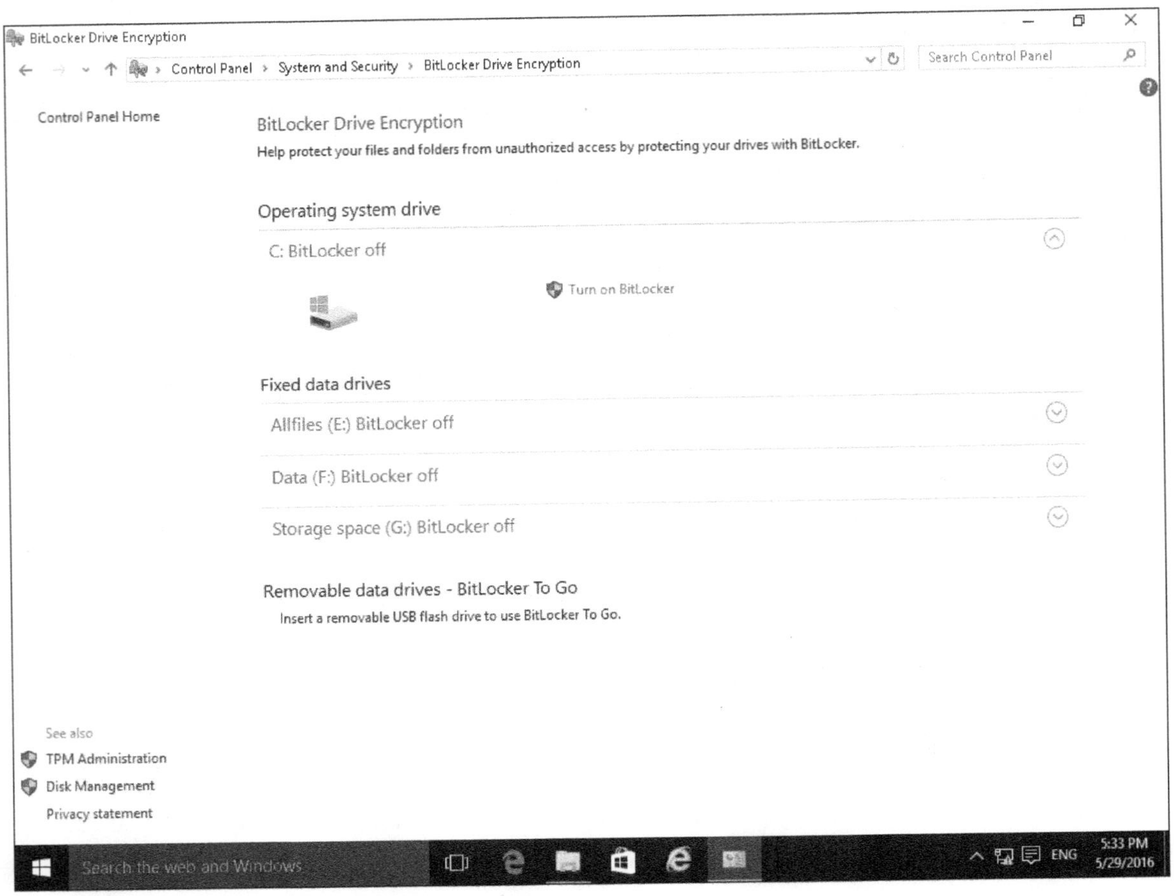

Figure 12-3
The BitLocker Drive Encryption window

3. Click the down arrow next to the Storage space (G:) drive and then click **Turn on BitLocker**. A BitLocker Drive Encryption (G:) window opens.

Question 7	*Which two methods can be used to unlock a drive?*

4. On the Choose how you want to unlock this drive page, select **Use a password to unlock the drive**. In the Enter your password text box and in the Reenter your password text box, type **Pa$$w0rd** and then click **Next**.

5. On the How do you want to back up your recovery key? page, click **Save to a file**.

6. In the Save BitLocker recovery key as dialog box, type **\\LON-DC1\Software** before BitLocker Recovery Key <GUID>.txt and then click **Save**. Click **Next**.

7. On the Chose which encryption mode to use page, the New encryption mode (best for fixed drives on this device) option is already selected. Click **Next**.

8. On the Are you ready to encrypt this drive? page, click **Start encrypting**.

9. Take a screen shot of the BitLocker Drive Encryption window by pressing **Alt+PrtScr** and then paste it into your Lab12_worksheet file in the page provided by pressing **Ctrl+V**.

10. Wait a couple minutes for the encryption to finish. Then for the G: drive, click **Turn off BitLocker**. When the BitLocker Drive Encryption warning appears, click **Turn off BitLocker**.

11. Wait a couple of minutes for the decryption to complete.

Close any open windows before you begin the Lab Challenge exercise.

Lab Challenge	Using Dynamic Access Control
Overview	In this challenge, you will configure Dynamic Access Control by enabling KDC support for claims and creating a resource property and resource rule.
Mindset	Dynamic Access Control (DAC), originally called claims-based access control, was introduced with Windows Server 2012, which is used for access management. It provides an automatic mechanism to secure and control access to resources.
Completion time	40 minutes

1. Log in to **LON-DC1** as **adatum\administrator** with the password of **Pa$$w0rd**.

2. On **LON-DC1**, in Server Manager, click **Tools > Group Policy Management**.

3. In the Group Policy Management console, expand **Adatum.com** and then expand **Domain Controllers**. Then right-click **Default Domain Controllers Policy** and select **Edit**.

4. In the Group Policy Management Editor, navigate to **Computer Configuration\Policies\Administrative Templates\System\KDC** and then double-click **KDC support for claims, compound authentication, and Kerberos Armoring**.

5. Click **Enabled**. Under Options, Supported is already selected.

6. Take a screen shot of the KDC support for claims, compound authentication and Kerberos armoring dialog box by pressing **Alt+PrtScr** and then paste it into your Lab12_worksheet file in the page provided by pressing **Ctrl+V**.

7. Click **OK** to close the KDC support for claims, compound authentication, and Kerberos armoring dialog box.

8. Close **Group Policy Management Editor**.

9. Close **Group Policy Management**.

10. On LON-DC1, using **Server Manager**, click **Tools > Active Directory Administrative Center**. The Active Directory Administrative Center opens.

11. Navigate to the **Dynamic Access Control** node and then click the **Claim Types** container, as shown in Figure 12-4.

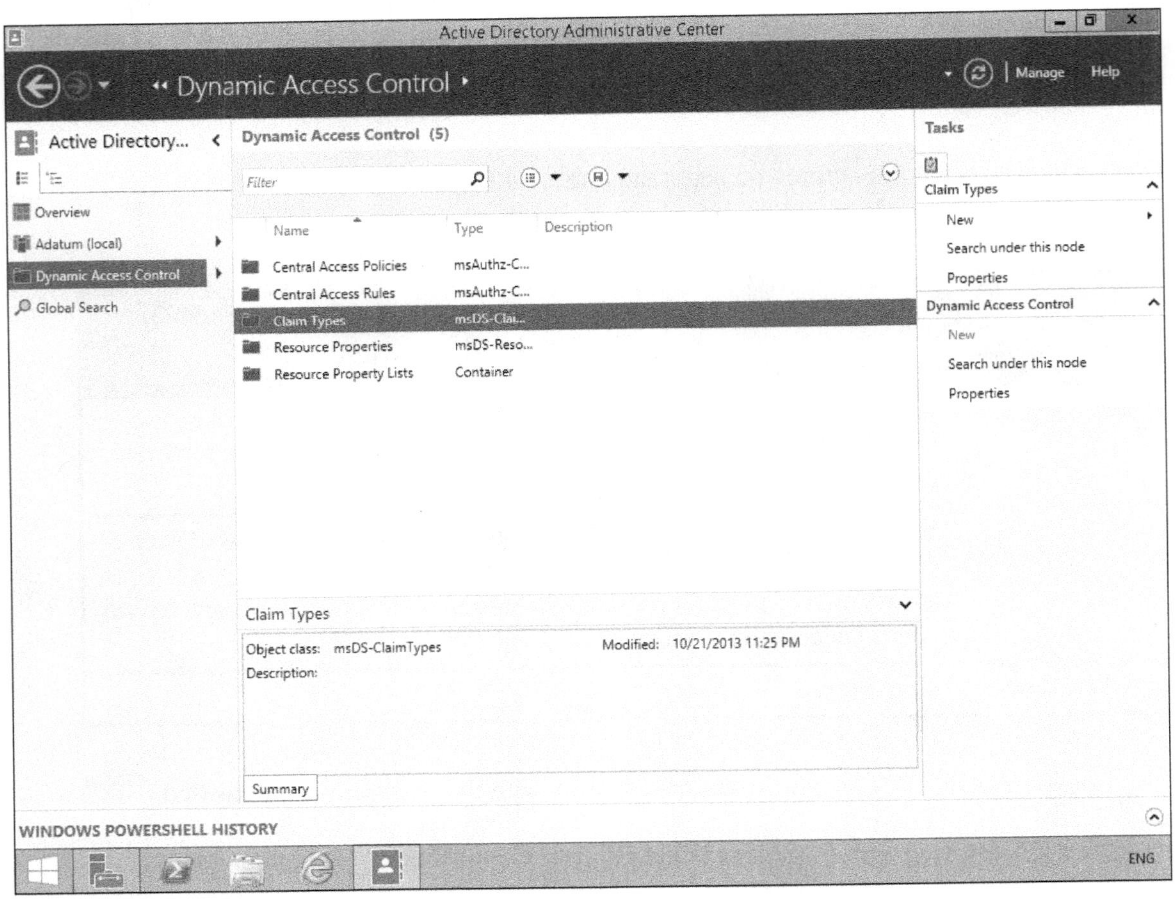

Figure 12-4
Opening Dynamic Access Control

12. In the Tasks pane, under Claim Types, click **New** and then click **Claim Type**. The Create Claim Type dialog box opens.

13. With User already selected on the right side of the dialog box, under Source Attribute, scroll down and click **department**.

Question 8	*What is the default display name?*

14. To close the Create Claim Type dialog box, click **OK**.

15. In the Tasks pane, under Claim Types, click **New** and then click **Claim Type**.

16. Under Source Attribute, scroll down and click **description**.

17. Click to deselect **User** and click to select **Computer**.

18. Click **OK** to close the Create Claim Type dialog box.

19. With Active Directory Administrative Center, click the **Dynamic Access Control** node and then double-click **Resource Properties**

20. To enable the Department resource property, under Resource Properties, right-click **Department** and choose **Enable**.

21. To enable the Confidentiality resource property, under Resource Properties, right-click **Confidentiality** and choose **Enable**. Close Resource Properties.

22. Close **Active Directory Administrative Center**.

23. Log in to LON-SVR1 as **adatum\administrator** with the password of **Pa$$w0rd**.

24. On **LON-SVR1**, using Server Manager, click **Manage > Add Roles and Features**. The Add Roles and Features Wizard opens.

25. Click **Next**.

26. On the Select Installation Type page, ensure that **Role-based or feature-based installation** is selected and then click **Next**.

27. On the Select destination server page, click **LON-SVR1.adatum.com** and then click **Next**.

28. On the Select server roles page, under Roles, expand **File and Storage Services** and then expand **File and iSCSI Services**. Click to select **File Server Resource Manager.** When you are prompted to add features, click the **Add Features** button. Then click **Next**.

29. On the Select features page, click **Next**.

30. On the Confirm installation selections page, click **Install**. When installation is complete, click **Close**.

31. On the taskbar, open File Explorer by clicking the **File Explorer** icon.

32. Create the **C:\DynamicShare** folder.

33. Open the **C:\DynamicShare**. Right-click the empty white space of the **DynamicShare** window, click **New**, and click **Rich Text Document**.

34. For the name of the document, type **Doc1** and press **Enter**.

35. On **LON-SVR1**, using **Server Manager**, click **Tools > File Server Resource Manager**.

36. In File Server Resource Manager, expand **Classification Management** and then click **Classification Properties**.

37. Right-click **Classification Properties** and choose **Refresh**.

Question 9	*What are the two classifications properties that have a global scope?*

38. Click **Classification Rules**.

39. Right-click **Classification Rules** and choose **Create Classification Rule**. The Create Classification Rule dialog box opens.

40. In the General tab, in the Rule name text box, type **Confidentiality**.

41. Click the **Scope** tab.

42. At the bottom of the dialog box, click **Add**. Browse to the **C:\DynamicShare** folder and then click **OK**.

43. Click the **Classification** tab.

44. The Classification method should already be Content Classifier and the property to be assigned to files and its value are, respectively, Confidentiality and High. To configure the Classification parameter, under Parameters, click **Configure**. The Classification Parameters dialog box opens.

45. Change the Regular expression to **String**. Under Expression, type **HR**, as shown in Figure 12-5. This means that if any of the documents have the string **HR**, it will be automatically be tagged as High confidentiality.

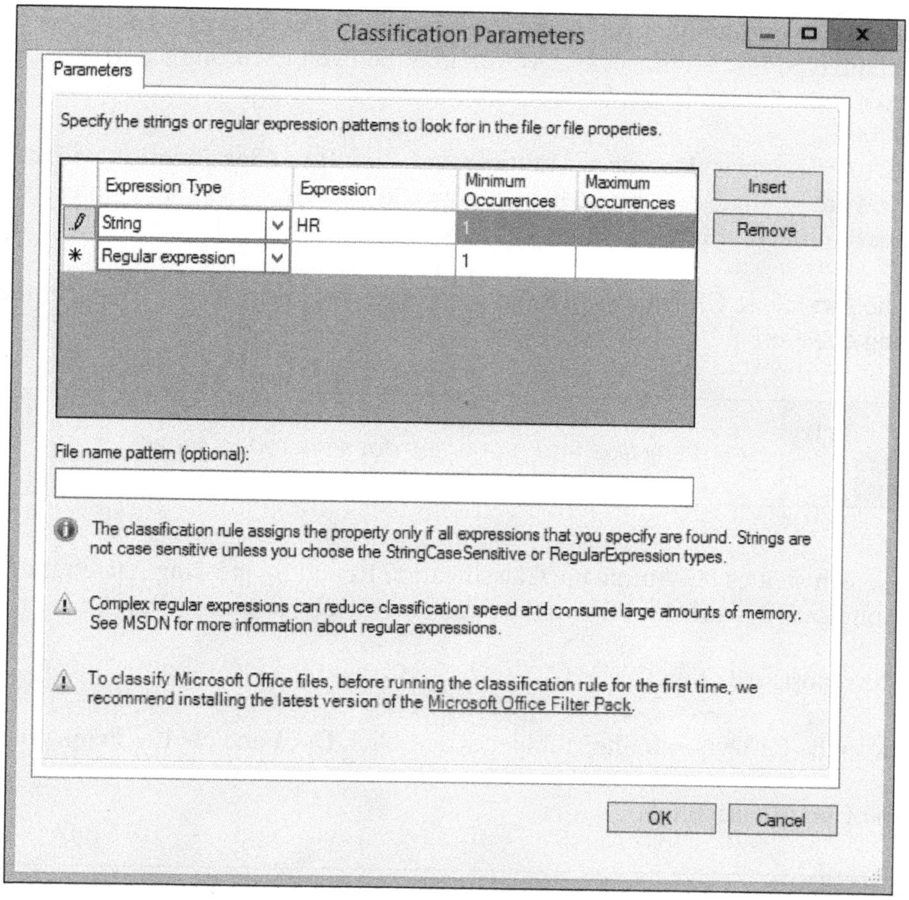

Figure 12-5
Defining a classification parameter

46. Click **OK** to close the Classification Parameters dialog box.

47. Click **Evaluation Type** tab.

48. **Click** to select **Re-evaluate existing property values.** Then select **Overwrite the existing value**.

49. Click **OK** to close the Create Classification Rule dialog box.

50. With File Server Resource Manager, under the Actions pane, click **Run Classification with All Rules Now**. When you are prompted to choose how you want to run the classification rules, click **Wait for classification to complete**.

51. When the Automatic Classification Report opens, answer the following question. Then review the results and close the report.

Question 10	*How many files and properties does the report show?*

52. Go to the **C:\DynamicShare** folder and double-click the **Doc1** document. When the Doc1 opens in WordPad, type **HR** and then close WordPad. When you are prompted to save the document, click **Save**.

53. Go back to **File Server Resource Manager** and click **Run Classification with All Rules Now**. When you are prompted to choose how you want to run the classification rules, click **Wait for classification to complete** and then click **OK**.

54. When the Automatic Classification Report opens, review the results and answer the following question.

Question 11	*How many files and properties does the report show?*

55. Take a screen shot of the Automatic Classification Report by pressing **Alt+PrtScr** and then paste it into your Lab12_worksheet file in the page provided by pressing **Ctrl+V**.

56. Close the report.

57. Go back to the **C:\DynamicShare** folder. Right-click **Doc1** and choose **Properties**.

58. Click the **Classification** tab.

Question 12	*What is the Confidentiality set to?*

59. Take a screen shot of the Doc1.rtf Properties dialog box by pressing **Alt+PrtScr** and then paste it into your Lab12_worksheet file in the page provided by pressing **Ctrl+V**.

60. Click **OK** to close the Properties dialog box.

61. Close **File Server Resource Manager**. Close all other open windows.

End of lab.

LAB 13
CONFIGURING SHARED RESOURCES

THIS LAB CONTAINS THE FOLLOWING EXERCISES AND ACTIVITIES:

Exercise 13.1 Configuring Printers

Lab Challenge Configuring Libraries

BEFORE YOU BEGIN

The lab environment consists of student workstations connected to a local area network, along with a server that functions as the domain controller for a domain called adatum.com. The computers required for this lab are listed in Table 13-1.

Table 13-1
Computers required for Lab 13

Computer	*Operating System*	*Computer Name*
Server (VM 1)	Windows Server 2012 R2	LON-DC1
Client (VM 2)	Windows 10	LON-CL1
Client (VM 3)	Windows 10	LON-CL2

In addition to the computers, you will also require the software listed in Table 13-2 to complete Lab 13.

Table 13-2
Software required for Lab 13

Software	***Location***
Lab 13 student worksheet	Lab13_worksheet.docx (provided by instructor)

Working with Lab Worksheets

Each lab in this manual requires that you answer questions, shoot screen shots, and perform other activities that you will document in a worksheet named for the lab, such as Lab13_worksheet.docx. You will find these worksheets on the book companion site. It is recommended that you use a USB flash drive to store your worksheets, so you can submit them to your instructor for review. As you perform the exercises in each lab, open the appropriate worksheet file, fill in the required information, and then save the file to your flash drive.

SCENARIO

After completing this lab, you will be able to:

- Install and configure printers
- Create and configure libraries

Estimated lab time: 30 minutes

Exercise 13.1	Configuring Printers
Overview	In this exercise, you will install a local printer on one system. You will then configure a printer with permissions. You will then install a printer on another system that points to the shared printer on the first system.
Mindset	One basic network service is network printing, in which multiple users can share the same printer. This is a cost-effective solution when you have several employees in different locations.
Completion time	20 minutes

1. Log in to **LON-CL1** as **adatum\administrator** with the password of **Pa$$w0rd**.
2. On **LON-CL1**, right-click the **Start** button and choose **Control Panel**.
3. Under Hardware and Sound, click **View devices and printers**. The Devices and Printers window opens, as shown in Figure 13-1.

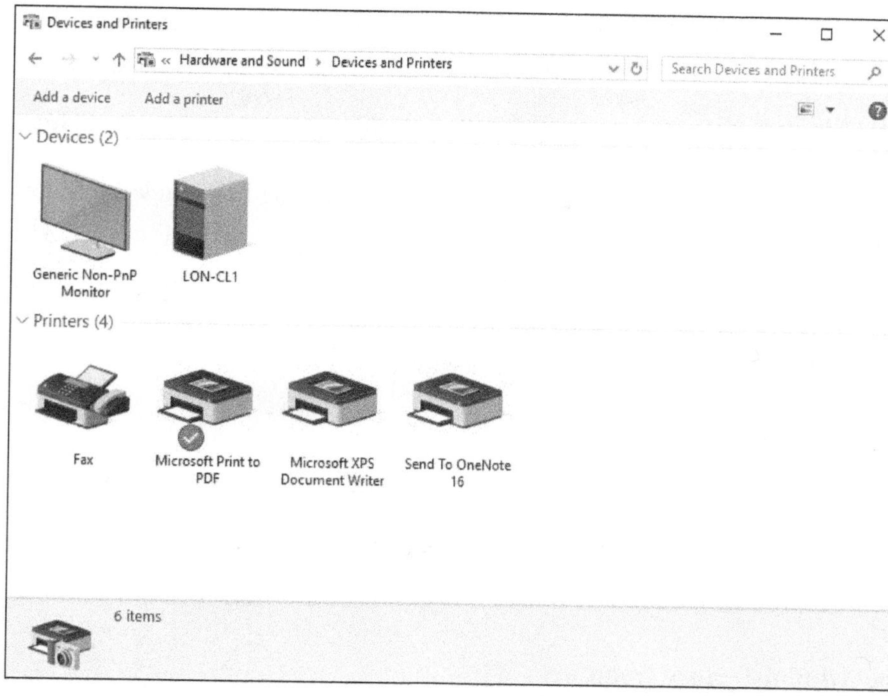

Figure 13-1
Viewing devices and printers

4. At the top of the window, click **Add a Printer**.
5. If there was a printer connected to a USB port, Windows would most likely find the printer. However, since we don't have a printer connected, wait until the search completes and then click **The printer that I want isn't listed**.
6. In the Add Printer wizard, select **Add a local printer or network printer with manual settings** and then click **Next**.
7. On the Choose a printer port page, answer the following question and then click **Next**.

Question 1	*Which port is the printer set to use?*

8. On the Install the printer driver page, for the Manufacturer, click **HP**. Then for the Printers, click **HP Color LaserJet 1600 Class Driver**. Click **Next**.
9. On the Type a Printer Name page, click **Next**.
10. On the Printer Sharing page, change the share name to **HPColorLJ1600** and then click **Next**.
11. Click **Finish**.

12. Take a screen shot of the Devices and Printers window by pressing **Alt+PrtScr** and then paste it into your Lab13_worksheet file in the page provided by pressing **Ctrl+V**.
13. Right-click the **HP Color LaserJet 1600 Class Driver** printer and choose **Printer Properties**.
14. In the HP Color LaserJet 1600 Class Driver Properties dialog box, click the **Sharing** tab. Notice the Share name.
15. For the printer to be listed in Active Directory, click to select **List in the directory**.
16. Click the **Ports** tab. Notice the port that is assigned.
17. Click the **Security** tab.

Question 2	*Who is allowed to print to this printer?*

18. Click the **Administrators** group.

Question 3	*Which permissions are assigned to administrator?*

19. Click **Everyone** again.
20. Select the **Allow Manage documents** permission.
21. Close the HP Color LaserJet 1600 Class Driver Properties dialog box by clicking **OK**.
22. Log in to **LON-CL2** as **adatum\administrator** with the password of **Pa$$w0rd**.
23. On **LON-CL2**, click the **Start** button. Type **\\LON-CL1** and press **Enter**.
24. Right-click the **HPColorLJ1600** printer and choose **Connect**.
25. Click the **Start** button and then click **Settings**.
26. In the Settings window, click **Devices**.
27. Take a screen shot of the Devices window by pressing **Alt+PrtScr** and then paste it into your Lab13_worksheet file in the page provided by pressing **Ctrl+V**.

End of exercise. Log off **LON-CL2**, but remain logged in to LON-CL1 for the next exercise.

Lab Challenge	Configuring Libraries
Overview	In this challenge, you will create a new library, which will combine multiple folders into the library.
Mindset	A library looks like an ordinary folder, but it is a virtual folder that simply points to files and folders in different locations on a hard disk, network drive, or external drive.
Completion time	10 minutes

1. On **LON-CL1**, to open File Explorer, on the Taskbar, click the **File Explorer** icon.
2. If the libraries are not showing in the navigation pane, select the **View** tab and then select **Navigation pane > Show libraries**, as shown in Figure 13-2.

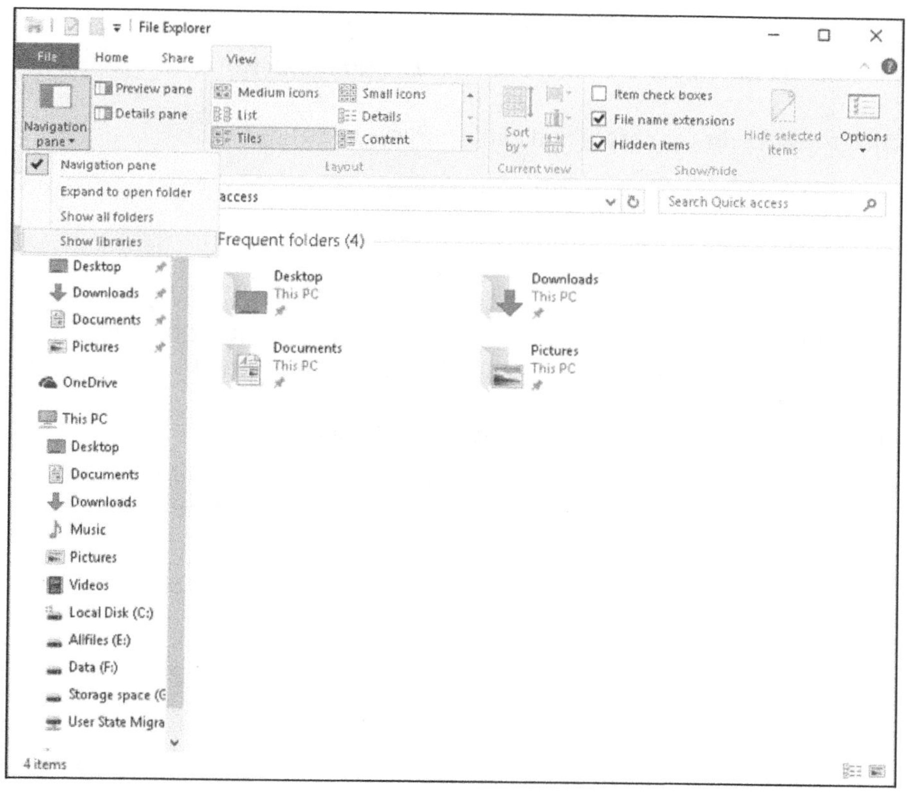

Figure 13-2
Showing libraries

3. In the navigation pane, click the **Libraries** node to select it.

Question 4	*Which libraries do you have?*

Question 5	*Why does the public library not show up?*

4. Then right-click **Libraries** and choose **New > Library**.
5. A Library node appears with the default name New Library. To rename the library, type **MyLibrary** and press **Enter**.
6. Double-click the new library. Then, because the library was just created and is empty, click the **Include a folder** button.
7. Click the **Documents** folder and then click the **Include folder** button.
8. Right-click the MyLibrary library and choose **Properties**.
9. In the MyLibrary Properties dialog box, click **Add**.
10. Click the **Desktop** folder and then click **Include folder**.
11. Take a screen shot of the MyLibrary Properties dialog box window by pressing **Alt+PrtScr** and then paste it into your Lab13_worksheet file in the page provided by pressing **Ctrl+V**.
12. Close the MyLibrary Properties dialog box by clicking **OK**.

End of lab.

LAB 14
CONFIGURING FILE AND FOLDER ACCESS

THIS LAB CONTAINS THE FOLLOWING EXERCISES AND ACTIVITIES:

Exercise 14.1 Using Disk Quotas

Exercise 14.2 Enabling Auditing

Lab Challenge Implementing Advanced Auditing

BEFORE YOU BEGIN

The lab environment consists of student workstations connected to a local area network, along with a server that functions as the domain controller for a domain called adatum.com. The computers required for this lab are listed in Table 14-1.

Table 14-1
Computers required for Lab 14

Computer	*Operating System*	*Computer Name*
Server (VM 1)	Windows Server 2012 R2	LON-DC1
Server (VM 2)	Windows Server 2012 R2	LON-SRV1
Client (VM 3)	Windows 10	LON-CL1

In addition to the computers, you will also require the software listed in Table 14-2 to complete Lab 14.

Table 14-2
Software required for Lab 14

Software	*Location*
Lab 14 student worksheet	Lab14_worksheet.docx (provided by instructor)

Working with Lab Worksheets

Each lab in this manual requires that you answer questions, shoot screen shots, and perform other activities that you will document in a worksheet named for the lab, such as Lab14_worksheet.docx. You will find these worksheets on the book companion site. It is recommended that you use a USB flash drive to store your worksheets, so you can submit them to your instructor for review. As you perform the exercises in each lab, open the appropriate worksheet file, fill in the required information, and then save the file to your flash drive.

SCENARIO

After completing this lab, you will be able to:

- Use disk quotas
- Enable auditing
- Implement advanced auditing

Estimated lab time: 100 minutes

Exercise 14.1	Enabling Disk Quotas
Overview	In this exercise, you will create disk quotas on Windows 10 that will limit how much disk space a user can use on a computer.
Mindset	To prevent users from filling up the C drive or other data drives, you can use Disk Quotas.
Completion time	10 minutes

1. On **LON-CL1**, log on using the **adatum\administrator** account and the **Pa$$word** password.

2. On **LON-CL1**, right-click the **Start** button and choose **Disk Management**. The Disk Management console opens, as shown in Figure 14-1.

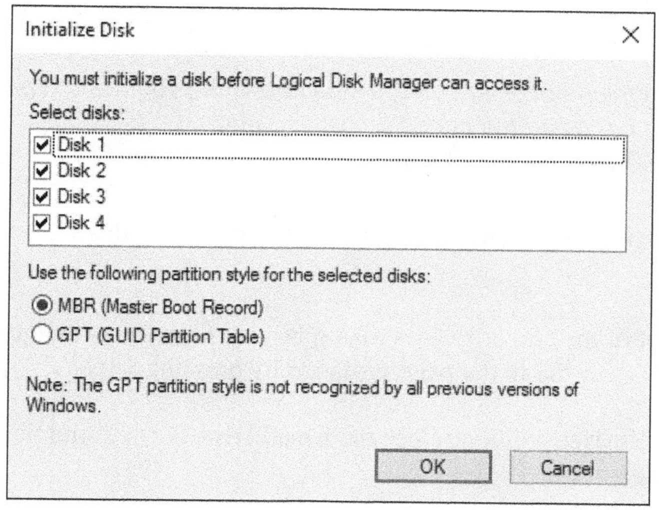

Figure 14-1
Opening Disk Management

3. Click **OK** to initialize the disks.

4. Right-click the **C** drive and choose **Properties**.

5. Click the **Quota** tab and then click **Enable Quota management**.

6. Select **Limit disk space to** and then type **500** in the field provided. Click the down arrow and select **MB**.

7. For the Set warning level to setting, type **300** in the field provided. Click the down arrow and select **MB**.

8. In the Select the quota logging options for this volume section, select both **Log event when a user exceeds their quota limit** and **Log event when a user exceeds their warning level.**

9. Take a screen shot of the Quota tab by pressing **Alt+PrtScr** and then paste it into your Lab14_ worksheet file in the page provided by pressing **Ctrl+V**.

10. Click **OK**.
11. After reading the disk quota message, click **OK**.
12. Right-click the **C** drive and choose **Properties**.
13. Click the **Quota** tab.

Question 1	*Which option should be selected when you want to prevent users from using the specified disk space?*

14. Click the **Quota Entries** button to see whether any user accounts are currently reaching their limits.
15. Take a screen shot of the Quota Entries dialog box by pressing **Alt+PrtScr** and then paste it into your Lab14_worksheet file in the page provided by pressing **Ctrl+V**.
16. Close the **Quota Entries** window, close the **Local Disk (C:) Properties** dialog box, and then close **Disk Management**.

End of exercise.

Exercise 14.2	Enabling Auditing
Overview	In this exercise, you will use standard Audit Policies to help keep track of who uses (and attempts to use) your network resources.
Mindset	Security can be organized according to three areas. Authentication is used to prove the identity of a user. Authorization gives access to the user who was authenticated. To complete the security picture, you need to enable auditing so that you can have a record of the users who have logged on, what the users accessed or tried to access, and which action the users performed (such as rebooting, shutting down a computer, or accessing a file).
Completion time	15 minutes

1. On **LON-CL1**, right-click the **Start** button and choose **Event Viewer**. The Event Viewer console opens, as shown in Figure 14-2.

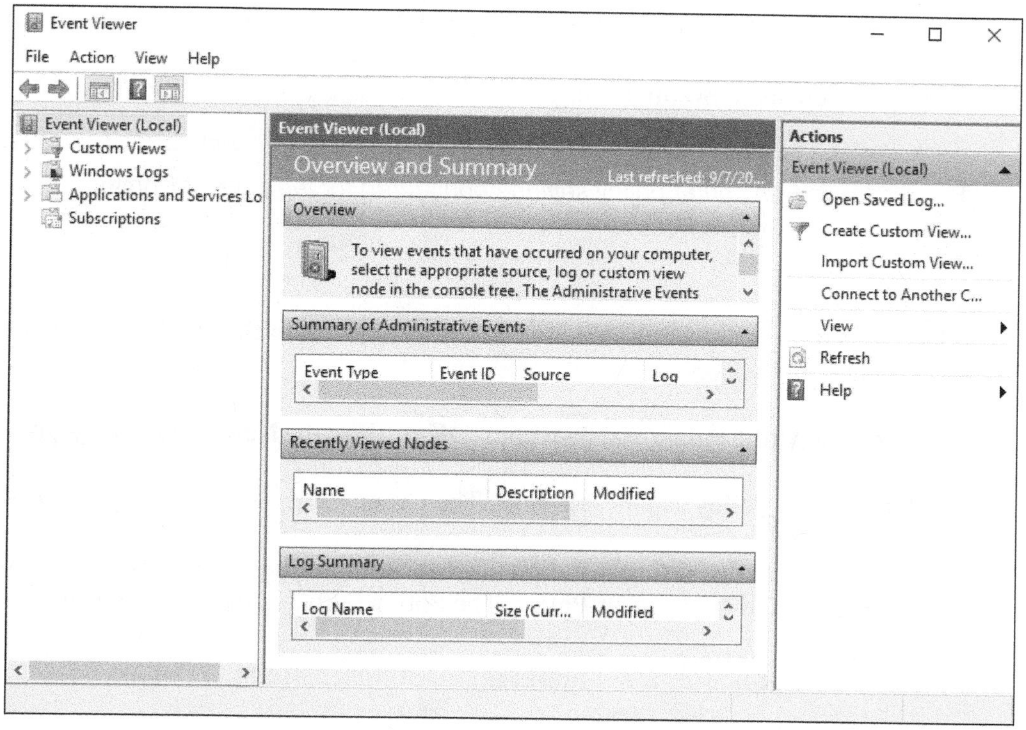

Figure 14-2
Opening the Event Viewer

2. Expand **Windows Logs** and then click **Security**.

Question 2	*By looking at the current logs, which security events are being captured?*

3. Log in to **LON-DC1** as **Adatum\Administrator** with the password of **Pa$$w0rd**. Server Manager automatically opens.

4. On **LON-DC1**, using Server Manager, click **Tools > Group Policy Management**. The Group Policy Management console opens.

5. Expand **Forest:adatum.com > Domains > adatum.com** and then click **Default Domain Policy**. If a Group Policy Management Console dialog box opens, read the message, click to select **Do not show this message again**, and then click **OK**.

6. In the right-pane, click the **Settings** tab.

Question 3	*Are any audit policy settings configured for the Default Domain Policy?*

7. Expand the **Domain Controllers** node and then click **Default Domain Controllers Policy**.

8. In the right-pane, click the **Settings** tab.

Question 4	*Are any audit policy settings configured for the Default Domain Controllers Policy?*

9. Right-click the **Adatum.com** node and choose **Create a GPO in this domain, and Link it here**. The New GPO dialog box opens.

10. For the name, type **Audit Policy** and then click **OK** to close the New GPO dialog box.

11. Right-click the **Audit Policy** and choose **Edit**. The Group Policy Management Editor opens.

12. Expand **Computer Configuration > Policies > Windows Settings > Security Settings > Local Policies** and then double-click **Audit Policy**. The Policy settings display, as shown in Figure 14-3.

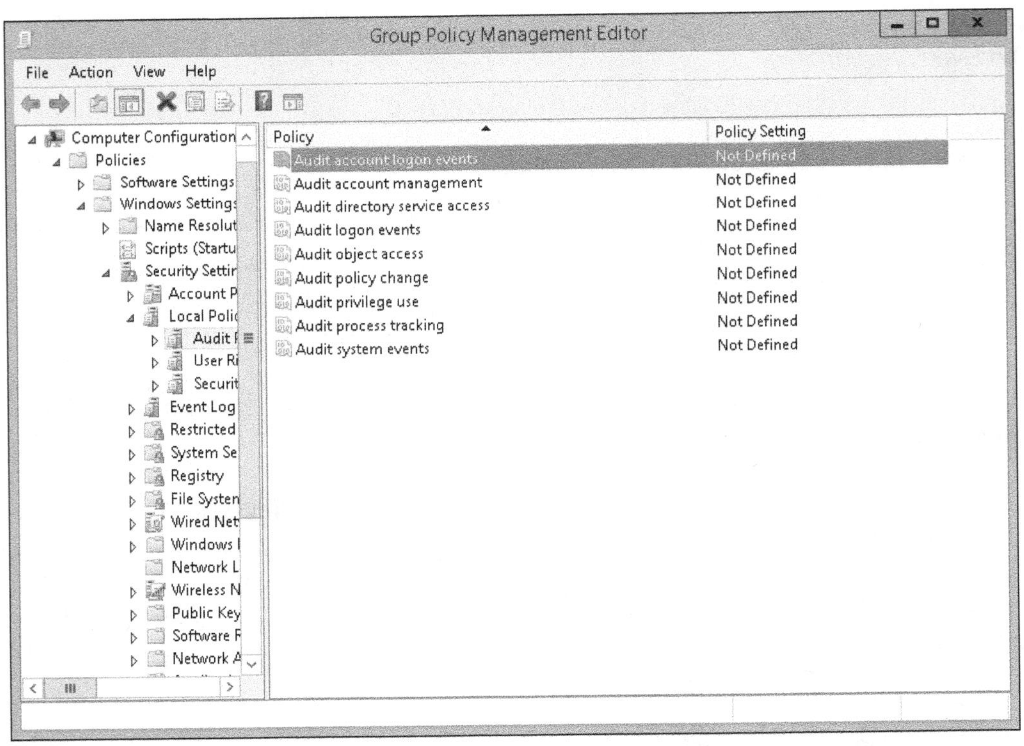

Figure 14-3
Configuring basic audit policies

13. Double-click **Audit account logon events**. The Audit account logon events Properties dialog box opens, as shown in Figure 14-4.

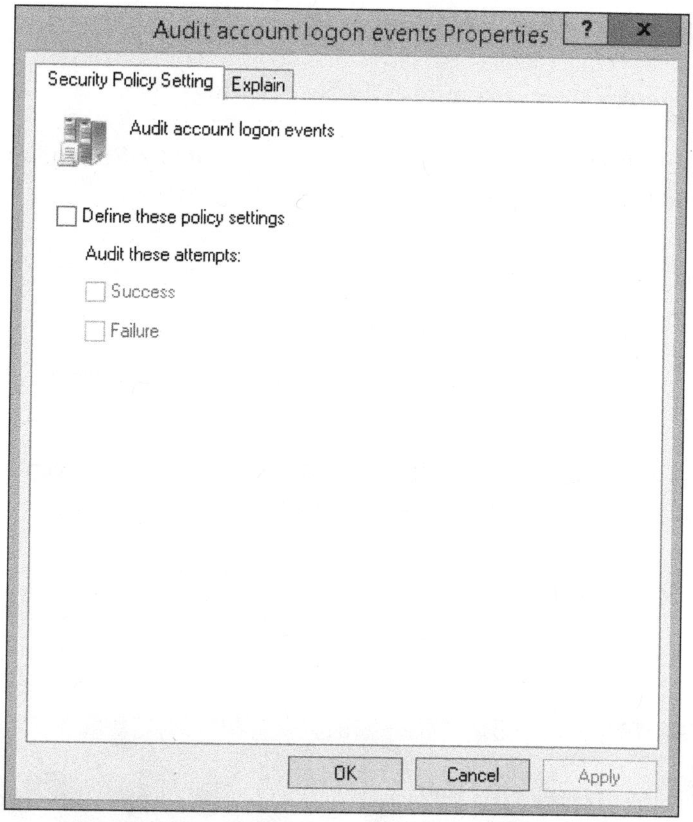

Figure 14-4
Enabling auditing of logon events

14. Click to select **Define these policy settings** and then select both **Success** and **Failure**. Click **OK** to close the Audit account logon events Properties dialog box.

15. Double-click **Audit Object** access. The Audit object access Properties dialog box opens.

16. Click to select **Define these policy settings** and then select both **Success** and **Failure**. Click **OK** to close the Audit object access Properties dialog box.

17. On **LON-CL1**, with the Event Viewer open and Security highlighted, press **F5** to refresh the Security logs.

18. Right-click the **Start** button and choose **Command Prompt (Admin)**. The Command Prompt opens.

19. Execute the following command:

```
gpupdate /force
```

20. Go back to the **Event Viewer** and refresh the Security logs again.

21. Take a screen shot of the Security window by pressing **Alt+PrtScr** and then paste it into your Lab14_worksheet file in the page provided by pressing **Ctrl+V**.

Question 5	*Which kinds of events appear now?*

22. Go back to **LON-DC1**. Open both **Audit object access** and **Audit account logon events** and then deselect the **Define these policy settings** check boxes.

Leave Group Policy Manager open for the next exercise.

Lab Challenge	Implementing Advanced Auditing
Overview	In this challenge, you will use standard Advanced Audit Policies to keep track of who uses (and attempts to use) your network resources.
Mindset	Advanced auditing provides you with more control over which events are recorded by using multiple subsettings instead of the traditional nine basic audit settings.
Completion time	20 minutes

1. On the **LON-DC1**, in the Group Policy Management Editor for Audit Policy, navigate to **Computer Configuration\Policies\Windows Settings\Security Settings\Advanced Audit Policy Configuration** and then click **Audit Policies**, as shown in Figure 14-5.

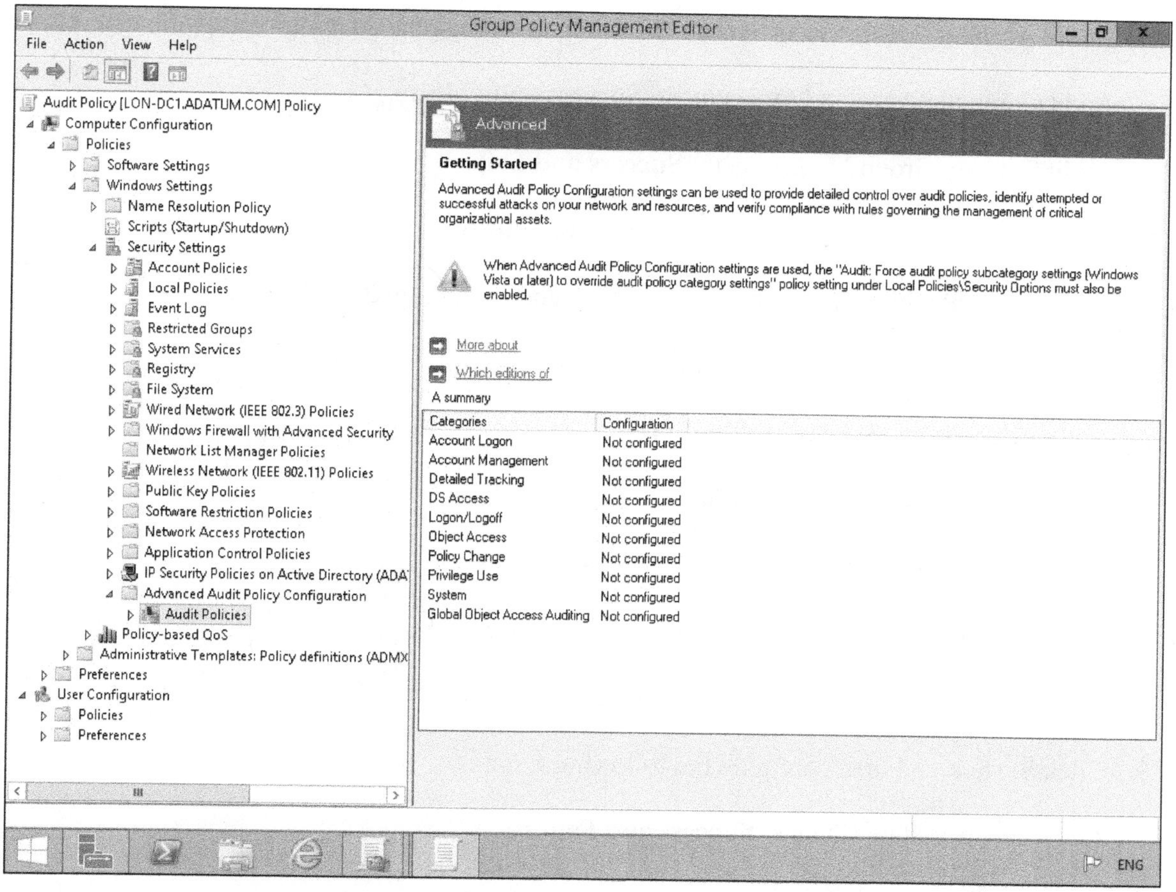

Figure 14-5
Configuring Advanced Audit Policy configuration settings

2. Under Audit Policies, double-click **Logon/Logoff**.

3. Double-click **Audit Account Lockout**. In the Audit Account Lockout Properties dialog box, click to select **Configure the following audit events** and then click to select the **Success** option. Click **OK** to close Audit Lockout Properties.

4. Now configure the following options:

   Audit Logoff: **Success**

   Audit Logon: **Success and Failure**

5. Take a screen shot of the Group Policy Management Editor window by pressing **Alt+PrtScr** and then paste it into your Lab14_worksheet file in the page provided by pressing **Ctrl+V**.

Question 6	*Which option is used to audit changes to Active Directory accounts?*

6. Under Account Policies, click **Account Management** and then configure the following settings:

   Audit Computer Account Management: **Success and Failure**

   Audit Security Group Management: **Success and Failure**

   Audit User Account Management: **Success and Failure**

7. Under Audit Policies, click **Object Access** and then configure the following settings:

   Audit File Share: **Success and Failure**

   Audit File System: **Success and Failure**

   Audit Registry: **Success and Failure**

   Audit SAM: **Success and Failure**

8. Click **Privilege Use** and then configure the following settings:

   Audit Sensitive Privilege Use: **Success and Failure**

9. Click **System** and then configure the following settings:

   Audit Security State Change: **Success and Failure**

10. Close the **Group Policy Editor**.

11. Go to **LON-CL1**, open a Command prompt windows, and then execute the following command:

    ```
    gpupdate /force
    ```

12. Go back to the **Event Viewer**. Then with the **Security** logs selected, press the **F5** key to refresh the security logs. Look for new security events.

13. To remove the GPO, go back to LON-DC1 and, using the Group Policy Management console, expand the **Group Policy Objects** node. Then right-click the **Audit Policy** GPO and choose **Delete**. When you are prompted to confirm that you want to delete this GPO and all links to it in this domain, click **Yes**.

End of lab.

LAB 15 CONFIGURING REMOTE CONNECTIONS

THIS LAB CONTAINS THE FOLLOWING EXERCISES AND ACTIVITIES:

Exercise 15.1 Configuring a VPN Client

Exercise 15.2 Using the Connection Manager Administration Kit (CMAK)

Exercise 15.3 Using Remote Desktop

Lab Challenge Configuring Split Tunneling

BEFORE YOU BEGIN

The lab environment consists of student workstations connected to a local area network, along with a server that functions as the domain controller for a domain called adatum.com. The computers required for this lab are listed in Table 15-1.

Table 15-1
Computers required for Lab 15

Computer	Operating System	Computer Name
Server (VM 1)	Windows Server 2012 R2	LON-DC1
Server (VM 2)	Windows Server 2012 R2	LON-RTR
Server (VM 3)	Windows Server 2012 R2	LON-SVR1
Client (VM 4)	Windows 10	LON-CL1

In addition to the computers, you will also require the software listed in Table 15-2 to complete Lab 15.

Table 15-2
Software required for Lab 15

Software	*Location*
Lab 15 student worksheet	Lab15_worksheet.docx (provided by instructor)

Working with Lab Worksheets

Each lab in this manual requires that you answer questions, shoot screen shots, and perform other activities that you will document in a worksheet named for the lab, such as Lab15_worksheet.docx. You will find these worksheets on the book companion site. It is recommended that you use a USB flash drive to store your worksheets, so you can submit them to your instructor for review. As you perform the exercises in each lab, open the appropriate worksheet file, fill in the required information, and then save the file to your flash drive.

SCENARIO

After completing this lab, you will be able to:

- Configure a VPN client
- Use the Connection Manager Administration Kit (CMAK)
- Use Remote Desktop
- Configure split tunneling

Estimated lab time: 90 minutes

Exercise 15.1	Configuring a VPN Client
Overview	Now that you have configured the VPN server, you need to configure a client to connect to the VPN server. In this exercise, you will use LON_CL1 to act as a VPN client.
Mindset	After the server is created, you have to go to each client and configure the VPN connection that can be used to connect to the VPN server.
Completion time	20 minutes

1. Log on to **LON-DC1** using the **adatum\administrator** account with the password of **Pa$$w0rd**.
2. On Server Manager, click **Tools > Active Directory Users and Computers**.

3. Expand **adatum.com**, if needed, and then click **Users**.

4. Right-click the **Users** node and choose **New > User**.

5. In the New Object – User wizard, fill in the following information and then click **Next**:

   First name: **Clark**

   Last name: **Wayne**

   Full name: **Clark Wayne**

   User logon name: **CWayne**

6. In the Password text box and the Confirm password text box, type **Pa$$w0rd**.

7. Deselect the **User must change password at next logon** option. Click **Next**.

8. Click **Finish**.

9. Double-click the **Clark Wayne** account. The Clark Wayne Properties dialog box opens.

10. Click the **Member Of** tab.

11. Click the **Add** button. In the Select Groups dialog box, type **Domain Admins**.

12. Click the **Dial-in** tab.

Question 1	*What is the default setting for Network Access Permission?*

13. In the Network Access Permission section, click to select **Allow access**.

14. Take a screen shot of the Administrator Properties window by pressing **Alt+PrtScr** and then paste it into your Lab15_worksheet file in the page provided by pressing **Ctrl+V**.

15. Close the Clark Wayne Properties dialog box by clicking **OK**.

16. On LON-CL1, log on using the **Adatum\CWayne** account with the password of **Pa$$w0rd**. It should take a couple minutes to create the CWayne profile.

17. On LON-CL1, right-click the **Network Status** icon and choose **Open Network and Sharing Center**.

18. In the Network and Sharing Center, choose **Set up a new connection or network**.

19. On the Set Up a Connection or Network page, choose **Connect to a workplace** and then click **Next**.

20. On the Connect to a Workplace page, click **Use my Internet connection (VPN)**.

21. If you are prompted to set up an Internet connection, click **I'll set up an Internet connection later**.

22. When you are prompted to type the Internet address to connect to, in the Internet address text box, type **172.16.0.13** and then click **Create**.

23. Click the **Network Status** icon (as shown in Figure 15-1) and then click **VPN Connection**. In the Settings window, click **VPN Connection** and then click **Connect**.

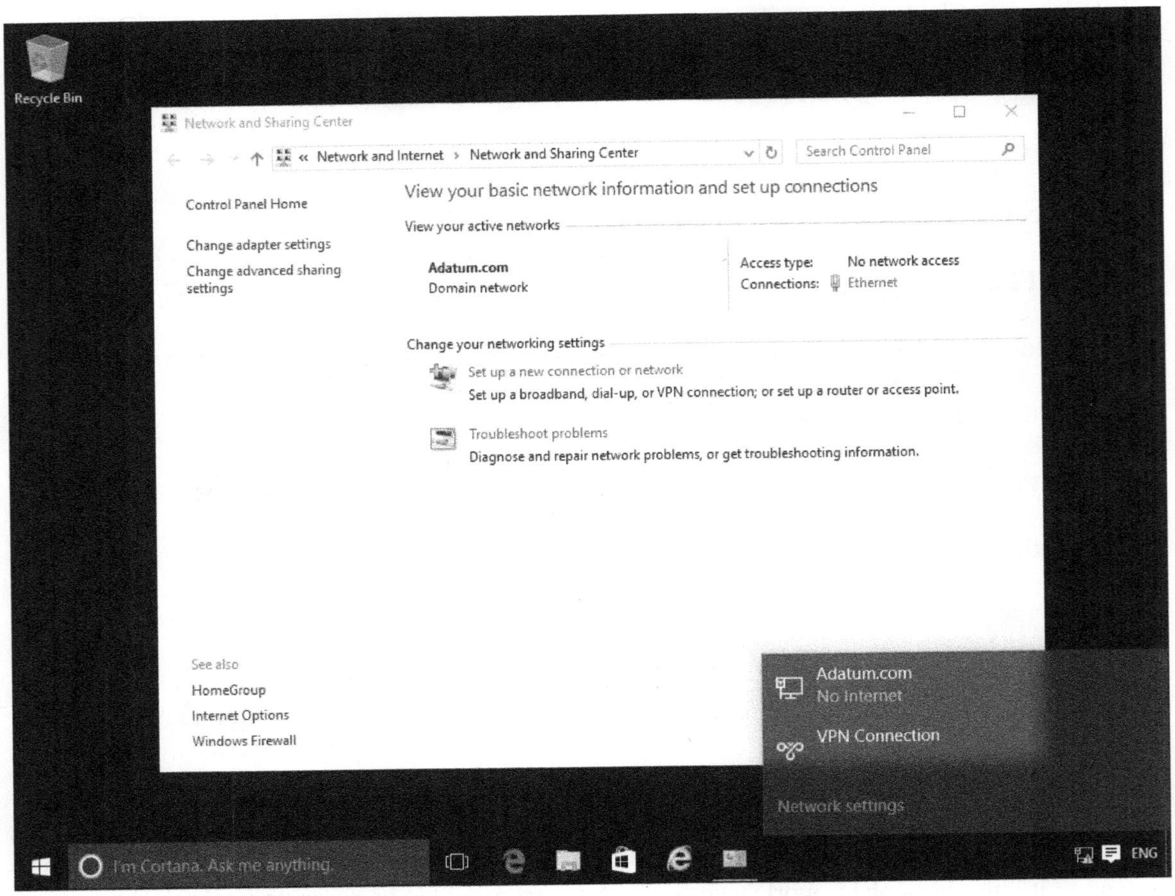

Figure 15-1
Clicking a VPN Connection

24. Log on using the **Adatum\CWayne** and **Pa$$w0rd** password. A minute or two might pass before you are connected.

25. Take a screen shot of the VPN page showing a successful connection by pressing **Alt+PrtScr** and then paste it into your Lab15_worksheet file in the page provided by pressing **Ctrl+V**.

Question 2	*A user says that he cannot connect to the VPN server from home. Since the client needs to connect over the Internet, what is the first thing that you should check that the client should be able to do?*

26. On the Settings page, click **Disconnect**.

27. Log off **LON-CL1**.

Exercise 15.2	Using the Connection Manager Administration Kit (CMAK)
Overview	In this exercise, to help deploy VPN connections to clients, you will use the Connection Manager Administration Kit (CMAK) to create an installation executable that can be deployed to clients that will contain a predefined VPN connection.
Mindset	The Connection Manager simplifies configuring a client computer's VPN connection by using profiles with connection settings that allow local computers to connect to a remote network. When done, you then distribute the created executable file to the client computers.
Completion time	40 minutes

1. Log on to **LON-CL1** as **adatum\administrator** with the password of **Pa$$w0rd**.

2. On **LON-CL1**, right-click the **Start** button and choose **Program and Features**.

3. The Program and Features page opens, as shown in Figure 15-2.

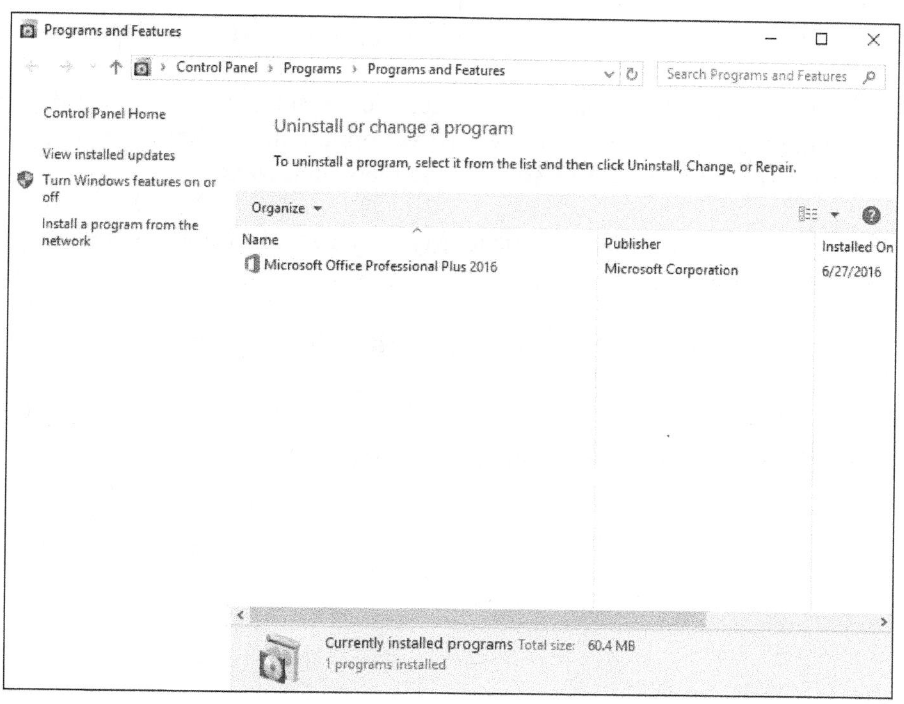

Figure 15-2
Managing programs and features

4. Click **Turn Windows features on or off**.
5. In the Windows Features dialog box, scroll down and select **RAS Connection Manager Administrator** (CMAK). Click **OK**.
6. When the feature has been installed, click **Close**.
7. Close **Program and Features**.
8. Click the **Start** button. Then type **CMAK** and press **Enter**. From the results, click **Connection Manager Administration Kit**. If you are prompted to confirm that you want to allow the cmak.exe app to make changes to your PC, click **Yes**.
9. In the Connection Manager Administration Kit Wizard, on the Welcome page, click **Next**.
10. On the Select the Target Operating System page, answer the following question and then click **Next**.
11. On the Create or Modify a Connection Manager profile page, click **Next**.

Question 3	*By choosing the first selection, list all of the operating systems that would be included.*

12. In both the Service name field and the File name field, type **MyVPN** and then click **Next**.
13. On the Specify a Realm Name page, click **Next**.
14. On the Merge Information from Other Profiles page, click **Next**.
15. On the Add Support for VPN Connections page, click to select the **Phone book from this profile**. With the Always use the same VPN server option already selected, in the Always use the same VPN server text box, type **172.16.0.13** and then click **Next**.
16. On the Create or Modify a VPN Entry page, MyVPN Tunnel <Default> is already highlighted. Click **Edit**.
17. In the Edit VPN Entry dialog box, click the **Security** tab.

Question 4	*By default, which authentication method is selected?*

18. Click the **Advanced** button. If you are required to use a preshared key, select the Use a preshared key option. For now, click **OK**.

19. Click the **Advanced** tab.

20. In the DNS suffix for this connection setting text box, type **adatum.com**. Click **OK**.

21. Back on the Create or Modify a VPN Entry page, click **Next**.

22. On the Add a Custom Phone Book page, deselect **Automatically download phone book updates** and then click **Next**.

23. On the Configure Dial-up Networking Entries page, click **Next**.

24. On the Specify Routing Table Updates page, click **Next**.

25. On the Configure Proxy Settings for Internet Explorer page, click **Next.**

26. On the Add Custom Actions page, click **Next**.

27. On the Display a Custom Logon Bitmap page, click **Next**.

28. On the Display a Custom Phone Book Bitmap page, click **Next**.

29. On the Display Custom Icons page, click **Next**.

30. On the Include a Custom Help File page, click **Next**.

31. On the Display Custom Support Information page, click **Next**.

32. On the Display a Custom License Agreement page, click **Next**.

33. On the Install Additional Files with the Connection Manager profile page, click **Next**.

34. On the Build the Connection Manager Profile and Its Installation Program page, select the **Advanced customization** option and click **Next**.

35. On the Make Advanced Customizations page, for the Section name, select **Connection Manager**.

36. In the Key Name box, type **ConnectionType**.

37. For the Value, type **1** and then click the **Apply** button. Then click **Next**.

Question 5	*Where is the executable stored?*

38. Take a screen shot of the Connection Manager Administration Kit Wizard by pressing **Alt+PrtScr** and then paste it into your Lab15_worksheet file in the page provided by pressing **Ctrl+V**.

39. Click **Finish**.

40. On the taskbar, click the **File Explorer** icon.

41. In File Explorer, navigate to the **C:\Program Files\CMAK\Profiles\Windows Vista and above** folder.

42. Double-click the **MyVPN** folder.

43. Right-click the **MyVPN** application and choose **Copy**.

44. Using File Explorer, open the **\\LON-DC1\software** folder.

45. Right-click the white space inside the software folder and choose **Paste**.

46. From the \\LON-DC1\Software folder, double-click **MyVPN.exe**. When you are prompted to confirm that you want to install MyVPN, click **Yes**.

47. In the MyVPN dialog box, select **All users**. If you are prompted to confirm that you want to allow this app to make changes to the PC, click **Yes**.

48. To close the MyVPN dialog box, click **OK**.

49. Take a screen shot of the Network Connections folder by pressing **Alt+PrtScr** and then paste it into your Lab15_worksheet file in the page provided by pressing **Ctrl+V**.

50. Double-click **MyVPN**.

51. In the Settings dialog box, click **MyVPN** and then click **Connect**.

52. Click the flashing icon on the taskbar, which opens the **MyVPN** dialog box.

53. Specify the following and then click **Connect**:

    User name: **CWayne**

    Password: **Pa$$w0rd**

    Logon domain: **adatum**

54. Take a screen shot of the Network Connections window by pressing **Alt+PrtScr** and then paste it into your Lab15_worksheet file in the page provided by pressing **Ctrl+V**.

55. Right-click the **MyVPN** connection and choose **Connect / Disconnect**.

Close all windows.

Exercise 15.3	Using Remote Desktop
Overview	In this exercise, you will check the settings that allow a remote desktop connection. You will then use the Remote Desktop Connection (RDC) program to access a server using various settings.
Mindset	The Remote Desktop Protocol (RDP) is a proprietary protocol developed by Microsoft to connect to another computer over a network connection using the same graphical interface that you would use if you were setting in front of the physical server. Typically, this would be done with Remote Desktop Connection (RDC), which would allow you to connect to a Remote Desktop Session Host or to a Remote Application.
Completion time	20 minutes

1. On **LON-CL1**, right-click the **Start** button and choose **System**.

2. In the System window, click **Remote settings**. The System Properties dialog box opens with the Remote tab selected, as shown in Figure 15-3.

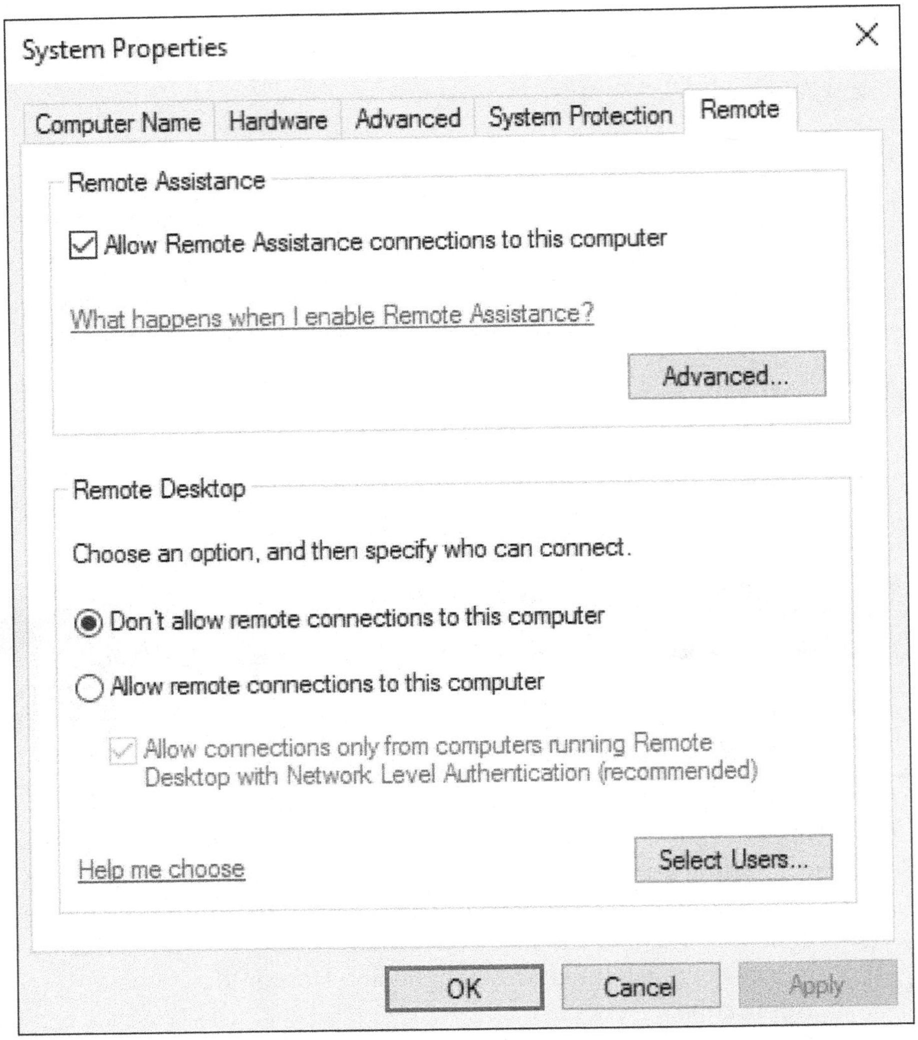

Figure 15-3
Managing Remote settings

Question 6	*Does LON-CL1 allow users to connect to the system remotely using RDP?*

3. Select the **Allow remote connections to this computer** option.

4. Click the **Select Users** button. The Remote Desktop Users dialog box opens.

Question 7	*Which users can connect to this computer using RDP?*

5. Close the Remote Desktop Users dialog box by clicking the **OK** button.

6. Close the System Properties dialog box by clicking the **OK** button.

7. Close the System window.

8. Log on to LON-SVR1 as **adatum\administrator** with the password **Pa$$w0rd**.

9. Right-click the **Start** button and choose **System**.

10. In the System window, click **Remote settings**.

11. In the System Properties dialog box, select the **Allow remote connections to this computer** option.

12. When a message indicates that a Remote Desktop Firewall exception will be enabled, click **OK.**

13. Close the System Properties dialog box by clicking **OK.** Then close the System window.

14. On LON-CL1, click the **Start** button. Type **remote desktop**. Then from the search results, click **Remote Desktop Connection.**

15. When the Remote Desktop Connection program opens, in the Computer text box, type **LON-SVR1** and then click the **Connect** button.

16. In the Windows Security dialog box, log on as **adatum\administrator** with the password of **Pa$$w0rd** and then click **OK.**

17. Take a screen shot of the Settings page showing the remote desktop connection by pressing **Alt+PrtScr** and then paste it into your Lab15_worksheet file in the page provided by pressing **Ctrl+V**.

18. Close the LON-SVR1 window and disconnect from the system by clicking the **x** at the top of the window and then clicking **OK**. The session will continue to run.

19. Click the **Start** button and then type **remote desktop**. From the search results, click **Remote Desktop Connection**.

20. Click the **Show Options** button.

21. When the dialog box expands, click the **Display** tab.

Question 8	*What is the display configuration set to?*

22. Change the display configuration to **800 by 600 pixels** by sliding the slide bar to the left.

23. Click the **Local Resources** tab.

24. Click the **More** button.

25. In the Local devices and resources dialog box, expand the **Drives** node, select the **Local Disk (C:)**, and then click **OK**.

26. Click the **Connect** button. When it you are prompted to confirm that you trust the remote connection, click **Connect**.

27. In the Windows Security dialog box, log on as **adatum\administrator** with the password of **Pa$$w0rd** and then click **OK**.

28. Take a screen shot of the Settings page showing the remote desktop connection by pressing **Alt+PrtScr** and then paste it into your Lab15_worksheet file in the page provided by pressing **Ctrl+V**.

29. In the LON-SVR1 Remote Desktop Connection window, open File Explorer by clicking **File Explorer** on the taskbar.

Question 9	*How does the Lon-CL1 C drive show up?*

30. Double-click **C on LON-CL1**. You are now browsing files on your LON-CL1.

31. Log off **LON-SVR1**.

Question 10	*During a Remote Desktop session, what would happen if you opened the Network Connections window on the remote computer and configured the network adapter to use a different IP address? Explain the result.*

Log off LON-CL1 for the next exercise.

Lab Challenge	Configuring Split Tunneling
Overview	In this challenge, you will configure a VPN client to allow split tunneling.
Mindset	By default, when you connect to a VPN using the previous configuration, all web browsing and network traffic goes through the default gateway on the remote network unless you are communicating with local home computers. Enabling this option helps protect the corporate network because all traffic also goes through firewalls and proxy servers, which prevents a network from being infected or compromised.
Completion time	10 minutes

1. On **LON-CL1**, log on as **adatum\CWayne** with the password of **Pa$$w0rd**.
2. On **LON-CL1**, right-click the **network status** icon on the taskbar and choose **Open Network and Sharing Center**.
3. In the Network and Sharing Center, click **Change adapter settings**.
4. Right-click **VPN Connection** and choose **Properties**.
5. Click the **Networking** tab.
6. Double-click the **Internet Protocol Version 4 (TCP/IPv4)**.
7. In the Internet Protocol Version 4 (TCP/IPv4) Properties dialog box, click the **Advanced** button.
8. In the Advanced TCP/IP Settings dialog box, deselect **Use default gateway on remote network**.
9. Take a screen shot of Advanced TCP/IP Settings dialog box by pressing **Alt+PrtScr** and then paste it into your Lab15_worksheet file in the page provided by pressing **Ctrl+V**.
10. Click **OK** to close the Advanced TCP/IP Settings dialog box.
11. Click **OK** to close the Internet Protocol Version 4 (TCP/IPv4) Properties dialog box.
12. Click **OK** to close the VPN Connection Properties dialog box.

End of lab.

LAB 16
CONFIGURING MOBILITY OPTIONS

THIS LAB CONTAINS THE FOLLOWING EXERCISES AND ACTIVITIES:

Exercise 16.1 Syncing Your Computer

Lab Challenge Using a Work Folder

BEFORE YOU BEGIN

The lab environment consists of student workstations connected to a local area network, along with a server that functions as the domain controller for a domain called adatum.com. The computers required for this lab are listed in Table 16-1.

Table 16-1
Computers required for Lab 16

Computer	*Operating System*	*Computer Name*
Server (VM 1)	Windows Server 2012 R2	LON-DC1
Server (VM 2)	Windows Server 2012 R2	LON-SVR2
Client (VM 3)	Windows 10	LON-CL1

In addition to the computers, you will also require the software listed in Table 16-2 to complete Lab 16.

Table 16-2
Software required for Lab 16

Software	*Location*
Lab 16 student worksheet	Lab16_worksheet.docx (provided by instructor)

Working with Lab Worksheets

Each lab in this manual requires that you answer questions, shoot screen shots, and perform other activities that you will document in a worksheet named for the lab, such as Lab16_worksheet.docx. You will find these worksheets on the book companion site. It is recommended that you use a USB flash drive to store your worksheets, so you can submit them to your instructor for review. As you perform the exercises in each lab, open the appropriate worksheet file, fill in the required information, and then save the file to your flash drive.

SCENARIO

After completing this lab, you will be able to:

- Configure Offline Files
- Use Sync Center
- Create and connect to a Work Folder

Estimated lab time: 55 minutes

Exercise 16.1	Syncing Your Computer
Overview	In this exercise, you will create a shared folder on a server and then configure a workstation to cache those files in an offline folder.
Mindset	When a computer is not connected to the network, the user will not be able to access files that are stored on a shared folder. If you want users to access a shared folder when offline, you can sync the files.
Completion time	30 minutes

1. On **LON-SVR2**, log on using the **Adatum\administrator** account and the **Pa$$word** password.
2. On the taskbar, click the **File Explorer** button to open File Explorer. Click **This PC** and then double-click **Local Disk (C:)**.
3. Right-click **Local Disk (C:)** in the left pane and choose **New > Folder**. For the folder name, type **Sales** and press **Enter**.
4. Right-click the **Sales** folder and choose **Properties**.
5. Click the **Sharing** tab.
6. Click the **Advanced Sharing** button.

7. In the Advanced Sharing dialog box, click to select the **Share this folder** option.

8. Click the **Permissions** button.

9. In the Permissions for Sales dialog box, for the Everyone group, select **Allow Full Control**. Click **OK** to close the Permission for Sales dialog box.

10. Click the **Caching** button.

Question 1	*If you have confidential information that you don't want to be available on a computer that is not actively connected to the organization network, should the information folder be cached or should it not cached?*

11. Select **All files and programs that users open the shared folder are automatically available offline**.

12. Click **OK** to close the Offline Settings dialog box.

13. Click **OK** to close the Advanced Sharing dialog box.

14. Click the **Close** button to close the Sales Properties dialog box.

15. On **LON-CL1**, log on as **Adatum\administrator** with password **Pa$$w0rd**.

16. On the taskbar, click the **File Explorer** button to open File Explorer.

17. Using **File Explorer**, navigate to **\\LON-SVR2**.

18. Right-click the **Sales** folder and choose **Always available offline**.

19. Take a screen shot of the LON-SVR2 window by pressing **Alt+PrtScr** and then paste it into your Lab16_worksheet file in the page provided by pressing **Ctrl+V**.

20. Double-click the **Sales** folder.

21. Right-click the empty white space of the Sales folder and choose **New > Text Document**.

22. Name the document **test.txt**.

23. In the top-left corner of the Sales folder, click the white document that displays a red checkbox icon (as shown in Figure 16-1).

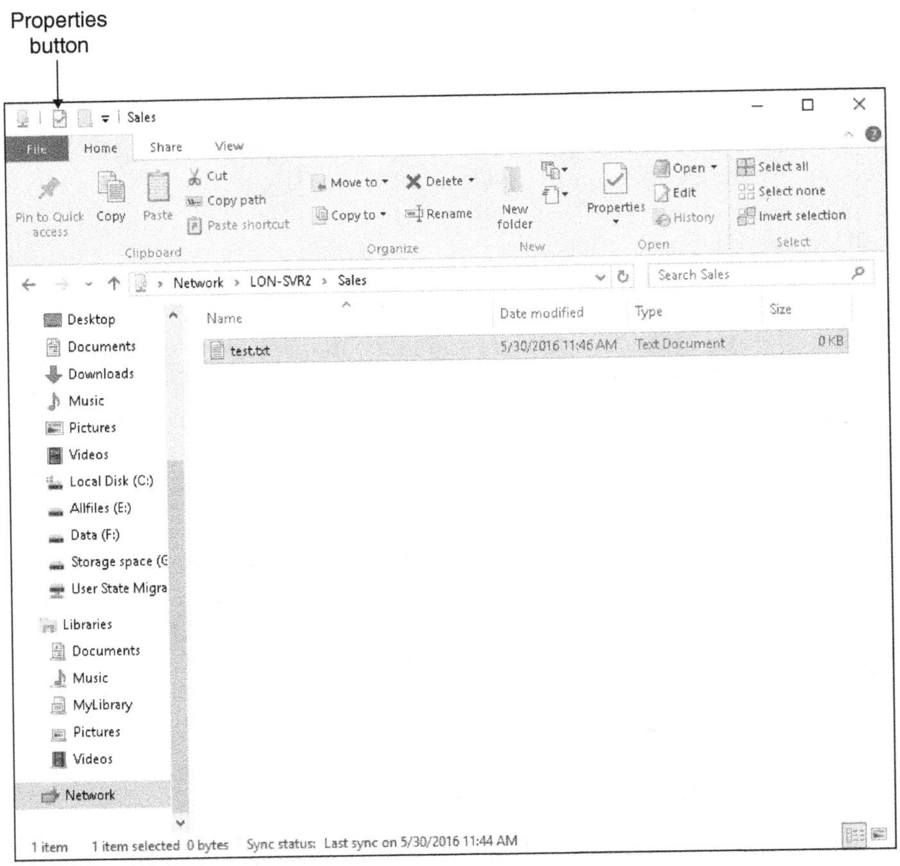

Figure 16-1
Clicking the Properties button (icon with red checkmark)

24. In the Sales (\\LON-SVR2) Properties dialog box, click the **Offline Files** tab.

25. Click the **Sync now** button.

26. Click **OK** to close the test.txt Properties dialog box.

27. Close the **Sales** folder.

28. On the taskbar, right-click the **Network Status** icon and choose **Open Network and Sharing Center**.

29. Click **Change adapter settings**.

30. In the Network Connections window, right-click **Ethernet** and choose **Disable**.

31. On the taskbar, click the **File Explorer** button to open File Explorer.

32. Open the **\\LON-SVR2\sales** folder.

33. Open the **test.txt** document. Type your name into the document and then save and close the document.

34. Go back to the Network Connections folder. Right-click **Local Area Connection** and choose **Enable**.

35. In the top-left corner of the Sales folder, click the white document that displays a red checkbox icon.

36. In the Sales Properties dialog box, click the **Offline Files** tab.

37. Click the **Sync now** button.

38. Take a screen shot of the Sales (\\LON-SVR2 Properties window by pressing **Alt+PrtScr** and then paste it into your Lab16_worksheet file in the page provided by pressing **Ctrl+V**.

39. Click **OK** to close the Sales (\\LON-SVR2) Properties dialog box.

40. Double-click the **test.txt** file and observe that your name has been synced into the Sales folder copy of test.txt. Close the test.txt file.

41. Close the **Sales** folder.

End of exercise. Close the Network Connections folder and the Network and Sharing Center on LON-CL1.

Lab Challenge	Using a Work Folder
Overview	In this challenge, you will create a Work Folder on LON-SVR2 and then configure workstation to access the Work Folder.
Mindset	Work Folders allow users to store and access work files on a sync share from multiple devices, including personal computers and devices (such as bring-your-own devices). Work Folders are for only individual data and do not support sharing files between users.
Completion time	25 minutes

1. On **LON-SVR2**, using **Server Manager**, click **Manage > Add Roles and Features**.

2. In the Add Role and Features Wizard, on the Before you begin page, click **Next**.

3. On the Select installation type page, click **Next**.

4. On the Select destination server page, click **Next**.

5. On the Select server roles page, select **File and Storage Services\File and iSCSI Services\Work Folders**.

6. When you are prompted to install additional features, click **Add Features**.

7. Back on the Select server roles page, click **Next**.

8. On the Select features page, click **Next**.

9. On the Confirm installation selections page, click **Install**.

10. When the installation succeeds, click **Close**.

11. Using Server Manager, click **File and Storage Services** and then click **Work Folders**, as shown in Figure 16-2.

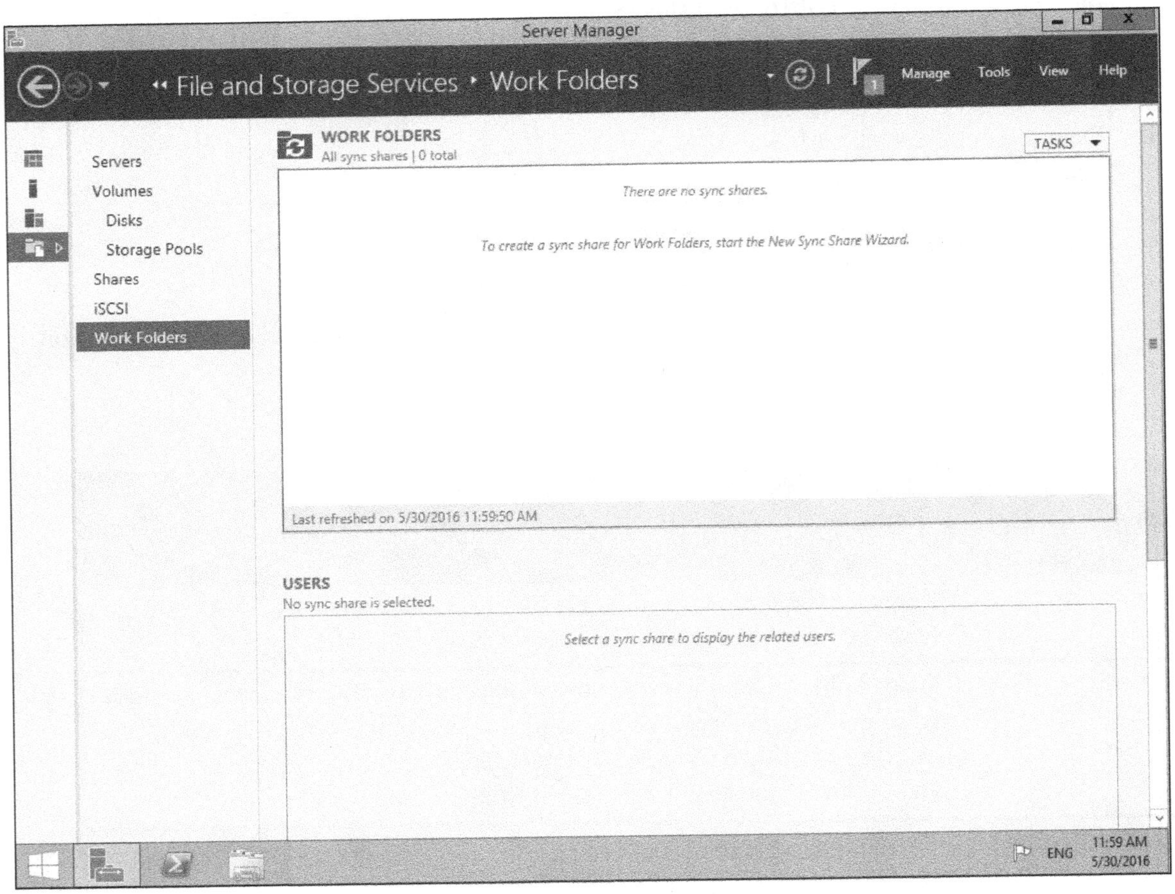

Figure 16-2
Opening the Work Folders page

12. Open **File Explorer**. Create a folder called **C:\CorpData**. Close **File Explorer**.

13. On the Work Folders page, click the **To create a sync share for Work Folders, start the New Sync Share Wizard** link.

14. In the New Sync Share Wizard, on the before you begin page, click **Next**.

15. On the Select the server and path page, under Enter a local path:, browse to the **C:\CorpData** folder and then click **Select folder**. Click **Next**.

16. On the Specify the structure for user folders page, with User alias already selected, click **Next**.

17. On the Enter the sync share name page, click **Next**.

18. On the Grant sync access to groups page, click **Add**. In the Select User or Group dialog box, type **Domain Users** in the Enter the object name to select and click **OK**. Back on the Grant sync access to groups page, click **Next**.

19. On the Specify device policies page, click **Next**.

20. On the Confirm selections page, click **Create**.

21. Take a screen shot of the New Sync Share Wizard page by pressing **Alt+PrtScr** and then paste it into your Lab16_worksheet file in the page provided by pressing **Ctrl+V**.

22. When the sync share is created, click **Close**.

23. On **LON-CL1**, to allow unsecure connections (http) with Work Folders, open a command prompt and execute the following command:

```
Reg add HKLM\Software\Microsoft\Windows\CurrentVersion\
WorkFolders /v AllowUnsecureConnection /t REG_DWORD /d 1
```

24. Close the Command Prompt window.

25. Open the **Control Panel**, click **System and Security**, and then click **Work Folders**.

26. On the manage Work Folders page, click **Set up Work Folders**.

Question 2	*You have defined Work Folders on multiple servers for hundreds of users. What is the easiest way to automatically set up Work Folders for your users?*

27. On the Enter your work email address page, click **Enter a Work Folders URL instead**.

28. On the Enter a Work Folders URL page, in the Work Folders URL text box, type **http://LON-SVR2.adatum.com**. Click **Next**.

29. On the Introducing Work Folders page, click **Next**.

30. On the Security policies page, select **I accept these policies on my PC** and then click **Set up Work Folders**.

31. Click **Close**.

32. Close the **Work Folders window**.

33. Take a screen shot of the Control Panel's Work Folders window by pressing **Alt+PrtScr** and then paste it into your Lab16_worksheet file in the page provided by pressing **Ctrl+V**.

34. Close the **Control Panel**.

End of lab.

LAB 17
DEPLOYING AND MANAGING AZURE REMOTEAPP

THIS LAB CONTAINS THE FOLLOWING EXERCISES AND ACTIVITIES:

Exercise 17.1 Using Remote Applications

Lab Challenge Removing Remote Desktop Services

BEFORE YOU BEGIN

The lab environment consists of student workstations connected to a local area network, along with a server that functions as the domain controller for a domain called adatum.com. The computers required for this lab are listed in Table 17-1.

Table 17-1
Computers required for Lab 17

Computer	Operating System	Computer Name
Server (VM 1)	Windows Server 2012 R2	LON-DC1
Server (VM 2)	Windows Server 2012 R2	LON-SRV1
Client (VM 3)	Windows 10	LON-CL1

In addition to the computers, you will also require the software listed in Table 17-2 to complete Lab 17.

Table 17-2
Software required for Lab 17

Software	*Location*
Lab 17 student worksheet	Lab17_worksheet.docx (provided by instructor)

Working with Lab Worksheets

Each lab in this manual requires that you answer questions, shoot screen shots, and perform other activities that you will document in a worksheet named for the lab, such as Lab17_worksheet.docx. You will find these worksheets on the book companion site. It is recommended that you use a USB flash drive to store your worksheets, so you can submit them to your instructor for review. As you perform the exercises in each lab, open the appropriate worksheet file, fill in the required information, and then save the file to your flash drive.

SCENARIO

After completing this lab, you will be able to:

- Use remote applications
- Remove Remote Desktop Services

Estimated lab time: 65 minutes

Exercise 17.1	Using Remote Applications
Overview	In this exercise, you will use the RemoteApp features to access and run an application on a remote server.
Mindset	To make an application available to users without actually installing the application on each client computer, users can run the application using the RemoteApp feature.
Completion time	50 minutes

First, you'll need to install PowerPoint Viewer by performing the following steps:

1. On **LON-SVR1**, log in as **adatum\administrator** with the password of **Pa$$w0rd**.
2. On **LON-SVR1,** click the **File Explorer** button on the taskbar to open File Explorer.
3. Using File Explorer, open the **\\LON-DC1\software** folder.

4. Double-click the **PowerPointViewer.exe** installation file. If a security warning prompts you to confirm that you want to run this file, click **Run**.

5. On the Microsoft Software License Terms page, select **Click here to accept the Microsoft Software License Terms** and then click **Continue**.

6. On the Microsoft PowerPoint Viewer Wizard page, click **Next**.

7. When you are prompted to confirm where to install the viewer, click **Install**.

8. When the installation is complete, click **OK**.

Next, install Remote Desktop Services by performing the following steps:

1. Reboot **LON-SVR1**, then log in as **Adatum\administrator** account and the **Pa$$w0rd** password.

2. On **LON-SVR1**, open Server Manager (if it is not open already) and then click **Manage > Add Roles and Features**.

3. On the Add Roles and Features Wizard page, click **Next**.

4. On the Select installation type page, click **Remote Desktop Services installation** (see Figure 17-1) and then click **Next**.

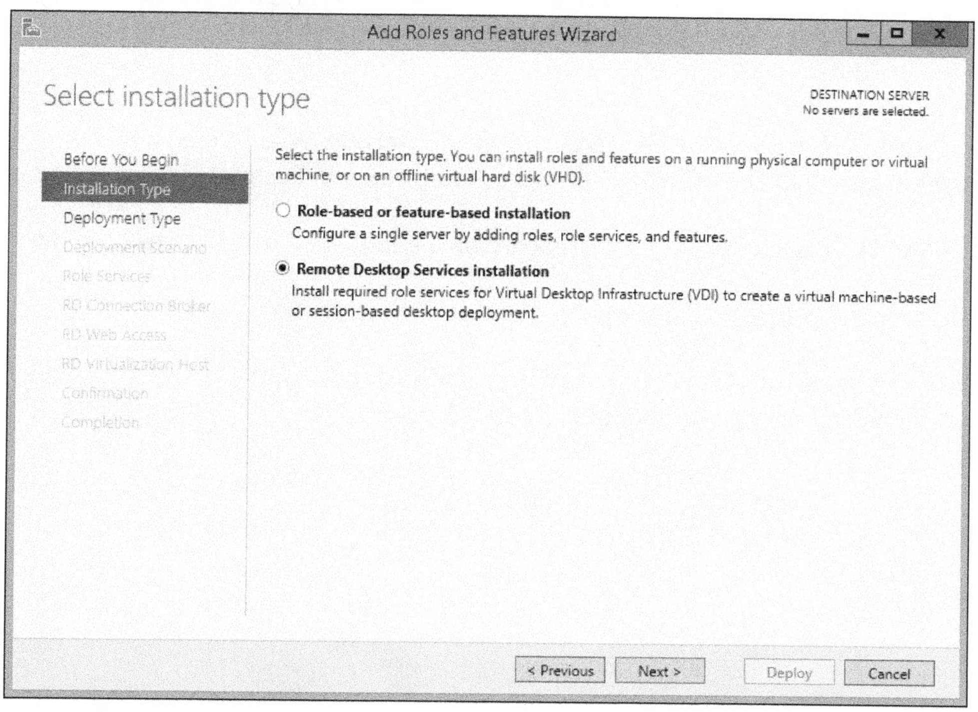

Figure 17-1
Specifying the Remote Desktop Services installation

5. On the Select deployment type page, click **Standard deployment** and then click **Next**.

6. On the Select deployment scenario page, click **Session-based desktop deployment** and then click **Next**.

7. On the Review role services page, click **Next**.

8. On the Specify RD Connection Broker server page, with **LON-SVR1.adatum.com** highlighted, click the > arrow button and then click **Next**.

9. On the Specify RD Web Access server page, with **LON-SVR1.adatum.com** highlighted, click the > arrow button and then click **Next**.

10. On the Specify RD Session Host servers page, with **LON-SVR1.adatum.com** highlighted, click the > arrow button and then click **Next**.

11. On the Confirm selections page, select **Restart the destination server automatically if required** and then click **Deploy**.

12. After LON-SVR1 reboots, log on to **LON-SVR1** using the **adatum\administrator** account and the **Pa$$w0rd** password. When Server Manager opens, the RD services will finish installing. If you get a Remote Desktop licensing mode is not configured popup, you can click the **x** button to close the popup. If Server Manager does not open, on the taskbar, click the Server Manger icon.

Question 1	*When Server Manager starts, how many days are available to use the Remote Desktop licensing mode?*

13. Shortly after you log on, the View progress window opens. When Remote Desktop Services role services is installed, click **Close** to close the Add Roles and Features Wizard dialog box.

14. Using Server Manager, under the Dashboard on the left, click **Remote Desktop Services**.

15. On the Overview page, in the left column, click **Collections**.

16. In the Collections section, click **Tasks > Create Session Collection**. You may need to scroll over to see the Tasks option, as shown in Figure 17-2.

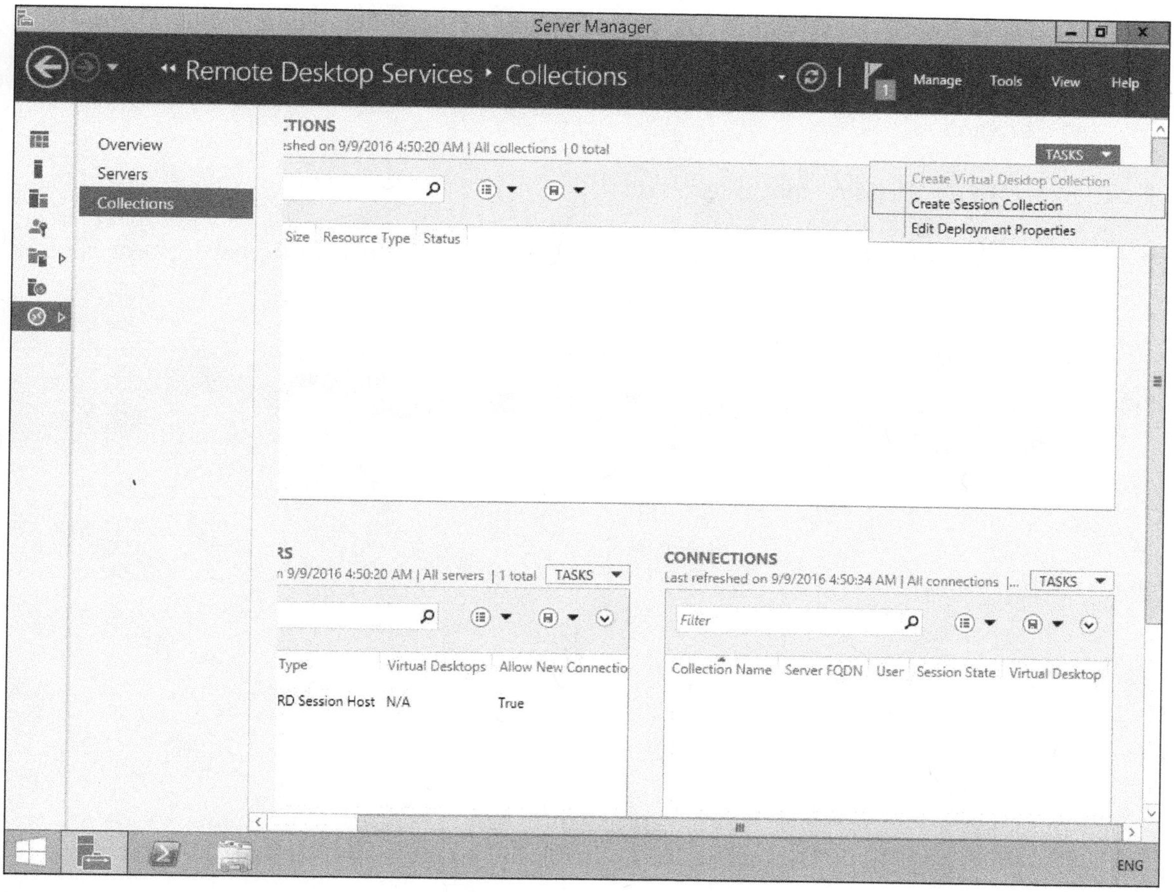

Figure 17-2
Showing the Collections Task option

17. On the Create Collection Wizard page, click **Next**.

18. On the Name the collection page, in the Name text box, type **LON-SVR1** and then click **Next**.

19. On the Specify RD Session Host servers page, with **LON-SVR1.adatum.com** highlighted, click the **>** arrow button and then click **Next**.

20. On the Specify user groups page, ADATUM\Domain Users is already added. Click **Next**.

21. On the Specify user profile disks page, in the Location of user profile disks text box, type **C:\UserProfile** and then click **Next**.

22. On the Confirm selections page, click **Create**.

23. When the collection is created, click **Close**.

24. Take a screen shot of the Collections page by pressing **Ctrl+PrtScr** and then press **Ctrl+V** to paste the image on the page provided in the Lab17_worksheet file.

Next, you'll need to configure RemoteApp Applications by performing the following steps:

1. On **LON-SVR1**, using Server Manager, click **Remote Desktop Services** at the top of the Server Manager window.
2. Click the **LON-SVR1** under Collections.
3. In the RemoteApp Programs section (see Figure 17-3), click **Publish RemoteApp programs**.

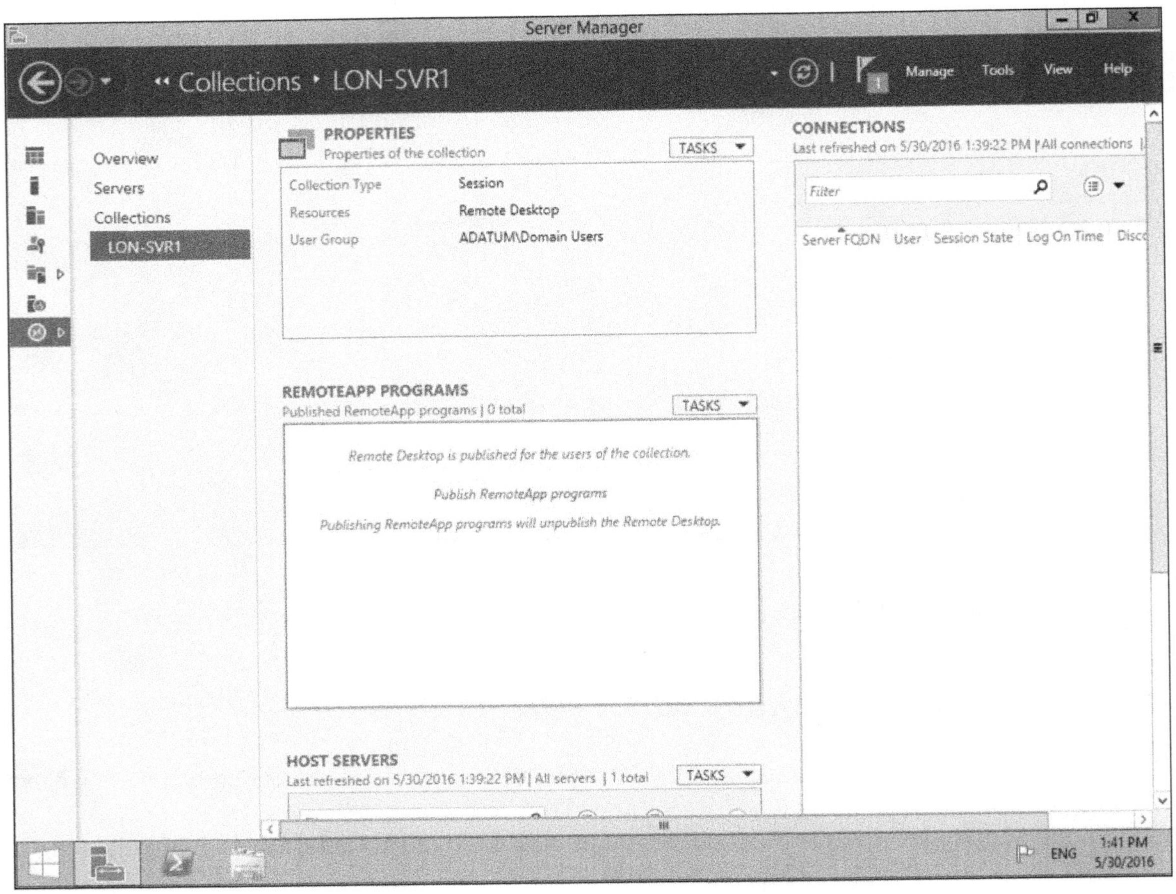

Figure 17-3
Accessing the RemoteApp Programs section

4. In the Publish RemoteApp Programs dialog box, click **Add**.
5. In the Open dialog box, double-click the **Program Files (x86)** folder, double-click **Microsoft Office** folder, double-click the **Office14**, and then click **PPTView**.
6. Answer the following question and then click **Open**.

Question 2	*What was the full path to the PPTView?*

7. Back on the Select RemoteApp programs page, click **Next**.
8. On the Confirmation page, click **Publish**.
9. Click **Close** to close the Publish RemoteApp Programs window.
10. Take a screen shot of the LON-SVR1 collection showing the RemoteApp Programs section by pressing **Ctrl+PrtScr** and then press **Ctrl+V** to paste the image on the page provided in the Lab17_worksheet file.
11. Click the **Start** button and then click **Administrative Tools**.
12. In the Administrative Tools folder, double-click **Internet Information Services (IIS) Manager**.
13. In Internet Information Services (IIS) Manager, expand **LON-SVR1** and then click **Application Pools**. If you are prompted to confirm whether you want to stay connected with the latest Web Platform Components, click **No**.
14. Right-click **RDWebAccess** and choose **Advanced Settings**.
15. If the Identity is configured to ApplicationPoolIdentity, click **ApplicationPoolIdentity**, then click the **. . .** button.
16. In the Application Pool Identity dialog box, change the Built-in account from Application Pool Identity to **NetworkService**. Close the Application Pool Identity dialog box by clicking **OK**.
17. Close the Advanced Settings dialog box by clicking **OK**.
18. Right-click **LON-SVR1** and choose **Stop**. Then right-click **LON-SVR1** and choose **Start**.
19. Close **Internet Information Services Manager**.

Next, you will use a RemoteApp application by performing the following steps:

1. On **LON-CL1**, log on using the **adatum\administrator** account and the **Pa$$w0rd** password.
2. Open **Internet Explorer** by clicking the **Internet Explorer** icon on the taskbar and then go to **https://LON-SVR1.adatum.com/rdweb**.
3. When a message indicates there is a problem with the website's security certificate, click **Continue to this website (not recommended)**.
4. At the bottom of the IE window, when you are prompted to run the Microsoft Remote Desktop Services Web Access Control, click **Allow**.
5. Click the **Certificate error** on the top of the IE window and then click **View certificates**.
6. In the Certificate dialog box, click **Install Certificate**.
7. On the Certificate Import Wizard page, click **Local Machine** and then click **Next**.
8. On the Certificate Store page, click **Place all certificates in the following store**.

9. Click the **Browse** button. In the Select Certificate Store dialog box, click **Trusted Root Certification Authorities** and then click **OK**.

10. Back on the Certificate Store page, click **Next**.

11. When the wizard is done, click **Finish**.

12. When The import was successful message appears, click **OK**.

13. Click **OK** to close the Certificate dialog box.

14. On the RemoteApp and Desktop Connection window, log in as **adatum\administrator** using the **Pa$$w0rd** password.

15. Take a screen shot of the RemoteApp and Desktops page showing the PPTVIEW icon by pressing Press **Ctrl+PrtScr** and then press **Ctrl+V** to paste the image on the page provided in the Lab17_worksheet file.

16. Double-click **PPTVIEW**.

17. In the RemoteApp dialog box, click **Connect**.

Question 3	*Where is the PowerPoint Viewer actually being executed?*

18. In the Microsoft PowerPoint Viewer dialog box, in the File name text box, type **\\LON-DC1\software** and then click **Open**. Double-click **Test PowerPoint Presentation**.

19. Take a screen shot of the Test PowerPoint Presentation window by pressing **Ctrl+PrtScr** and then press **Ctrl+V** to paste the image on the page provided in the Lab17_worksheet file.

20. Close the **PowerPoint Viewer** and then close the **Test PowerPoint Presentation** window.

21. Close **Internet Explorer**.

Leave LON-SVR1 open for the Lab Challenge. Log off LON-CL1.

Lab Challenge	Removing Remote Desktop Services
Overview	In this challenge, you will remove the Remote Desktop Services that you installed in Exercise 17.1.
Mindset	To keep the system clean for future exercises, you should remove services that will no longer be used.
Completion time	15 minutes

1. On LON-SVR1, using Server Manager, click **Manage > Remove Roles and Features**.
2. In the Remote Roles and Features Wizard, on the Before You Begin page, click Next.
3. On the Server Selection page, click **Next**.
4. On the Remote Server Roles page (as shown in Figure 17-4), deselect **Remote Desktop Services**.

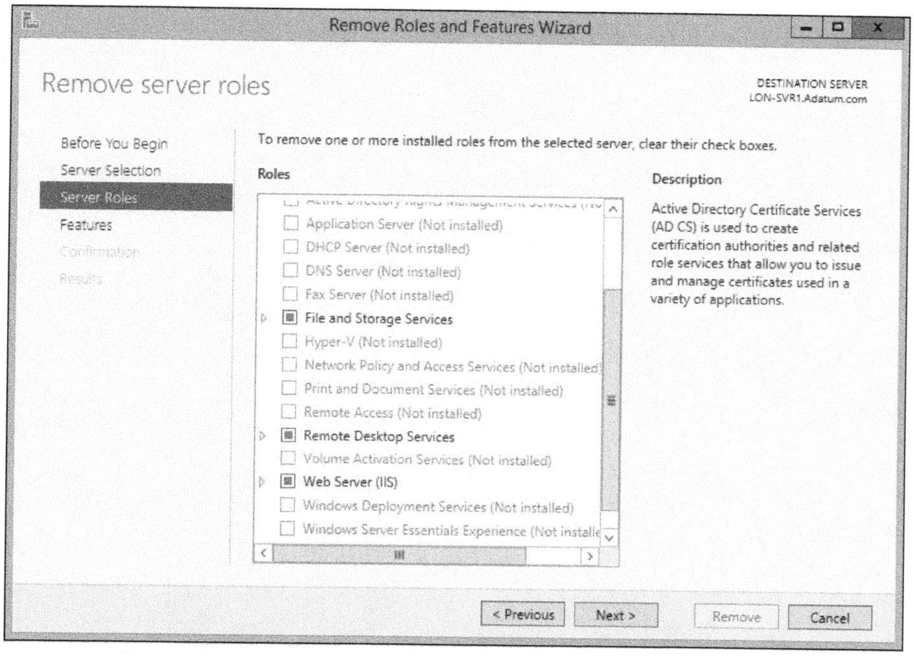

Figure 17-4
Deselecting Remote Desktop Services

5. When you are prompted to confirm that you want to remove features, click **Remove Features**.
6. Back at the Server Roles page, click **Next**.
7. On the Features page, click, **Next**.
8. On the Confirmation page, click **Remove**.
9. Take a screen shot of the Removal progress page by pressing **Ctrl+PrtScr** and then press **Ctrl+V** to paste the image on the page provided in the Lab17_worksheet file.
10. When the removal is complete, reboot LON-SVR1.

End of lab.

LAB 18
SUPPORTING DESKTOP APPS

THIS LAB CONTAINS THE FOLLOWING EXERCISES AND ACTIVITIES:

Exercise 18.1 Installing and Using the Application Compability Toolkit (ACT)

Exercise 18.2 Deploying Desktop Applications Using Microsoft Intune

Lab Challenge Removing the Microsoft Intune Client

BEFORE YOU BEGIN

The lab environment consists of student workstations connected to a local area network, along with a server that functions as the domain controller for a domain called adatum.com. The computers required for this lab are listed in Table 18-1.

Table 18-1
Computers required for Lab 18

Computer	*Operating System*	*Computer Name*
Server (VM 1)	Windows Server 2012 R2	LON-DC1
Server (VM 2)	Windows Server 2012 R2	LON-SRV2
Client (VM 3)	Windows 10	LON-CL1

In addition to the computers, you will also require the software listed in Table 18-2 to complete Lab 18.

Table 18-2
Software required for Lab 18

Software	*Location*
Lab 18 student worksheet	Lab18_worksheet.docx (provided by instructor)

Working with Lab Worksheets

Each lab in this manual requires that you answer questions, shoot screen shots, and perform other activities that you will document in a worksheet named for the lab, such as Lab18_worksheet.docx. You will find these worksheets on the book companion site. It is recommended that you use a USB flash drive to store your worksheets, so you can submit them to your instructor for review. As you perform the exercises in each lab, open the appropriate worksheet file, fill in the required information, and then save the file to your flash drive.

SCENARIO

After completing this lab, you will be able to:

- Install and use the Application Compatibility Toolkit (ACT)
- Deploy a desktop application using Microsoft Intune
- Remove the Microsoft Intune Client

Estimated lab time: 60 minutes

Exercise 18.1	Installing and Using the Application Compatibility Toolkit (ACT)
Overview	In this exercise, you will install SQL Express and then install the Application Compatibility Toolkit.
Mindset	The Application Compatibility Toolkit (ACT) helps determine whether applications, devices, and computers within your organization can run with newer versions of Windows.
Completion time	35 minutes

1. On **LON-SVR2**, log on as **adatum\administrator** with the password of the **Pa$$w0rd**.

2. On **LON-SVR2** open **File Explorer** and then open the **\\LON-DC1\software** or **\\LON-DC1\software\Windows Kits\10\ADK** folder where the adksetup program is located. Then double-click **adksetup**. If you are prompted to confirm that you want to run the file, click **Run**.

3. On the Specify Location page, click **Next**.

4. On the Windows Kits Privacy page, click **Next**.

5. On the License Agreement page, click **Accept**.

6. On the Select the features you want to install page (see Figure 18-1), deselect all features except Application Compatibility Toolkit (ACT). Click **Install**.

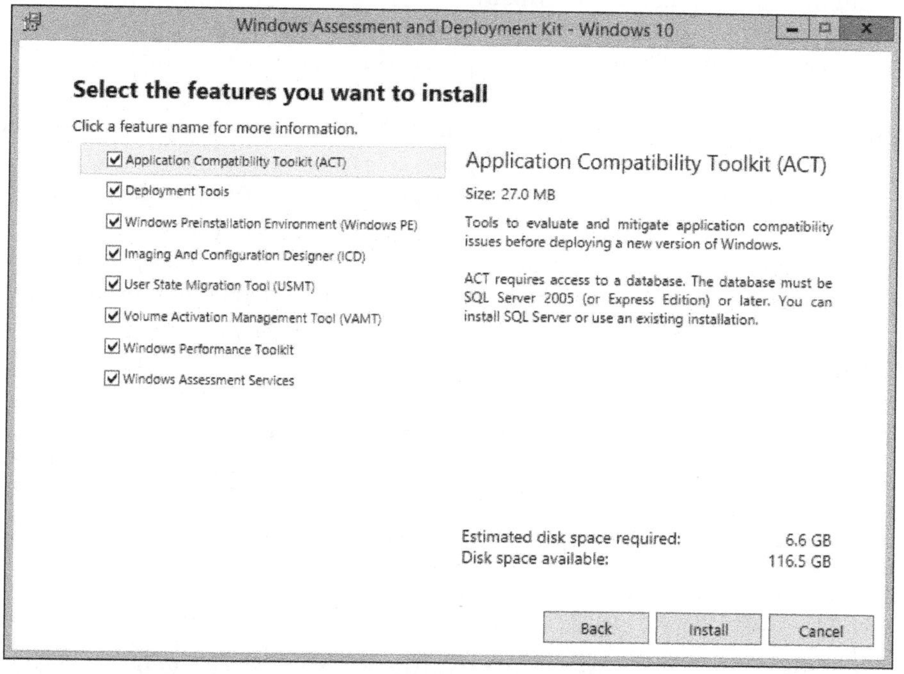

Figure 18-1
Selecting Windows ADK features

7. Take a screen shot of the Welcome to the Windows Assessment and Deployment Kit - Windows 10! screen by pressing **Alt+PrtScr** and then paste it into your Lab18_worksheet file in the page provided by pressing **Ctrl+V**.

8. Click **Close**.

9. Click the **Start** menu. Then, on the Start screen, type **acm**. From the Results list, click **Application Compatibility Manager**. The Application Compatibility Manager opens.

10. In the Welcome to the ACT Configuration Wizard, click **Next**.

11. On the Do you want to use this computer to run an ACT Log Processing Service? page, click **Next**.

12. On the Configure Your ACT Database Settings page, for the SQL Server setting, select **(local)\ADK** and then click **Connect**. In the Database: text box, type **ACT** and then click **Next**.

13. On the Configure Your ACT Database Settings page, click **Next**.

14. On the Configure Your Log File Location dialog box, click **Browse**.
15. In the Browse for Folder dialog box, expand **This PC** and then click **Local Disk (C:)**. Click **Make New Folder** and then create a folder called **Logs**. With Logs highlighted, click **OK**.
16. Back on the Configure Your Log File Location page, click **Next**.
17. On the Configure Your ACT Log Processing Service Account page, click **Next**.
18. On the Congratulations page, click **Finish**.
19. In the left pane of the Application Compatibility Manager window, click **Collect**.
20. On the menu at the top of the screen, click **File > New**.
21. On the Choose the type of package to create page, click **Inventory collection package**.
22. Take a screen shot of the Set up your inventory package dialog box by pressing **Alt+PrtScr** and then paste it into your Lab18_worksheet file in the page provided by pressing **Ctrl+V**.
23. Click **Create.**
24. Read the Save Data Collection Package dialog box and then answer the following question.

Question 1	*Where is the package going to be saved?*

25. In the File name text box, type **\\LON-DC1\software\New_Package.msi**. Click **Save**.

Question 2	*What are the next steps for your inventory collection package?*

26. Click **Finish**.
27. Close **Collect - Microsoft Application Compatibility Manager**.
28. Click the **Start** button.
29. On the Start page, click the **Apps** down arrow button. Then under Windows Kits section, click **Compatibility Administrator (64-bit)**. Note: You will need to scroll over to see the Windows Kits section and you must hover the mouse over the applications to find the Compatibility Administrator (64-bit) tile.

30. In the Compatibility Administrator (64-bit) window, under the System Database (64-bit) node, expand **Applications** and then click **Adobe Photoshop CS4 (64 Bit)**.

Question 3	*How many fixes are available for Adobe Photoshop CS4 (64 Bit)?*

Question 4	*Which Compatibility Modes setting is available for Photoshop?*

Close Compatibility Administrator (64-bit). Log off LON-SVR2.

Exercise 18.2	Deploying Desktop Applications Using Microsoft Intune
Overview	In this exercise, you will deploy the PowerPointViewer.exe program using Microsoft Intune.
Mindset	Microsoft Intune is an integrated, cloud-based client management solution for managing computers, tablets, and phones. You can deploy software to PCs and other devices, track software licenses, and manage software licenses.
Completion time	20 minutes

NOTE	*If you are using the MOAC Labs Online system, you will not be able to perform this exercise. Instead, you need to use a computer running Windows 10 with access to the Internet. If your classroom has a dedicated Windows Server 2012 R2 or Windows Server 2016, you can use a virtual machine running Windows 10.*

1. Log on to a computer running Windows 10 that is connected to the Internet.

2. Launch **Internet Explorer** and go to the **Microsoft Intune Account Portal** (**http://portal.office.com**). Log in with your Intune account.

3. Click the **Admin centers** workspace (last workspace) and then click **Intune**.

4. Click the **APPS** workspace.

5. Under Tasks, click **Add Apps**. If you are prompted to log in again, log in with your Microsoft Intune account.

6. In the Add Software – Microsoft Intune Software Publisher wizard, on the Before you begin page, click **Next**.

7. On the Software setup page (as shown in Figure 18-2), click the **Browse** button and then browse to and select the **C:\Software\PowerPointViewer.exe** file used in Lab 1. Then click **Open**. Although the PowerPointViewer.exe is a Microsoft file, and not a third-party program, the procedure is still the same.

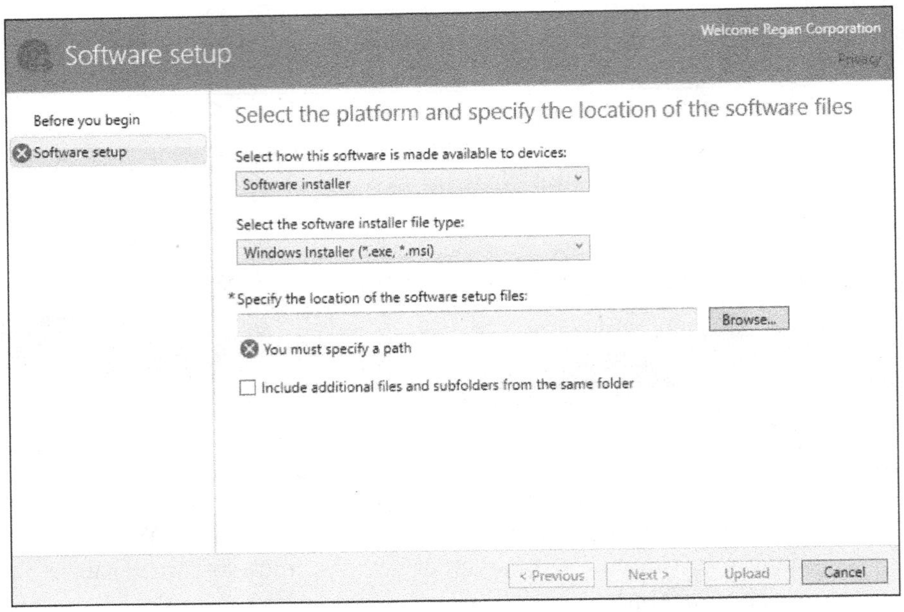

Figure 18-2
Adding Software to Microsoft Intune

Question 5	*Which file types are supported by the Software installer?*

8. Click **Next**.

9. On the Software description page, in the Publisher text box, type **Microsoft**. Click **Next**.

10. On the Requirements page, click **Next**.

11. On the Detection rules page, select the **Use the default detection rules** option and then click **Next**.

12. On the Command Line Arguments page, click **Next**.

13. On the Return codes page, select **No**. Click **Next**.

14. On the Summary page, take a screen shot by pressing **Alt+PrtScr** and then paste it into your Lab18_worksheet file in the page provided by pressing **Ctrl+V**.

15. Click **Upload**.

16. When the upload is complete, click **Close**.

17. Under **Apps**, which is above Volume-Purchased Apps.

18. Right-click **PowerPointViewer.exe** and choose **Manage Deployment**.

19. In the PowerPointViewer.exe window, on the Select Groups page, select **My Test Group** and then click **Add**. Click the **Next** button.

20. On the Deployment Action page, under the Deployment column, select **Required Install**. Click **Finish**.

21. To remove an application, right-click the **PowerPointViewer.exe** file and choose **Delete**. When you are prompted to confirm, click **Yes**.

Leave the Microsoft Explorer/Microsoft Intune console open for the next exercise.

Lab Challenge	Removing the Microsoft Intune Client
Overview	In this challenge, you will remove the Microsoft Intune Client from the compture by retiring the computer.
Mindset	If you do not want to manage the computer using Microsoft Intune, you must remove the Microsoft Intune client. The easiest way this is done is by retiring the computer using the Microsoft Intune console.
Completion time	20 minutes

NOTE	*If you are using the MOAC Labs Online system, you will not be able to perform this exercise. Instead, you need to use a computer running Windows 10 with access to the Internet. If your classroom has a dedicated Windows Server 2012 R2 or Windows Server 2016, you can use a virtual machine running Windows 10.*

1. On the Windows 10 computer that is connected to the Internet, using the Internet Explorer/ Microsoft Intune console, click the **GROUPS** workspace.

2. Click **All Computers**. Your device should show up, as shown in Figure 18-3.

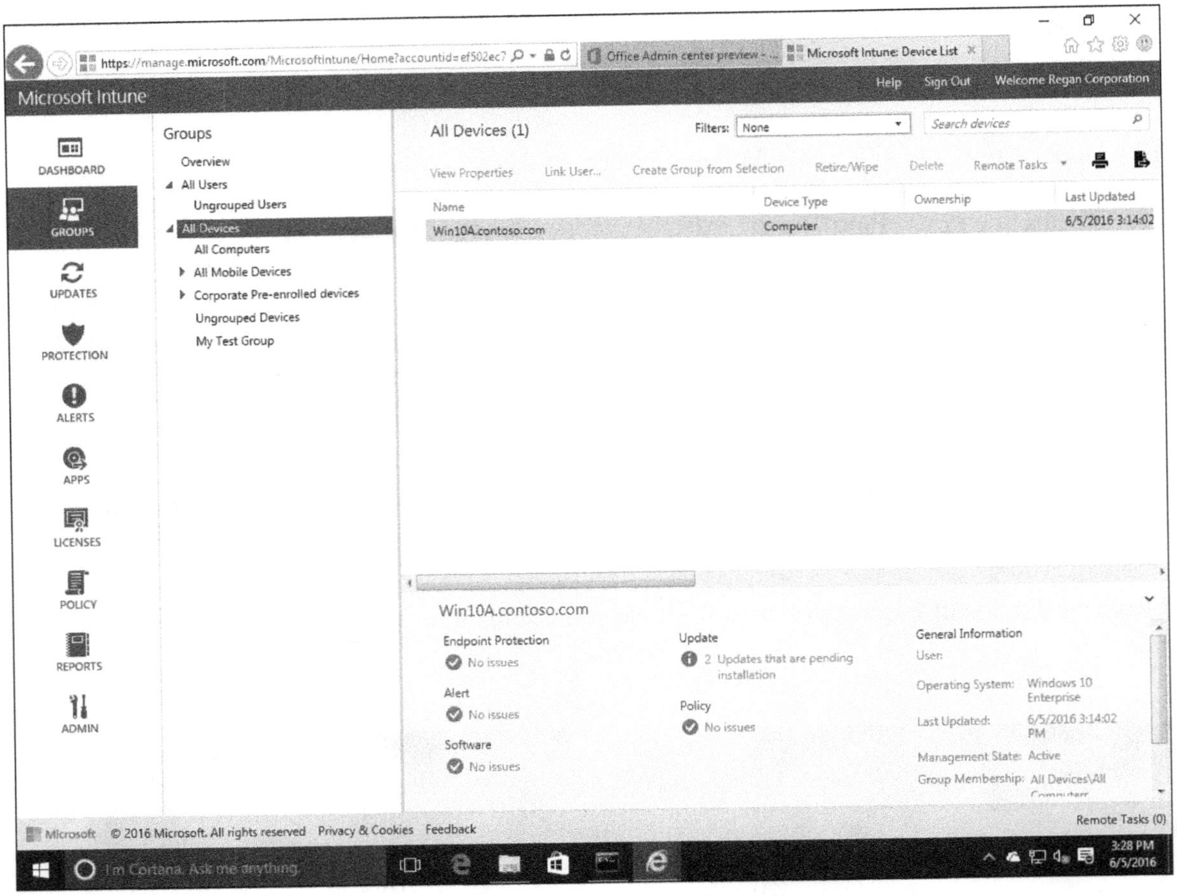

Figure 18-3
Managing devices

3. Right-click your device and choose **Retire/Wipe**.

Question 6	*In the Retire Device dialog box, which option is selected?*

4. Click **Yes**.

5. Take a screen shot of the All Devices page showing that the device is being deleted by pressing **Alt+PrtScr** and then paste it into your Lab18_worksheet file in the page provided by pressing **Ctrl+V**.

End of lab.

LAB 19
CONFIGURING SYSTEM RECOVERY

THIS LAB CONTAINS THE FOLLOWING EXERCISES AND ACTIVITIES:

Exercise 19.1 Configuring and Using a Restore Point

Lab Challenge Rolling Back a Device Driver

BEFORE YOU BEGIN

The lab environment consists of student workstations connected to a local area network, along with a server that functions as the domain controller for a domain called adatum.com. The computers required for this lab are listed in Table 19-1.

Table 19-1
Computers required for Lab 19

Computer	*Operating System*	*Computer Name*
Server (VM 1)	Windows Server 2012 R2	LON-DC1
Client (VM 2)	Windows 10	LON-CL1

In addition to the computers, you will also require the software listed in Table 19-2 to complete Lab 19.

Table 19-2
Software required for Lab 19

Software	*Location*
Lab 19 student worksheet	Lab19_worksheet.docx (provided by instructor)

Working with Lab Worksheets

Each lab in this manual requires that you answer questions, shoot screen shots, and perform other activities that you will document in a worksheet named for the lab, such as Lab19_worksheet.docx. You will find these worksheets on the book companion site. It is recommended that you use a USB flash drive to store your worksheets, so you can submit them to your instructor for review. As you perform the exercises in each lab, open the appropriate worksheet file, fill in the required information, and then save the file to your flash drive.

SCENARIO

After completing this lab, you will be able to:

- Configure and use system restore points
- Perform a driver rollback

Estimated lab time: 35 minutes

Exercise 19.1	Configuring and Using a Restore Point
Overview	In this exercise, you will create a restore point, which can be used to roll back to a previous state.
Mindset	Sometimes when you install an application or perform an upgrade, the installation or upgrade causes major problems with Windows. In these situations, you can use a restore point to restore the system back to its original state before the upgrade.
Completion time	20 minutes

1. On **LON-CL1**, log in as **adatum\administrator** with the password of **Pa$$w0rd**.
2. On **LON-CL1**, right-click the **Start** button and choose **Control Panel**.
3. In the Search Control Panel text box, type **Create a Restore point**. Under System, click **Create a restore point**. The System Properties dialog box displays (see Figure 19-1).

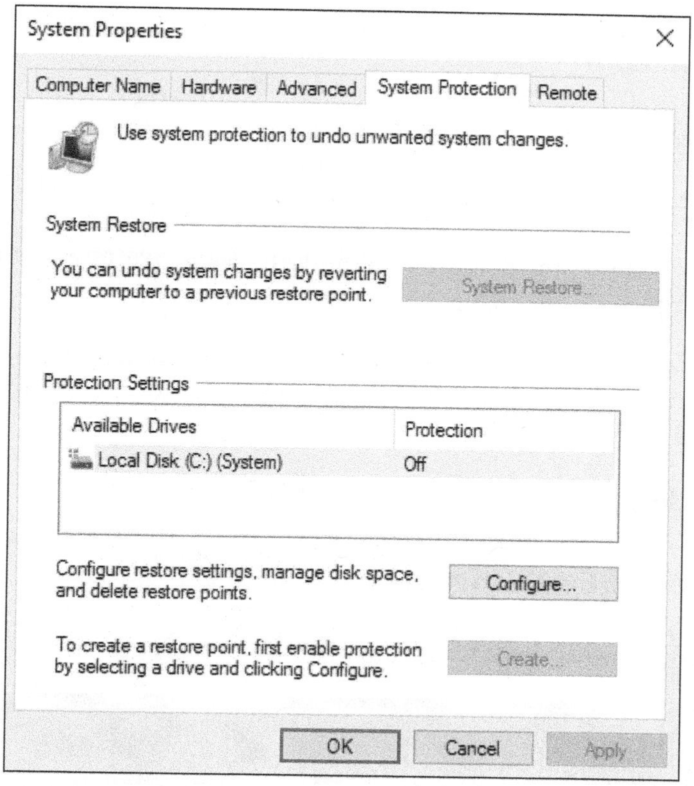

Figure 19-1
The *System Properties* dialog box

Question 1	*Which drive is already protected?*

4. Click **Local Disk (C:)** and then click **Configure.**
5. In the System Protection dialog box, click **Turn on system protection**. Click **OK.**
6. To create a restore point, click **Create**.
7. In the System Protection dialog box, in the text box, type **Test** and then click **Create**.
8. When the restore point is created, take a screen shot of the The restore point was created successfully message dialog by pressing **Alt+PrtScr** and then paste it into your Lab19_worksheet file in the page provided by pressing **Ctrl+V**.
9. Click **Close**.
10. In the System Properties dialog box, click **System Restore**.
11. On the System Restore Wizard page, click **Next**.

12. When a list of current restore points is displayed, click the Test restore point that you just made and then click **Next**.

13. On the Confirm your restore point page, click **Finish**.

14. When a warning indicates that the system restore cannot be interrupted, click **Yes** to continue.

15. After LON-CL1 reboots, log on using the **Adatum\administrator** account and the **Pa$$w0rd** password.

16. When the system restore finishes, take a screen shot of the System Restore dialog box by pressing **Alt+PrtScr** and then paste it into your Lab19_worksheet file in the page provided by pressing **Ctrl+V**.

17. Click **Close** to close the System Restore dialog box.

Leave LON-CL1 logged in for the next exercise.

Lab Challenge	Rolling Back a Device Driver
Overview	In this challenge, you will use Device Manager to roll back a device driver.
Mindset	Sometimes when you upgrade or load a device driver, the device that the device driver is used for stops working or causes other problems with Windows. With Device Manager, you can roll back a device driver to the previous device driver.
Completion time	15 minutes

1. On **LON-CL1**, right-click the **Start** button and choose **Device Manager**.

2. Expand the **Ports (COM and LPT)** node and then click **Communications Port (COM2) port**.

3. Right-click **Communications Port (COM2) port** and choose **Update Driver Software**.

4. On the How do you want to search for driver software? page, click **Search automatically for updated driver software**.

Question 2	*Which driver was located and what information was provided about the driver?*

5. Click **Close** to close the Update Driver Software – Communications Port (COM2) dialog box.

6. Right-click **Communications port (COM2)** and choose **Properties**.

7. Click the **Driver** tab.

Question 3	*Which driver version is being used by Communicaton Port (COM2)?*

8. Click **Update Driver**.

9. On the How do you want to search for driver software? page, click **Browse my computer for driver software**.

10. On the Browse for driver software on your computer page, click **Let me pick from a list of device drivers on my computer**.

11. On the Select the device driver you want to install for this hardware page, click to deselect the **Show compatible hardware**.

NOTE	*This is for demonstration purposes only. Normally, you want to use drivers that are compatible.*

12. For the Manufacturer, click **Trimble** and then click **Trimble PCMCIA GPS Adapter (Rev. B)**. Click **Next**.

13. When an update driver warning is displayed, click **Yes**.

14. When the driver has been installed, click **Close**.

15. Take a screen shot of the Trimble PCMCIA GPS Adapter (Rev. B) (COM2) Properties dialog box by pressing **Alt+PrtScr** and then paste it into your Lab19_worksheet file in the page provided by pressing **Ctrl+V**.

16. Click **Close** to close the Trimble PCMCIA GPS Adapter (Rev. B) (COM2) Properties dialog box.

17. Right-click the **Trimble PCMCIA GPS Adapter (Rev. B) (COM2)** port and choose **Properties**. Then click the **Driver** tab.

18. Click **Roll Back Driver**.

Question 4	*Which option would you have clicked to manually pick a driver to install?*

19. When you are prompted to confirm that you are sure you would like to roll back to the previously installed driver software, click **Yes**.

20. Take a screen shot of the Communications Port (COM2) Properties dialog box by pressing **Alt+PrtScr** and then paste it into your Lab19_worksheet file in the page provided by pressing **Ctrl+V**.

21. Close the Communications Port (COM2) Properties dialog box by clicking **Close**.

22. Close the Device Manager on LON-CL1.

End of lab.

LAB 20
CONFIGURING FILE RECOVERY

THIS LAB CONTAINS THE FOLLOWING EXERCISES AND ACTIVITIES:

Exercise 20.1 Scheduling a Windows 10 Backup

Exercise 20.2 Performing a File Restore

Exercise 20.3 Using File History

Lab Challenge Recovering Files from OneDrive

BEFORE YOU BEGIN

The lab environment consists of student workstations connected to a local area network, along with a server that functions as the domain controller for a domain called adatum.com. The computers required for this lab are listed in Table 20-1.

Table 20-1
Computers required for Lab 20

Computer	*Operating System*	*Computer Name*
Server (VM 1)	Windows Server 2012 R2	LON-DC1
Client (VM 3)	Windows 10	LON-CL1

In addition to the computers, you will also require the software listed in Table 20-2 to complete Lab 20.

Table 20-2
Software required for Lab 20

Software	*Location*
Lab 20 student worksheet	Lab20_worksheet.docx (provided by instructor)

Working with Lab Worksheets

Each lab in this manual requires that you answer questions, shoot screen shots, and perform other activities that you will document in a worksheet named for the lab, such as Lab20_worksheet.docx. You will find these worksheets on the book companion site. It is recommended that you use a USB flash drive to store your worksheets, so you can submit them to your instructor for review. As you perform the exercises in each lab, open the appropriate worksheet file, fill in the required information, and then save the file to your flash drive.

SCENARIO

After completing this lab, you will be able to:

- Schedule a Windows 10 backup
- Perform a file restore
- Use File History
- Recover files from OneDrive

Estimated lab time: 60 minutes

Exercise 20.1	Scheduling a Windows 10 Backup
Overview	In this exercise, you will perform a backup and then schedule a backup using the Windows 7 File Recovery utility.
Mindset	The best method in disaster recovery is to have a good backup. A disaster could be small or could be major. But if you have a backup of your data, you can restore to a computer and continue with the work that needs to be done.
Completion time	30 minutes

1. On **LON-DC1**, log on using the **Adatum\administrator** account and the **Pa$$w0rd** password.
2. Open **File Explorer** by clicking the **File Explorer** icon on the taskbar.
3. Under This PC, click **Local Disk (C:)**.
4. Right-click **Local Disk (C:)** and choose **New > Folder**. For the folder name, type **BAK** and then press **Enter**.
5. Right-click the **C:\BAK** folder and choose **Properties**.
6. In the BAK Properties dialog box, click the **Sharing** tab.
7. Click the **Advanced Sharing** button.
8. In the Advanced Sharing dialog box, click to select the **Share this folder**.

9. Click the **Permissions** button.
10. Click to select **Allow Full Control Permission** for the Everyone group.
11. Click **OK** to close the Permissions for BAK dialog box.
12. Click **OK** to close the Advanced Sharing dialog box.
13. Click **Close** to close the BAK Properties dialog box.
14. On **LON-CL1**, log on using the **Adatum\administrator** account and the **Pa$$w0rd** password.
15. Right-click the **Start** button, and click **Control Panel** .
16. In the Search Control Panel text box, type **File Recovery**. From the search results, click **Backup and Restore (Windows 7)**. The Backup and Restore (Windows 7) page displays (see Figure 20-1).

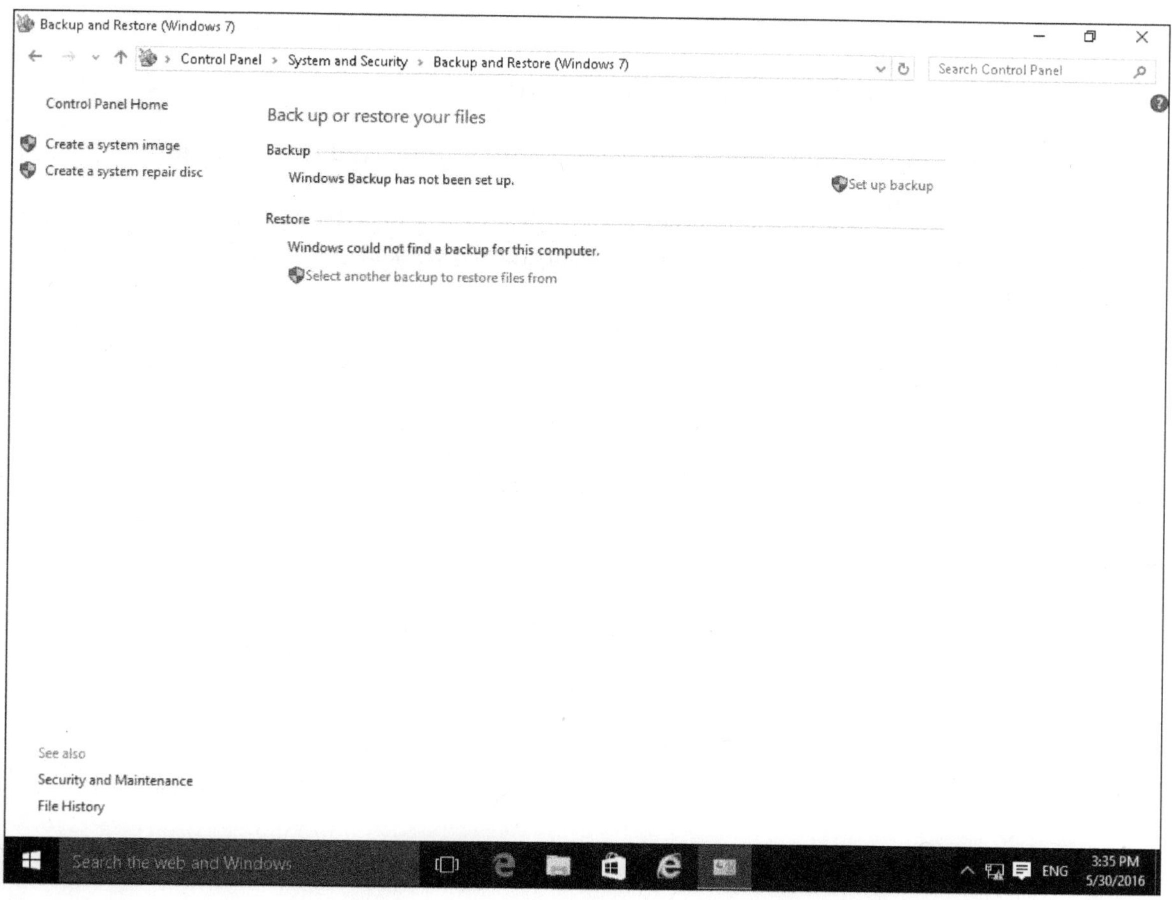

Figure 20-1
The *Windows 7 File Recovery* page

17. Click **Set up backup**.
18. On the Set up backup page, answer the following question.

Question 1	*Which backup destination is already available?*

19. Click **Save on a network**.
20. In the Set up backup page, in the Network location text box, type **\\LON-DC1\BAK**.
21. In the Username text box, type **adatum\administrator**. In the Password text box, type **Pa$$w0rd**. Click **OK**.
22. Back on the Set up backup page, ensure **\\LON-DC1\BAK** is selected and then click **Next**.
23. On the What do you want to back up? page, select **Let me choose** and then click **Next**.

Question 2	*By default, which items are selected for backup?*

24. Deselect **Include a system image of drives: System Reserved, (C:)** and then click **Next**.
25. On the Review your backup settings page, click **Save settings and run backup**.
26. When the backup finishes, take a screen shot of the Backup and Restore (Windows 7) page by pressing **Alt+Prt Scr** and then paste it into your Lab20_worksheet file in the page provided by pressing **Ctrl+V**.
27. Under Schedule, click **Change settings**.
28. On the Select where you want to save your backup page, click **Next**.
29. On the What do you want to back up? page, click **Next**.
30. On the What do you want to back up? second page, click **Next**.
31. On the Review your backup settings page, click **Change schedule**.

Question 3	*When is the backup scheduled?*

32. Change the time to **8:00 PM** and then click **OK**.
33. On the Review your backup settings page, take a screen shot by pressing **Alt+PrtScr** and then paste it into your Lab20_worksheet file in the page provided by pressing **Ctrl+V**.
34. Click **Save settings and exit**.

Leave the Backup and Restore (Windows 7) window open for the next exercise.

Exercise 20.2	Performing a File Restore
Overview	In this exercise, you will restore a file that was backed up last exercise.
Mindset	When you have a backup, you will need to know how to restore files from the backup. As a reminder, you should always test your backups from time to time by performing a restore of some files.
Completion time	10 minutes

1. On **LON-CL1**, using Backup and Restore (Windows 7), under the Restore section, click the **Restore my files** button.

Question 4	*When you want to use the current backup of all of the files, which option should be selected?*

2. In the Restore Files window (see Figure 20-2), click **Browse for folders**.

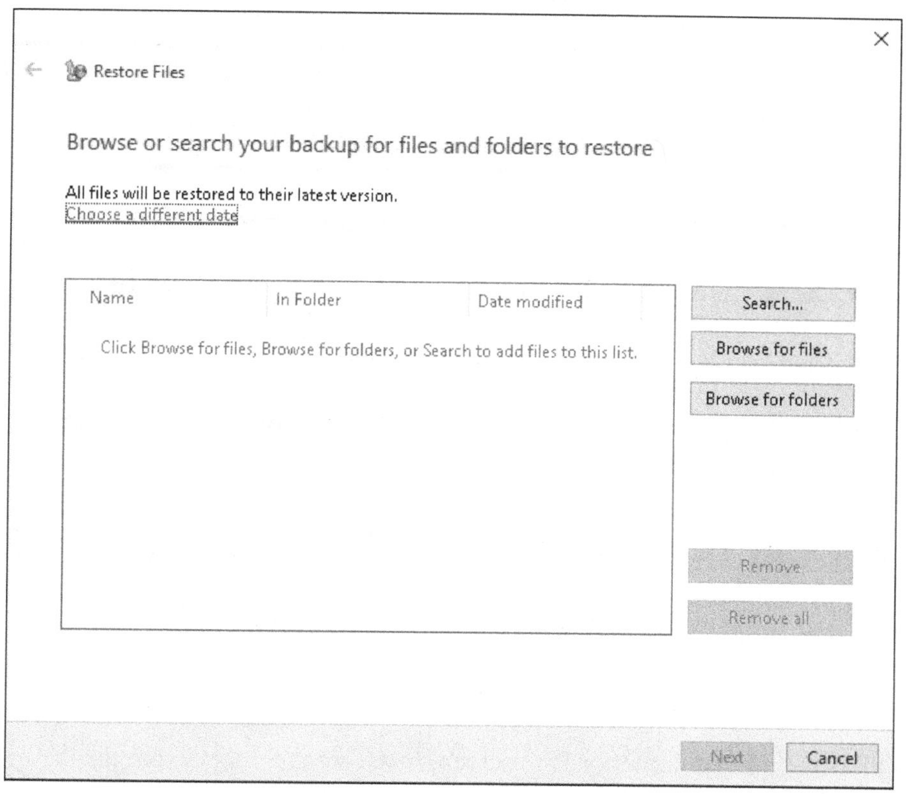

Figure 20-2
The Restore Files window

3. In the Browse the backup for folders or drives dialog box, click **Administrator's backup** and then click **Add folder**.

4. Back on the Browse or search your backup for files and folders to restore page, click **Next**.

5. When you are prompted to identify where you want to restore the files, In the original location is already selected. Click **Restore**.

6. In the Copy file dialog box, click to select the **Do this for all conflicts** option and then click **Copy and Replace**.

7. When the restore has been completed, take a screen shot of the Your files have been restored page by pressing **Alt+Prt Scr** and then paste it into your Lab20_worksheet file in the page provided by pressing **Ctrl+V**.

8. Click **Finish**.

9. To run off the schedule, click the **Turn off schedule** option.

10. Close **Backup and Restore (Windows 7)**.

Exercise 20.3 Using File History

Overview	In this exercise, you will restore a file that is saved in File History.
Mindset	File History in Windows periodically makes a copy of a data folder and keeps several copies of those files. Then you can restore the files from File History using any of the saved copies.
Completion time	10 minutes

1. On **LON-CL1**, open File Explorer by clicking File Explorer on the tasbar.

2. If you do not have an E drive, use the following steps:

    a. Right-click the **Start** button and choose **Disk Management**. Disk Management opens.

    b. If you are prompted to initialize disks, click **OK**.

    c. Right-click the 10 GB Unallocated disk and choose **New Simple Volume**.

    d. In the New Simple Volume Wizard, on the Welcome screen, click **Next**.

    e. On the Specify Volume Size page, click **Next**.

    f. On the Assign Drive Letter or Path screen, make sure that the assign the driver letter is **E** and then click **Next**.

    g. On the Format Partition screen, in the Volume label text box, type **Data**. Click **Next**.

    h. On the Completing the New Simple Volume Wizard screen, click **Finish**.

i. When a Microsoft Windows dialog box opens asking to format the disk, click **Cancel**.

j. Close the File Explorer New Volume (E:) window.

k. Close **Disk Manager** and then close the other **File Explorer**.

3. Right-click the desktop and choose **New > Text Document.** Name the document **Test**.

4. Right-click the **Start** button and choose **Control Panel**.

5. In the Search Control Panel text box, type **File History**. When the File History option is displayed, click **File History**. The File History page displays (see Figure 20-3).

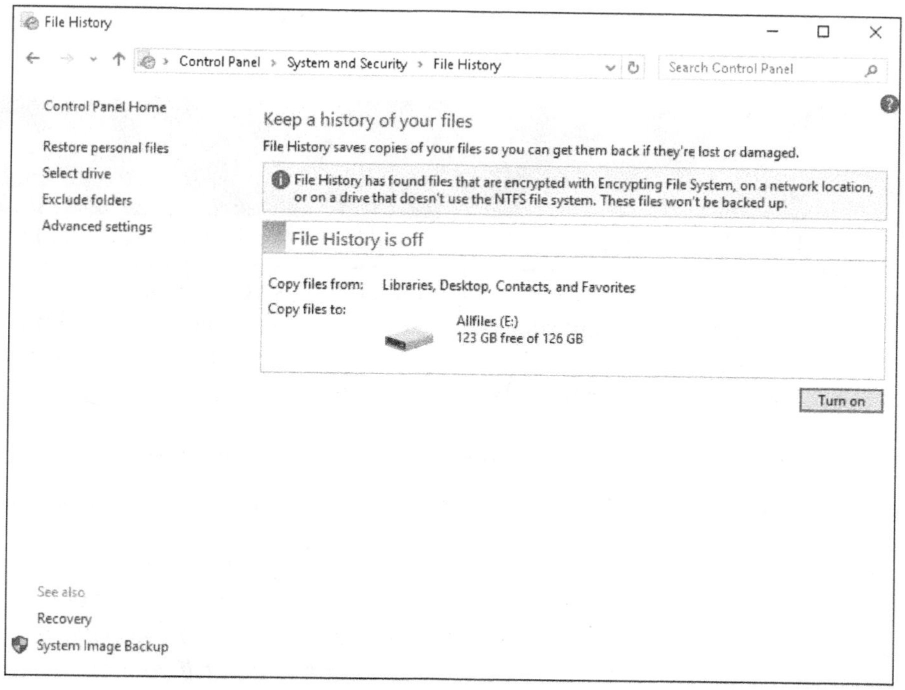

Figure 20-3
The File History page

6. Click the **Turn on** button.

Question 5	*Where are the files being copied to?*

7. After a few seconds, click **Run now**.

8. Take a screen shot of the File History page by pressing **Alt+PrtScr** and then paste it into your Lab20_worksheet file in the page provided by pressing **Ctrl+V**.

9. In the left pane, click **Restore personal files**.
10. In the Home - File History window, double-click **Desktop**.
11. Click **Test** and, at the bottom of the window, click the (green) **Restore to original location** button.
12. In the Replace or Skip Files dialog box, click **Replace the file in the destination**.
13. Close the **Desktop** window.
14. Close the **Desktop - File History** dialog box.
15. Close the **File History** window.

Lab Challenge	Recovering Files from OneDrive
Overview	In this challenge, you will restore a deleted file in Microsoft OneDrive.
Mindset	OneDrive is a file-hosting service that allows you to store and create files and folders and share them with other users and groups. Similar to deleting local files in Windows 10, when you delete a file, you have 30 days to recover from the OneDrive Recycle Bin, which is a temporary storage place of deleted items.
Completion time	10 minutes

NOTE	*If you are using the MOAC Labs Online system, you will not be able to perform this exercise. Instead, you need to use a computer running Windows 10 with access to the Internet. If your classroom has a dedicated Windows Server 2012 R2 or Windows Server 2016, you can use a virtual machine running Windows 10.*

1. Log in to a Windows 10 computer that is connected to the Internet.
2. Launch Internet Explorer and go to **http://onedrive.live.com**. If you are not automatically logged in, click **Sign In** and sign in with your Office 365 credentials. When you are logged in, you should see a page similar to what is shown in Figure 20-4.

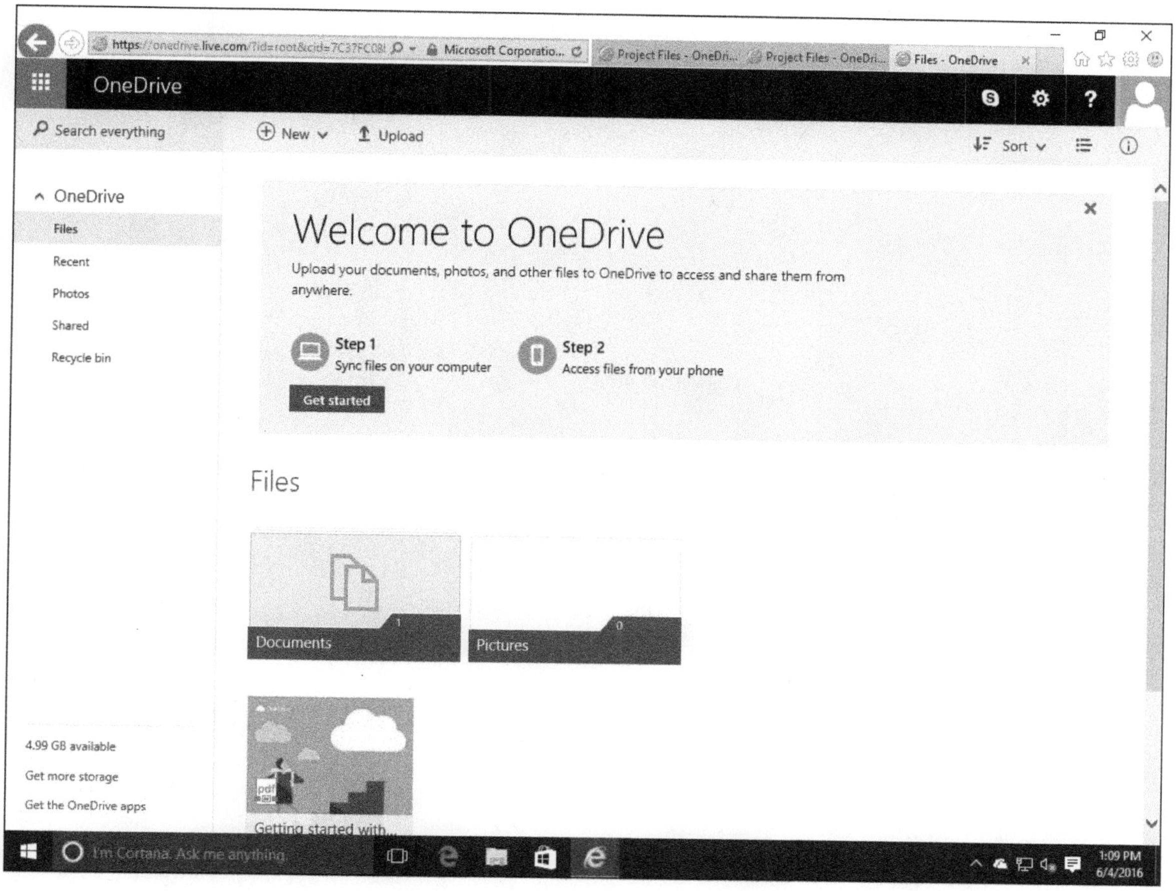

Figure 20-4
The OneDrive web page

3. Click the **Documents** folder and then click the **Project Files** folder.

4. Right-click the Project Scope.docx file and choose **Delete**.

5. Click the **Recycle bin** link.

6. Right-click a ProjectScope.docx document and choose **Restore**.

7. Navigate back to the Project Files folder; you will see the document is returned to the folder.

8. Take a screen shot of the OneDrive page by pressing **Alt+Prt Scr** and then paste it into your Lab20_worksheet file in the page provided by pressing **Ctrl+V**.

End of lab.

LAB 21
CONFIGURING AND MANAGING UPDATES

THIS LAB CONTAINS THE FOLLOWING EXERCISES AND ACTIVITIES:

Exercise 21.1 Configuring Windows 10 Updates

Lab Challenge Configuring Windows Update Policies

BEFORE YOU BEGIN

The lab environment consists of student workstations connected to a local area network, along with a server that functions as the domain controller for a domain called adatum.com. The computers required for this lab are listed in Table 21-1.

Table 21-1
Computers required for Lab 21

Computer	*Operating System*	*Computer Name*
Server (VM 1)	Windows Server 2012 R2	LON-DC1
Client (VM 2)	Windows 10	LON-CL1

In addition to the computers, you will also require the software listed in Table 21-2 to complete Lab 21.

Table 21-2
Software required for Lab 21

Software	*Location*
Lab 21 student worksheet	Lab21_worksheet.docx (provided by instructor)

Working with Lab Worksheets

Each lab in this manual requires that you answer questions, shoot screen shots, and perform other activities that you will document in a worksheet named for the lab, such as Lab21_worksheet.docx. You will find these worksheets on the book companion site. It is recommended that you use a USB flash drive to store your worksheets, so you can submit them to your instructor for review. As you perform the exercises in each lab, open the appropriate worksheet file, fill in the required information, and then save the file to your flash drive.

SCENARIO

After completing this lab, you will be able to:

- Configure Windows 10 updates
- Configure Windows update policies

Estimated lab time: 35 minutes

Exercise 21.1	Configuring Windows 10 Updates
Overview	In this exercise, you will configure Windows 10 updates and then review updates that already been installed.
Mindset	Windows Update provides your Windows 10 users with a way to keep their computers current by checking a designated server. The server provides software that patches security issues, installs updates that make Windows and your applications more stable, fixes issues with existing Windows programs, and provides new features.
Completion time	15 minutes

1. Log in to **LON-CL1** as **adatum\administrator** with the password of **Pa$$w0rd**.
2. Click the **Start** button and then click **Settings**.
3. In the Settings window, click **Update & security**. The Windows Update page opens (see Figure 21-1).

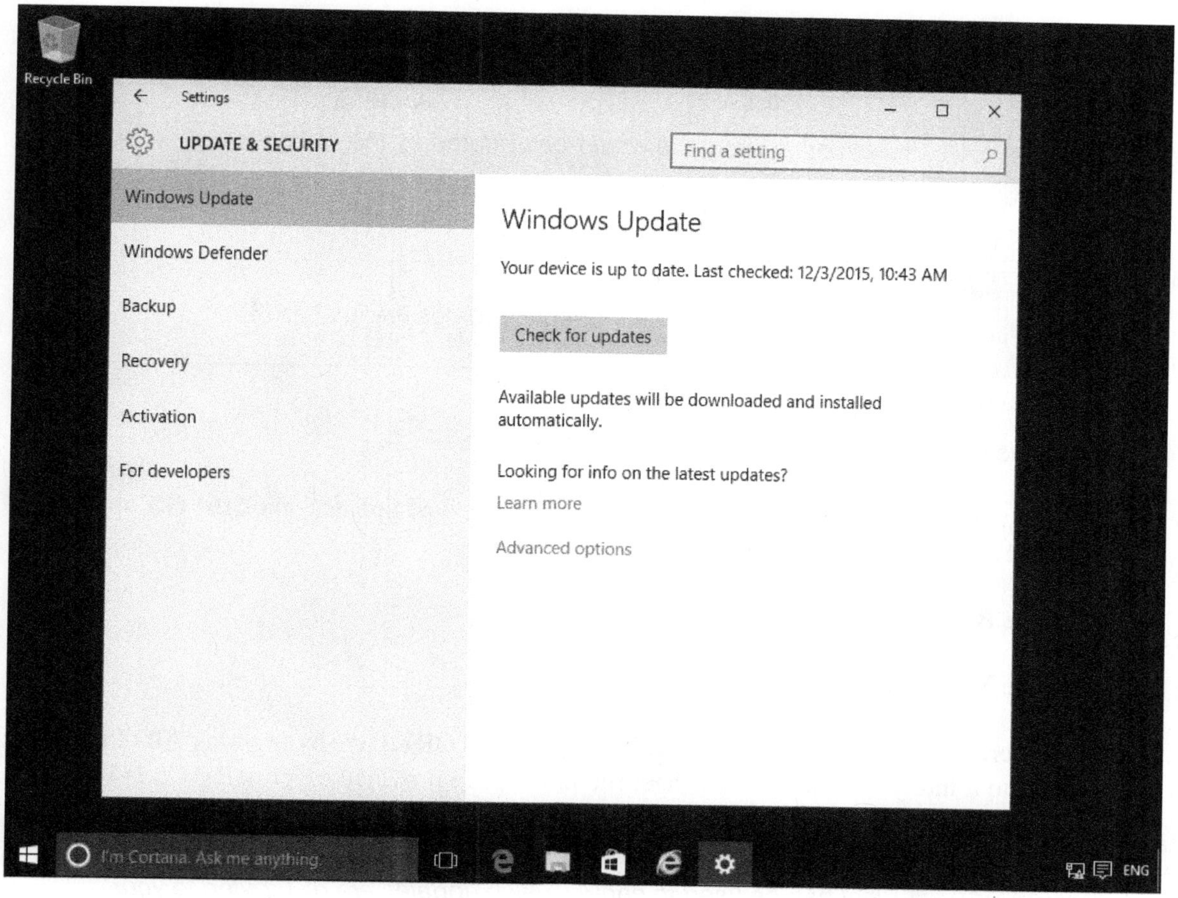

Figure 21-1
Managing Windows updates

Question 1	*When was the last time the system was updated?*

Question 2	*Would the date shown in Question 1 present a potential security risk? Why or why not?*

4. Click **Check for updates**.

Question 3	*Did the updates work?*

5. Click the **Advanced options** option.

6. Select the **Give me updates for other Microsoft products when I update Windows** option.

Question 4	*Which other products would be updated by this option?*

Question 5	*Which option is selected for how updates are installed?*

7. Select the **Choose how updates are delivered** option.
8. To get updates from nearby computers that already received updates, click the **Off** option. It should change to On.
9. Click the **Back** button.
10. Click the **View your update history** option.
11. Take a screen shot of the VIEW YOUR UPDATE HISTORY page by pressing **Alt+PrtScr** and then paste it into your Lab21_worksheet file in the page provided by pressing **Ctrl+V**.

Question 6	*What can be used to control which updates are distributed to your corporate clients running Windows 10?*

Lab Challenge	Configuring Windows Update Policies
Overview	In this challenge, you will create a Group Policy Object (GPO) that will configure Windows update settings for domain systems.
Mindset	Normally, you do not need to create a domain GPO to support Configuration Manager software updates. However, if you use a GPO to perform a Configuration Manager client agent installation, you must also configure the Windows Update server update options for clients to use the active software update point.
Completion time	20 minutes

1. Log in to **LON-DC1** as **adatum\administrator** with the password of **Pa$$w0rd**.
2. In the Server Manager console, click **Tools > Group Policy Management**.
3. Right-click the **Group Policy Objects** folder (as shown in Figure 21-2) and choose **New**.

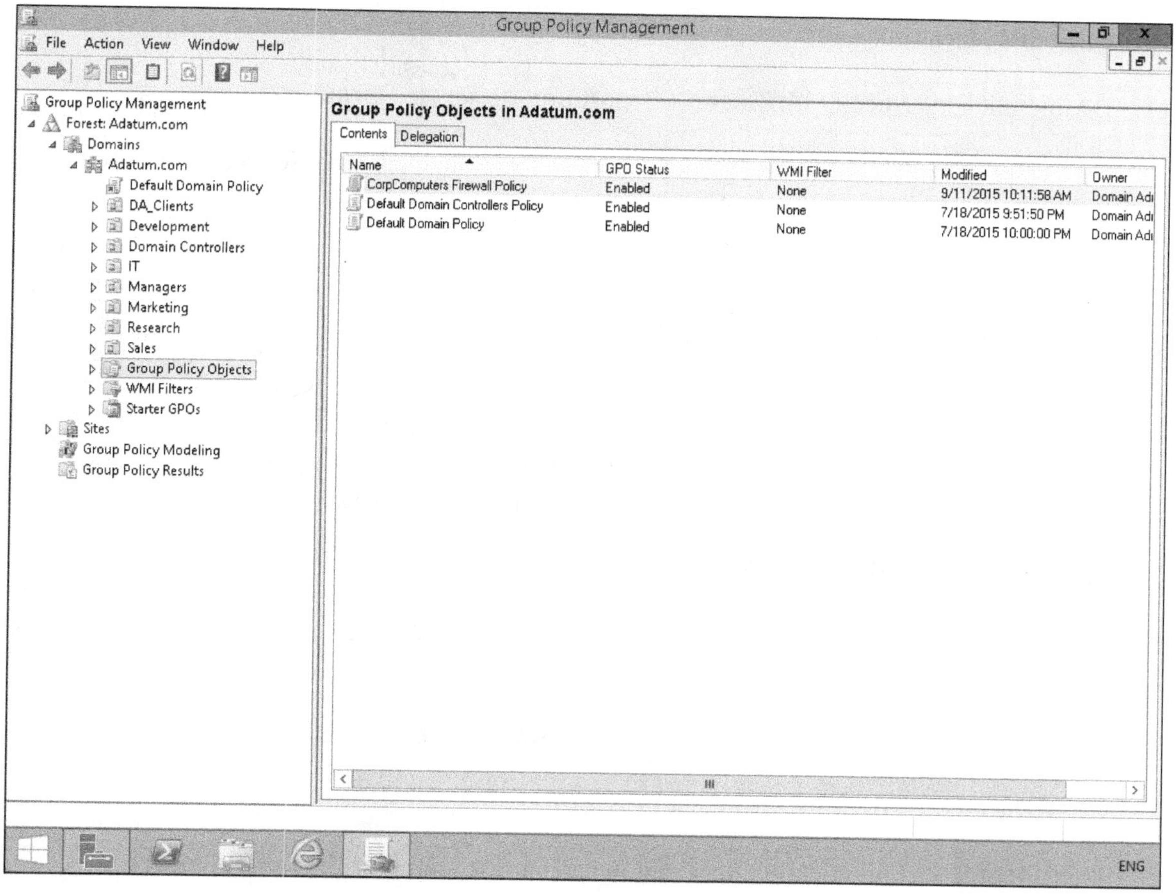

Figure 21-2
Managing GPOs

4. In the Name field, type **WSUS AutoUpdate** and then click **OK**.

5. Expand the Group Policy Objects folder and then right-click the **WSUS AutoUpdate** GPO and choose **Edit**.

6. In the Group Policy Management Editor opens, expand the **Computer Configuration > Policies > Administrative Templates > Windows Components > Windows Update**.

7. In the details pane, double-click **Configure Automatic Updates**.

8. Under Configure Automatic Updates, click **Enabled**. Under Configure Automatic updating, review the options.

9. Under Configure automatic updating, make sure **3 - Auto download and notify for install** is visible. Read the information in the help panel to understand how this setting works.

Question 7	*What is the scheduled install time?*

10. Click **OK** when finished.

11. Double-click the **Specify intranet Microsoft update service location** option.

12. Under Specify intranet Microsoft update service location, click **Enabled** and then type the following URL of the upstream WSUS server.

    http://LON-DC1:8530

13. For the intranet statistics server, type the same information.

14. Click **OK**.

15. Take a screen shot of the Group Policy Management Editor page by pressing **Alt+PrtScr** and then paste it into your Lab21_worksheet file in the page provided by pressing **Ctrl+V**.

16. Close the Group Policy Management Editor window.

17. Back in the Group Policy Management console, right-click the **Adatum.com** node and choose **Link an existing GPO**.

18. In the Select GPO dialog box, choose **WSUS AutoUpdate** and then click **OK**.

19. Close the Group Policy Management console.

20. On **LON-CL1**, right-click the Start button and choose **Command Prompt (Admin)**.

21. From the Command Prompt window, type **gpresult /r** and then press **Enter**.

22. The WSUS AutoUpdate GPO should appear under the **Computer Settings > Applied Group Policy Objects** section of the report. If it does not, type **gpupdate /force** and then try **gpresult /r** again.

23. Type **wuauclt /detectnow** and then press **Enter**. This forces the Windows 10 computer to contact the WSUS server immediately.

End of lab.

Printed in the USA
K03B1G5SCI122116 01S29053000000001687